Tourism: Marketing and Advertising

Tourism: Marketing and Advertising

By

V.S. Dahiya

2008

CYBER TECH PUBLICATIONS
4264/3, Ansari Road, Daryaganj, New Delhi-110002 (India)
Ph.: 011-23244078. Fax: 011-23280028
E-Mail: cyberpublicationsdelhi@yahoo.com

TOURISM: MARKETING AND ADVERTISING

V.S. Dahiya

First Edition 2008

Published by :

G.S. Rawat for Cyber Tech Publications
4264/3, Ansari Road, Daryaganj, New Delhi-110002 (India)
Ph.: 011-23244078. Fax: 011-23280028
E-Mail: cyberpublicationsdelhi@yahoo.com

Printed at : **Asian Offset Printers**

Preface

Tourism as an industry is making tremendous headway in many countries of the world including India. Growth of tourism brings benefits to an economy in a number of ways such as generation of income, expansion of employment opportunities, mobilization of foreign exchange, social integration, cultural transformation and development of commerce.

The Ministry of Tourism, Government of India, functions as the nodal agency for the development of tourism within the country and for attracting foreign tourists. It has now come out with a National Tourism Policy which pledges, inter alia, to make tourism and travel an important instrument for sustainable human development, poverty alleviation, and employment generation.

In this highly advanced world every thing whether product or service is hard to sell without advertising and marketing. The present book is designed in such a manner as to bring together service providers in the tourism industry, government officials, policy makers, researchers and academia for sharing experience and generating new knowledge in the thrust area of tourism.

Taking into account the importance of tourism industry, I have taken utmost care in selecting papers for this volume which are focused on new paradigms of tourism marketing, eco-tourism and evil effects of tourism from an international perspective, giving emphasis on Indian environment.

—Author

Contents

1

INDIAN TOURISM: 'INCREDIBLE INDIA'

The caselet gives an overview of the 'Incredible India' campaign undertaken by the Government of India (GoI) to promote tourism in India. It highlights the measures taken by the Tourism Department of India in various countries across the world to promote 'Brand India'. It also deals with the public relations exercise undertaken by the GoI to restore tourists' confidence in view of the tsunami that hit the country in 2004.

Issues: Integrated Marketing Communications in tourism promotion.

INTRODUCTION

Till 2002, Indian tourism was promoted through delegates at the Indian tourist offices located globally. These promotional campaigns were not too effective as the promotional approach was unorganized, varied, and limited by the skills and capabilities of the delegates. Realizing the need for a consistent approach, the Tourism Department of India appointed Ogilvy and Mather (O&M), Delhi, to develop a print campaign and Enterprise Nexus, Mumbai, to create a television commercial. The media account was handled by WPP Group's Maximize India, and Grey Interactive was briefed to work on the official website www.tourismofindia.com.

In September 2002, the Tourism Department unveiled a new campaign called 'Incredible India' to promote Indian tourism globally. The first phase of the campaign, for a period of three months, was jointly funded by the Government of India and Experience India Society, an association of travel agents in India. The campaign focused on the Himalayas, wildlife, yoga, and ayurveda and was widely promoted in the print media, television, and the Internet. The television campaign was telecast on CNN, BBC, and other popular channels across the world.

WAYS TO MARKET TOURISM

India receives three million foreign tourists a year while a small country like Thailand, with much more limited geographic and historical attraction, receives more than three times that number and they plan to double it to 20 million tourists in the next decade.

The importance of tourism is not only the foreign exchange it brings in but, more importantly, in the employment it generates at several locations and in several layers of society — ranging from airline staff to hotel employees and scooter-taxi wallahs.

India is yet to be marketed to its full potential as a tourist destination. Let us explore some possible ways of marketing India in new ways.

The first step in any marketing exercise is to identify the customer and his or her needs and inclinations. Tourism is a leisure occupation for those who can afford it.

The major sources of such tourists are the three richest regions of the world, viz. the US, Western Europe, and Japan. And in those regions, the target groups we have to attract are people who have the time and the money.

These are usually people who have retired and can afford to explore the world outside their own immediate reach. The younger backpackers or student-type tourists are not sufficiently well funded.

Therefore, they are not our primary target group although they should also be encouraged and welcomed to this country as they can be our brand ambassadors to the older generations of their countrymen and one day when they can afford it, they may come back with their own families.

Taking our primary target group of retired people, there is one common characteristic among such people throughout the world. They like to play golf and explore history, religions, and arts, for which they had little time when they were busy with their careers.

So far, the Indian tourism industry has focused on selling ancient, medieval, and Mughal India, the temples and forts of ancient days. This is good but it isn't enough.

We need to explore opportunities for leisure tourism, and for playing games like golf. There are people who will come to enjoy India's winter sun, and so Goa has been marketed, but India has many more beaches.

More recently, Kerala has successfully marketed itself for everything — from the ayurvedic massage to its backwaters. India's hill states can easily attract more tourists than Nepal does, especially now that Nepal is in trouble, but Nepal is much better organised for trekkers and mountain-lovers than Uttaranchal or Himachal Pradesh.

The Japanese and Chinese will willingly do the Buddhist circuit in much greater numbers, if we can organise a pleasant experience for them in Bihar. Then, our colonial history presents its own opportunities.

Fortunately, in my opinion, we as a nation have become confident enough in our own standing and achievements that we can rise above anti-colonial feelings and talk about the colonial period without inhibitions or resentment.

Although the Mughals colonised India and even converted our people to their religion four centuries ago, today we take pride in showing tourists monuments like the Taj Mahal as the pride of India.

With the passage of time, the same is happening to the monuments and cities built by our European colonisers — the Portuguese, the Dutch, the French, and the British.

For a European tourist it is often more interesting to see remnants of the adventurers from their own countries. Even for the Americans, it is easier to relate to such sites as most of them are descendants of Europeans.

Fortunately, we have several such monuments and sites bearing witness to the history of our European colonisers. We should use them to market our country. Take Pondicherry. It has several French remnants, including the use of the French language. In France schoolchildren are still taught about the French empire in India, which consisted of Pondicherry, Mahe, Karaikkal, and Chandannagar.

Of these, Pondicherry is probably the most attractive and easily accessible from Madras. If our tourism ministry produced a film in French about Pondicherry and showed it as an advertisement on French television, it would boost French tourism to India.

From Pondicherry a French tourist can go to Mysore, where Tipu Sultan, an ally of the French, fought the British along with the French. The story of Vasco da Gama, the first European to reach our shores by sea, will be of immense interest to most Europeans.

He was buried in Cochin in a church which is still standing.

But perhaps the people who have most historical connections with India are the British and through them their cousins from the US. The British East India Company began its operations in Madras.

Inside the walls of Fort St George in Madras, there is a small church, St Mary's, where Clive, the founder of the British Empire, was married. St. Thomas Mount and Santhome Cathedral in Madras are other historical monuments from Portuguese times.

The other legacy of the British is the plantations of the Nilgiris on the Eastern side and Munnar on the Western side. The pioneering British planters braved malaria and wild animals to create the rubber, coffee, and tea estates which are totally Indian-owned today. A drive from Ooty and Conoor over the hills to Munnar can combine history with some of the most beautiful sights of nature in India. On the way one can see how wild elephants are captured and trained systematically and humanely to become useful vehicles for the movement of heavy timber in difficult terrain.

There are very few locations in the world where this can be seen. A travel film on this section of India in itself can be a great advertisement for India. The drive from Munnar to Cochin is an essay in the beauty of nature. Tea plantations give way to coffee estates and then to rubber estates as we descend and suddenly we break out into plains with rice fields and coconut groves.

We can end up in some fine hotels, located on the shores of the vast backwaters of Kerala, the like of which one can never see anywhere else in the world.

But perhaps the least exploited among our cities is Mumbai as a creation of the British. Until about 300 years ago, Mumbai was a collection of fishing villages inhabited by Kohlis, who were local fisherfolk.

It was only when it was gifted to the British as part of the dowry of Charles II, who married the Portuguese princess Catherine of Braganza, that Mumbai came to the notice of the British.

They shifted their western base from Surat to this collection of fishing villages, which they discovered were bordering a deep-sea harbour.

They built a fort and a church, as they did everywhere they settled. The church is still in existence as St Thomas Cathedral, the fort gate to which was called Churchgate (after which a whole part of Mumbai is called even today).

But if you ask anyone today where is this church in Churchgate, no one can recognise St Thomas Cathedral as it is dwarfed by high-rise buildings.

The other gates in the fort were Bazargate facing North, and Apollo Gate, leading to Apollo Bunder in the South.

Mumbai Castle, which they inherited from the Portuguese, still exists within the Naval dockyard.

There is a whole treasure trove of British history woven around South Mumbai.

In short, if we were to look at different parts of India against the canvas of the history of the European merchants in India, we can create a whole saga of great interest to Western tourists.

No other country in Asia has this asset and it is time for us to exploit it by marketing this part of our history.

INDIAN TOURISM LAUNCHED AGGRESSIVE MARKETING CAMPAIGN

Department of Tourism has planned a number of measures and events to boost tourism in the country. Since tourist season in the county is about to set in and most of the countries have withdrawn or diluted travel advisories regarding travel to India issued May/June this year after 11th September 2001, these measures will help to project India as an absolutely safe, secure, warm and friendly destination and lead to increased arrivals

ITTM-2002 The 4th International Travel and Tourism Mart is schedules to be held during September 27-29, 2002 at Pragati Maidan. About 400 buyers and sellers representing various streams of tourism, travel and trade from all over the world are expected in the mart. So far, 250 registrations have been made for the participation. The mart will offer an opportunity to showcase various aspects of India tourism and to sell various destinations. Simultaneously, it will also be an occasion for foreign buyers to tap the Indian tourism market. The mart will also be followed by a similar event in Kerala. Foreign participants will also be able to attend the Kerala mart.

Andhra Pradesh, Goa and Uttaranchal are participating as partner States in the ITM while Rajasthan and Tamil Nadu are participating as focus States. As many as 30 States and Union Territories are participating in the Mart. Tafcon Projects is the Event Manager for the mart and it has the support from premier tourism bodies like PATA, WTTC, FHRAI, HAI, TAAI, IATO and IAAPI etc. The ITM will also coincide with celebrations of World Tourism Day on 27th September and the annual convention of the Federation of Hotel and Restaurants Associations, one of the largest bodies of the hospitality industry. Thus, these three days will provide an opportunity to tourism experts to discuss various issues related with tourism.

Eco Tourism Promotion

World Tourism Organisation has declared 2002 as the Year of Eco Tourism and Mountains. In view of this, Department of

Tourism has taken up various activities to create awareness about eco-tourism which include on the spot painting competitions for children in each State capital. The Department of Tourism has provided Rs. 50,000 to each State for this purpose. In Delhi, such competitions will be organized at the Delhi School of Art by Delhi Tourism Development Corporation.

As a unique experiment, the Department of Tourism in collaboration with Uttaranchal Government has invited 22 well known artists from all over the country to paint 'Different Moods of Himalayas' and their perceptions about mountains, during their one week stay at Ananda Resort in the Garhwal in Uttaranchal. Later these paintings have been displayed at the tea lounge of Ashok Hotel Lobby.

Indian Interline Golf Championship

Golf is an eco-sport, popular the world over. To project India as an ideal Golf destination as the Department of Tourism is organizing a 2-day Golf tournament on 28-29 September for senior executives of International Airlines and major tour operators around the world. So far, 61 confirmations have been made for the participation. Most of the expenditure for this activity will be borne by various sponsors from trade and industry.

Global Media Presentation: In a significant initiative, Department of Tourism has invited about 250 foreign media travel writers and tour operators to see for them selves that India is safe, secure and friendly destination and to let them have its first hand experience. These travel writers and tour operators will get an opportunity to see various Indian destinations which ultimately lead to better marketing of these destinations. The Indian hospitality industry along with the Department of Tourism will host these guests. Most of the guests are being provided hospitality include hotel stay by the industry. All these measures being taken are expected to create better understanding and right perspective of Indian tourism in the coming months.

India's travel and tourism market was valued at US$42 billion in 2005, and is growing rapidly. India emerged as the fifth most preferred destination by the world's travellers in a survey conducted across 134 countries. India also figures in the Annual Readers' Travel Awards 2005, which were announced by the prestigious magazine Conde Nast Travellers UK in its September 2005 edition. A 5,000 year history, culture, religion and alternative medicine fascinate both budget and luxury travellers alike.

The Department of Tourism's resolve in promoting Indian tourism has strengthened as it recognises its potential. Tourism in India is the third largest foreign exchange earner, accounting for 2.5% of GDP. It also makes a direct contribution to economy with significant linkages with agriculture, horticulture, handicrafts and construction. The outlay on tourism development rose to Rs7,860 million in 2005/2006, from Rs 3,500 million in 2003/2004, and continued to focus on the "Atithi Devo Bhavah" campaign, targeted at the inbound foreign tourists in the country. Translated literally this means "Guest is God".

Domestic Tourism Driving the Industry

With 390 million Indians on the move in 2005, it is little wonder that it is domestic travellers that sustain the travel and tourism business. Domestic business travel and visiting family/ friends, as well as pilgrimages, contributed to the 13% growth in number of trips within the country that year.

Outbound Gets Interesting

The number of outbound travellers from India grew by 15% to 6.2 million in 2005. This was almost twice the number of arrivals witnessed by the country. A booming economy, with GDP growth of more than 7%, rising disposable incomes, higher aspirations, cheaper air travel to countries such as Malaysia, Thailand and Singapore and better products from the industry enticed Indian travellers. This has prompted a number of global tour operators to enter the Indian tourism market either directly or through strategic alliances.

Arrivals and Tourism Earnings Growth Slow Down

Growth in arrivals and incoming tourism earnings slowed down substantially in 2005, to 14% and 19%, respectively. The slowdown followed a particularly good performance in 2004, with global travel recovering from various health and natural disaster scares in the previous two years. Returning Indians constitute a significant proportion of incoming arrivals and as both the country and long haul travel became more expensive, they chose other holiday destinations instead of returning to their home country.

Destinations with Overseas Indians Top List of Arrivals

The UK and the US lead arrivals into the country. Combined, they accounted for 33% of total arrivals in 2005. The Middle East, including Dubai, the UK and the US were the favourite destinations in terms of departures. Popular new destinations for Indians include Southeast Asian countries such as Singapore, Thailand, Malaysia and Hong Kong. Cheaper airfares and competitive holiday packages have made these favoured vacation spots.

US Popularity Diminishes

The US Patriot Act has led to a number of changes, as the American government becomes more stringent about its visa rules. As a result, there were huge delays and backlogs for visa processing, with some instances of visa call dates for tourist visas being given four months after the travel date. Hence the country's popularity as an outbound destination diminished in 2005, with European destinations, particularly the UK, favoured instead. However, the number of departures to the US still remained ahead of those to the UK.

Budget Airlines New Kid on the Block in Air Travel

At Rs1,103 billion in 2005, India's transportation industry is the largest sector of the travel and tourism industry. The sector outperformed the review period CAGR performance in 2005, with 15% sales value growth. Investment in international quality roads, the launch of low cost carriers as well as the expansion of the railways were responsible for driving growth.

Six new low cost carriers were launched in India in 2005, and there seemed to be room for more. SpiceJet Ltd was the outstanding success during the year. As competition heated up, prices came down, making the Indian consumer the winner in all respects. Promotional fares as low as Rs1 were launched, but this was limited to short periods, as fuel price hikes and taxes made it difficult for companies to sustain these fares. Tier II city routes that were earlier sidelined or ignored were taken note of and serviced. The airline subsector outperformed the growth of the transportation sector as a whole in 2005.

After Low Cost Carriers it is Budget Hotels Next

Travel accommodation in India accounts for only 12% of the travel and tourism industry in value terms. The skewed nature of hotel accommodation in India is evident from the fact that it constituted 5% of the accommodation market in terms of number of outlets, but accounted for 28% of sales value. The hotel subsector achieved growth of 18% in current value terms in 2005, which was driven by increasing demand, notably in business travel. The huge gap between demand and supply of hotel rooms drove up occupancy levels and average room rates (ARRs) to new highs during the review period. Hotels generally cater to foreign visitors, corporate business clients and high-end Indian travellers, as hotel accommodation is out of the reach of the average Indian. Indians are increasingly seeking world-class facilities, such as clean and comfortable accommodation, Internet connection, and perhaps even fitness facilities, at local prices. In response to changing consumer needs, leading luxury and business hotels player Indian Hotels Company Ltd shifted its focus to budget hotels and rolled out the first indiOne hotel, its budget brand, in Bangalore in South India. Interglobe Enterprises signed a joint venture with Accor, in March 2005, to develop budget hotels in India under the brand name Ibis.

The travel retail sector constituted 17% of the travel and tourism industry in 2005, and was the second largest sector, valued at Rs274 billion. With 25% growth in 2005, it was responsible for driving much of the value growth in the overall market. Sensing opportunities in this area, with Indian travellers becoming more Internet savvy, dropping costs of broadband and a general increase in access to information, on-line travel retail intermediary MakemyTrip.com shifted its focus from returning Indians primarily from the American market to Indians within the country.

Low Cost Carriers and Indian Railways Popularise the Internet

E-ticketing and e-travel in India took off as a result of efforts by Indian Railways in late 2004, accompanied by good deals offered by new generation budget airlines, which sell most of their stock through the Internet. An estimated 7,000 tickets with an average price of Rs1,500 each are sold each day on the Indian Railways website. However, in terms of value sales, Internet rail transportation constitutes a lower proportion of the total than air transportation.

Consumers sought out Internet access through various means and made sure they did not get left out of the benefits-usually price discounts. On-line hotel reservations in India have also picked up, but constitute just 3% of the business. According to the Internet and Mobile Association of India, 16% of on-line shoppers spent in the Rs10,000 plus range, including spending on computers, hotel rooms, jewellery, airline tickets and home appliances.

Company-owned sites, as well as specialised travel portals, drew in travellers in thousands. Travel agents also recognised the importance of the Internet as a means to distribute and market various deals, drawing in 7% of business from this medium. Much of it is still, however, not real-time.

Outlook well on Way to Growth

By 2020, the government of India expects travel and tourism to contribute Rs8,500 billion to GDP, almost four times the value in 2005. With successive governments committed to reform, a strong manufacturing sector and a private sector that already has a critical mass that is needed to drive growth, it is unlikely that the strong growth in GDP is likely to be reversed. The rising middle class is also becoming increasingly affluent, mobile, Internet savvy and more sophisticated in terms of what is demanded in terms of tourism products and services, and more importantly the price they are willing to pay for it.

A boom is expected in travel accommodation, as more serviced apartments, budget hotels (2-star category) and highway motels are established.

Significant changes are expected in travel retail, with the arrival of more international players, such as Le Passage and Cox & Kings, particularly in outbound travel. British company Cox & Kings plans to relocate its corporate headquarters from London to Mumbai as a result of its being bought out by its Indian arm in late 2005. Global interest also includes the American millionaire Alfred Ford with plans to set up a Himalayan ski resort. Internet intermediaries are expected to expand significantly and grow the market without significantly adding to volume growth. Rural tourism and medical tourism for inbound tourists will also give rise to new products and services in this sector.

Until recently, not much emphasis had been given to the maintenance and development of the historical and heritage sites in India, which resulted in a large number of tourists staying away from these. However, the Indian government's increasing investment in the upgrading and modernisation of infrastructure will translate into better facilities, amenities and access to the leading tourist attractions and sites.

Internet holds much Promise

According to International Data Corporation (IDC), India is expected to record the highest compound annual growth rate (CAGR), of 84%, among Asia-Pacific countries in e-commerce revenues between 2003 and 2008, exceeding the CAGR of 81% expected in China. It is estimated that travel will account for one third of this. Much of the growth is expected to be driven by intermediaries.

By 2010, India is expected to have 100 million Internet users, with the majority of them aged 25-39. Transportation and accommodation transactions will grow as they seek out newer experiences and get more comfortable with the medium.

Across all the sectors, much higher growth is expected from the Internet in contrast to bricks-and-mortar business operations. 16% of travel retail business in 2010 is expected to be sourced through the Internet, as the nascent dynamic packaging subsector picks up due to the efforts of on-line retailers.

While there is no direct danger of bird flu at the moment, it is definitely a potential threat as India sees a significant number of migratory birds from China, Tibet, Mongolia and Russia. Having said that, India's pharmaceutical industry is more than sufficiently equipped to provide supplies of medicine for the purpose. A significant proportion of India's poultry industry is small scale and scattered, translating to a low level of threat.

UNTAPPED POTENTIAL IN THE MEDICAL TOURISM MARKET

The Indian healthcare market is Rs 15 billion and growing at over 30 per cent every year. Indian private hospitals are increasingly finding a mention in the travel itineraries of foreigners, with the trend of medical tourism catching up in the country. If industry estimates are to be believed, the size of the medical tourism industry stands at Rs 1,200-Rs 1,500 crore (Rs 12-15 billion).

A recent CII-McKinsey study on healthcare says medical tourism alone can contribute Rs 5,000-Rs 10,000 crore (Rs 50-100 billion) additional revenue for upmarket tertiary hospitals by 2012, and will account for 3-5 per cent of the total healthcare delivery market. Compared to countries like the UK or the US, procedures like heart bypass surgery or angioplasty come at a fraction of the cost in India, even though the quality of doctors and medical equipment is comparable to the best in the world.

A heart bypass surgery in India costs USD 3,000-6,000, while in the US it costs between USD 15,000 and USD 40,000. The Indian Health Care Federation (IHCF), an association of the healthcare delivery sector that includes the Escorts Heart Institute, Apollo Hospitals Group, Fortis Healthcare among others and CII, under the leadership of Dr Naresh Trehan, executive director, Escorts Heart Institute and Research Centre (EHIRC), New Delhi have also decided to project India as a major healthcare destination. Even travel agents are aggressively promoting India as a destination for medical tourism. This is a huge, untapped market, not just for therapeutic medical tourism like ayurveda, but also for curative treatment.

The benefit to tourism industry could be of the order of Rs 1,000 crore (Rs 10 billion). Indian NRIs, Asians and tourists from around the world are beginning to realise the potential of modern and traditional Indian medicine. Health and medical tourism is perceived to be one of the fastest growing segments in marketing 'Destination Incredible India' today. While this area has so far been relatively unexplored, we now find that not only the ministry of tourism, Government of India, but also the various state tourism boards are all promoting health and medical tourism as a segment with tremendous potential for future growth. Indian hospitals have also realised the potential of this niche market and have begun to tailor their services for foreign visitors. Visitors, especially from the west and the middle-east, find Indian hospitals as an affordable and a viable option rather than grappling with health insurance and national medical systems in their native lands.

- Areas where Indian healthcare excels
- Clinical outcomes being on par with the world's best centres.
- Internationally qualified and experienced doctors.
- Technology edge.
- Competitive costs-1/5th to 1/10th of costs in the west.
- Quality of service.
- No waiting time.
- Patient-centric care.
- Exotic experience, increasing popularity as a tourist destination.
- Eastern healthcare wisdom along with the expertise of western medicine.
- Areas where Indian healthcare has to focus
- Accreditation norms to be adopted by all major hospitals.
- Hospitals must conform to a code of ethics.
- Provision of a uniform price band for major specialities especially for health insurance majors.
- Handling of medico-legal issues.

Working with Indian tourism ministry and tour operators to promote medical tourism overseas. Cross-border travel for healthcare reasons is still a highly disorganised movement, but countries are slowly waking up to its potential. In some places, the governments have taken a lead. In others, travel agents specialising in medical tourism are driving the trend.

In India, private hospitals are trying to attract patients on their own and by showcasing Indian healthcare overseas through CII-IHCF led overseas missions. Developed nations will benefit majorly as costs and waiting time come down for a significant chunk of their population. Developing countries benefit through medical tourism as it brings in revenues and provides the right spur to improve their overall healthcare sector, apart from reducing brain drain in their medical fraternities. Least developed countries, too, benefit as they lack facilities for cutting-edge treatment. The situation was so dismal that in 2002, the National Health Services(NHS) in UK started a pilot scheme for 'overseas treatment' to see if surgery services abroad could be bought to shorten the waiting lists. The project focused mainly on facilities available in the European Union.

Meanwhile, many British patients take the initiative to seek their own treatment abroad without waiting for the NHS to sort out its problems. A Rs 15-billion-plus market growing at over 30 per cent per year throws up huge opportunities for anyone smart enough to tap it. Thus, India not only offers world class cardiac bypass surgery, hip replacements, organ transplants, but also cosmetic, dental surgery and vision correction etc and alternative healthcare which is a significant niche opportunity.

Healthcare insurers in the developed countries are aware of the fact that the option of medical treatment in countries like India could help them reduce premiums and offer options to people who are currently uninsured. Over the next few years, insurance firms are expected to provide a fillip to the medical tourism business in India.

Big Tourism Marketing Push in the U.S.

India's Ministry of Tourism has launched an aggressive advertising campaign in the United States, designed to lure more American tourists. The tagline: Incredible India. India adopted a new National Tourism Policy in 2002, in order to "position India as a global brand to take advantage of the burgeoning global travel trade and the vast untapped potential of India as a destination." The National Tourism Policy "acknowledges the critical role of private sector with government working as a pro-active facilitator and catalyst."

The award-winning Incredible India! campaign has been aimed at persuading affluent travelers from the US, Europe, the Asia Pacific and the Middle East to visit India.

According to this report, the Incredible India campaign going forward will continue to target the US, Canada, the Asia Pacific region (including the Middle East and Australia) and Europe, and the Indian government Ministry of Tourism has budgeted Rs 75-80 crore for the international advertising campaign. One Indian crore is equivalent to the number 10 million, so 75-80 crore rupees is 750-800 million rupees-or $16.4-$17.5 million in U.S. currency at current currency conversion rates.

The media mix will include television, press and outdoor advertising.

The ministry has decided to use various popular sites such as the Times Square in New York on New Year's Eve (where a huge crowd tends to gather) or outdoor sites that have been booked near prominent international airports such as London, Paris, Dubai and Singapore.

Besides outdoor and print, this year Ministry of Tourism has also included television in its media plan, which is also expected play a crucial role. As far as television goes, Incredible India ads will run on major international channels in various markets. Some of these channels include BBC, CNN, Discovery (including D Max in Germany), National Geographic Channel, Sky News, Fox, Travel Channel (in Germany and France) and Euro News (in Europe).

The press plan is that there will be more emphasis on magazines than on newspapers. Within the magazine genre, lifestyle, travel, business and consumer magazines will be targeted.

According to the U.S. Department of Commerce Office of Travel & Tourism Industries, the number of tourists visiting the United States from India-308,845-was down 12 percent from the 344,926 who visited in 2004.

Although India is not currently one of the United States' largest sources of international visitors-it would rank around 14th, on par with Venezuela-the number of people from India visiting the U.S. has grown in recent years, from 228,000 in 1998. And India, a pro-Western multi-cultural democracy with its huge population and middle class, would seem to offer a huge potential market that could be reached by an American tourism marketing push.

But the United States government currently does no tourism marketing in India.

2

STATE ENDEAVOURS

LAKSHADWEEP

One of the world's most spectacular tropical island systems, Lakshadweep, with an area of 32 square kilometres, is an archipelago consisting of 12 atolls, three reefs and five submerged banks. It is comprised of ten inhabited islands, 17 uninhabited islands, four newly formed islets and five submerged reefs. The islands are surrounded by 4,200 square kilometres of lagoon rich in marine wealth.

An extremely fragile eco-system supports Lakshadweep's ecological and cultural heritage. The inhabited islands are Kavaratti, Agatti, Amini, Kadmat, Kiltan, Chetlat, Bitra, Andrott, Kalpeni and Minicoy. They are located 220 to 440 kms away from the coastal city of Kochi in Kerala, in the Arabian Sea. More than 93 per cent of the population who are indigenous, are Muslims and majority of them belong to the Shafi School of the Sunni Sect. Malayalam is spoken in all the islands except Minicoy where people speak Mahl which is written in Divehi script and is spoken in Maldives also.

The marine life of the sea is quite elaborate and difficult to condense. The commonly seen vertebrates are cattle and poultry. Oceanic birds generally found in Lakshadweep are Tharathasi (Sterna fuscata) and Karifetu (Anous solidus). They are generally found in one of the uninhabited islands known as Pitti. This island has been declared as a bird sanctuary.

The money cowrie (cypraea monita) are also found in abundance in the shallow lagoons and reefs of the islands. Other cypraeds found here are cypraca talpa and cyprea maculiferra. Among crabs, the hermit crab is the most common. Colourful coral fish such as parrot fish (Callyedon sordidus), Butterfly fish (chaetodon auriga), Surgeon fish (acanthurus lineotus) are also found in plenty.

With fishing, coconut cultivation and coir twisting being the predominant occupations of the region, tourism is fast emerging as a major industry.

COMING OF AGE

Lakshadweep has consciously followed a middle path between tourism promotion and environmental conservation. The environmental impact of coastal tourism is carefully monitored. Steps have been taken to promote tourism in a manner consistent with ecological concerns.

To avoid pressure on the ecological environment, tourism promotion has been synchronised with the carrying capacity of the islands. Though all the islands are endowed with the beauty of coral reefs, sandy beaches, unpolluted and clear water and hospitable settings, most of these differ in terms of facilities and services offered. Some have been promoted for diving and water sports while others have been developed so that people enjoy the charm of relaxation and natural enjoyment. Due to scarcity of land area, the administration's policy has been to promote water-based tourism where the motto, admire but don't exploit the natural beauty, is followed with commitment.

Due to the dispersed nature and small sizes of the islands, they have been forced to import almost all requirements. Lakshadweep has looked at this constraint as an asset and is encouraging quality tourism rather than mass or quantity tourism. This has the added advantage of having minimal impact on the natural and cultural environment.

The thrust is therefore on an extremely low volume, high value added specialised tourism.

Going the Distance

The objective and policies with regard to tourism promotion are looked after by the Tourism Department and a society named Society for Promotion of Recreational Tourism and Sports

(SPORTS) which is the tourism promotion Agency of Lakshadweep Administration.

SPORTS: THE DRIVER OF LAKSHADWEEP TOURISM

Sports (Society for Promotion of Nature Tourism and Sports), a registered Society established in 1982, is the nodal agency for promotion of tourism in Lakshadweep. Lakshadweep Administration has also recognised Sports as the implementing agency for various tourism activities in the islands.

The organisation has a number of Beach Resorts in Lakshadweep. At present there are six islands open for tourism viz. Minicoy, Kavaratti, Kadmat, Kalpeni, Agatti and Bangaram. Of these three islands viz. Bangaram, Agatti and Kadmat are open for international tourists. Sports has leased out Bangaram Beach Resorts to private entrepreneurs for operation. The resorts in the four other islands except Agatti are being managed by Sports. The carrying capacity of each island has been assessed depending on potable water, density of population in the islands and other available resources.

Day excursion trips are encouraged and organised by Sports so that the tourists do not deplete already limited resources. In such trips, tourists stay on board the ship and during the day time, they get down to the island for sightseeing etc. The ship MV Tipu Sultan can carry a maximum number of 160 tourists per trip. On an average, 30 such packages are operated in a year.

The main source of income for Sports is operation of tour packages to different islands. For this a number of packages are operated to Kavaratti/ Kalpeni/ Minicoy/ Kadmat.

Following are the tour packages undertaken by Sports.

(a) Coral Reef (Kavaratti, Minicoy, Kalpeni)

(b) Marine Wealth Awareness Programme (Kadmat)

(c) Tarathashi (Kavaratti)

(d) Swaying Palm (Minicoy)

(e) Coconut Grove (Kalpeni)

(f) Scuba Diving Package (Kadmat)

Apart from these, private cottages at Minicoy and Kalpeni are also marketed by Sports. Over the years a number of tourists have visited the islands in different packages. The tourism packages are totally dependent on the ships-MV Tipu Sultan and MV Bharath Seema. Shipping services and tourism performance in Lakshadweep are interrelated. Due to the island's topography, shipping services are vital to tourism.

Hence for smooth operation of the packages, a proper ship service is a prerequisite. Sports has started transporting tourists by new ships MV Amindivi and M.V. Minicoy.

All the focal islands are surrounded by vast lagoons ideal for water sports. Sports has established a number of water sport facilities such as a water sports institute in Kadmat, along with kayaking, canoeing, windsurfing, yachting and glass bottomed boats in almost all the focal islands. Scuba diving facilities with competent instructors are available at Bangaram and Kadmat. A new scuba diving centre has opened at Kavaratti also.

As an organisation committed to the welfare of the people of Lakshadweep, Sports has employed around 72 persons in different capacities directly and has generated many employment opportunities indirectly. Further whatever items available are purchased locally so that the local population is benefited.

During 2001-2002, around 2992 domestic tourists and 871 international tourists visited the islands. Despite many bottlenecks, Sports has been able to generate a decent revenue for the year 2001-2002. The cost of operation of the package has also come down considerably to around 33 per cent against 60 per cent during previous years. During current year, the total turnover stood at Rs 2.98 crore. Sports has undertaken catering on board MV Amindivi and MV Minicoy.

There are 6 units of Sports at Kalpeni, Minicoy, Kavaratti, Kadmat, Andrott and Kochi. All the units in the islands except Andrott are looking after the activities of the tourists in the respective islands. Andrott Unit has recently been created for coordination of the activities connected with the running of the hostel mess of Mahatma Gandhi Sr Sec School Hostel. The

Kochi unit has been functioning for booking, coordination and as the procurement branch of the Sports.

ECO-FRIENDLY INITIATIVES

Some of the initiaves by the Lakshadweep Tourism Department to promote eco-friendly tourism are as follows:

- Most tourist accommodations have thatched huts and tiled roof All tourism properties have largely PVC solar streetlights. Tourists are encouraged to live in harmony with nature.
- Use of compact fluorescent lamps
- Electric power supplied by solar plants during the day
- The islanders are educated to adopt eco-friendly ways like burning of coconut husks to tackle mosquitoes and pests instead of pesticide

Bio-mass gasfires is proposed to be set up at Kavaratti on an experimental basis to utilise coconut waste and eventually generate electricity at a cheaper rate and also save the environment from pollution

- A film is shown to the tourist once they board the ship on way to Lakshadweep islands informing them about the islands, its environment, the coral reefs and its management, the ban on picking up of corals, plastics etc. and ways to keep the islands clean and enjoy the beauty without disturbing or destroying it.
- Being a restricted area, entry is allowed only after issue of permits and therefore overcrowding in the islands is easily taken care of
- Fishing in Lakshadweep is carried out by pole and line method only. It is acknowledged all over the world that the pole and line method is the most eco friendly method of tuna fishing.
- Islanders are being trained in scuba diving so that they not only know about marine wealth but also contribute in maintaining the ecology of the islands and work as eyes and ears of the administration.

The administration has initiated steps to document the bio-diversity of the island with the help of the MS Swaminathan Foundation and the local staff.

- The Lakshadweep Building Development Board has been constituted to import and provide construction materials so that locals do not collect it from the island and damage the ecology.

THRUST ON ECOLOGICAL TOURISM

The ecological policy thrust is very much evident from the fact that only 3587 tourists visited the islands during the financial year 1998-99. The policies and guidelines prepared by the Union Territory of Lakshadweep to promote sustainable tourism can be categorised into four groups.

1. Impacts on physical environment
2. Impact on ecological environment
3. Impacts on human use values, and
4. Impacts on quality of life values.

Physical Environment

In order not to adversely affect the physical environment, the administration's emphasis is to promote tourism only in those islands that can sustain it. The facilities there are developed in such a way that they do not result in loss of bio-diversity. No development is permitted in geologically unstable zones. An adequate buffer zone has been provided between development areas and the existing shoreline. The construction of high-rise structures are banned. It has been ensured that construction materials and methods are compatible with environment and height, shape and location of buildings merge with the natural vegetation.

The administration has imposed a total ban on the removal of any material from the coral reef and lagoons. Construction of structures that enhance the erosion process has been totally regulated, the administration has taken steps to stop the erosion by identifying the danger areas and has taken up anti-sea erosion measures like creating rubble walls, concrete block spurs, tetra pods, sea walls etc. All new buildings are required to have a rainwater harvesting system. Community rainwater harvesting systems are also being set up.

Ecological Environment

Keeping in view the fragile ecology of the islands, the tourism promotion policy has been tuned to protecting the ecology. Lakshadweep in totality has been declared a 'no plastic zone'. With the help of voluntary organisations, a scheme of collection of all non-biodegradable wastes is being carried out. The soil of Lakshadweep is porous, low in organic matter and water-holding capacity. Hence the use of chemicals pose a threat to the ecology. To counter this problem, it has been decided since 1997 to minimise the use of chemical fertilisers and switch over to organic manure. Coral reefs form one of the primary tourist attractions. The corals are damaged either intentionally or out of ignorance, primarily due to fishing activities, besides tourism related activities and seawater pollution. In order to protect the coral reefs, the administration has regulated entry and exit of boats in the lagoon area.

Human use Values

It has been the constant endeavour of the administration to preserve the human use values which includes water supply, beach access, landscape and natural beauty.

Quality of Life Values

Quality of life, particularly of the local community, is another area that is affected by the growth of tourism. The impacts are related to health, and socio-cultural aspects. Inadequate and inefficient solid and liquid waste disposal system poses a health hazard for the locals. In order to counter the pressure, the tourism department has laid more emphasis on promoting day tourism where tourists visit the islands in the day and travel during the night in ship. Only small resorts are allowed to be set up.

Power supply (especially during the day) to the resorts are through grid interactive solar plants. These have already been set up at Kadmat and Bangaram and are being installed at

Minicoy and Agatti. To minimise sound pollution, the administration has initiated action for the procurement of silent generators. In order to protect the socio-cultural fabric of islands, development of accommodations are encouraged away from local habitation areas and from uninhabited islands. Prohibition is enforced in all islands except Angaram.

All tourism development schemes are first analysed from environmental impact point of view and only if they meet the norms is implementation taken up.

Interactive Ventures

The administration also conducts training courses, workshops, seminars, sports festivals/ competitions and studies to promote sustainable development tourism. Some of them are:

- Workshops organised for employees of Lakshadweep Tourism in collaboration with the Department of Science, Technology and Environment appraised by District Judge, Lakshadweep, and magistrate dealing with the Environmental Protection Act.
- Workshops organised for interaction of the Tourism Officers with Joint Secretary, Ministry of Environment and Forest. National Seminar on status and protection of coral reef was conducted at Kadmat.
- Under the auspices of global Coral Reef Monitoring Network South Asia a workshop on socio-economic monitoring for coral reef was conducted in September 1998.
- The Administration with the help of National Institute of Oceanography, National Remote Sensing Agency, Centre for Marine and Fishery Research Institute and Department of Ocean Development, besides the Ministry of Environment and Forests is formulating a 25 year strategy and Action Plan for protection of coral reefs and lagoons.
- As the islands have a very fragile ecology, it is important that people living here and those visiting the islands realise the importance of preserving the system. With

this aim regular awareness programs are organised besides imparting information through pamphlets and brochures.

- Project for cleaning the lagoons by involving non-governmental organisations (NGOs) is in place. NGOs have been set up with the idea of cleaning the lagoons of various non-bio-degradable wastes that have accumulated for the past so many years. The project would be implemented in a phased manner with the help of financial assistance from the administration and Ministry of Environment and Forests.
- Pollution Awareness Committees have been constituted in all the islands to detect and monitor any environmental degradation. The Committee would also work for the general enhancement of the quality of environment.
- An international seminar unanimously recommended the case of Lakshadweep for world heritage status as a natural site. UNESCO in Paris has given a positive response and an application to this effect is being sent through Government of India.

TOURISM POLICY-SALIENT FEATURES

- Preserve fragile ecological and environmental structure
- Preserve local culture and social fabric
- High value and low volume tourism
- Sustainable tourism based on the "carrying capacity" of islands
- Sea based ship tourism for larger numbers
- Air based airline/helicopter tourism for high value tourists only
- Local features:
    * No violation of prohibition
    * Promotion of folk art and culture
    * Eco friendly water sports, mainly non mechanised
    * Promotion of scuba-diving.

* Promotion of Solar Power and Biological toilets.
* Collection of non biodegradable waste
* Disposal of kitchen waste in open sea
* Promotion of smokeless "Chula" in kitchen
* Discouragement to diesel generation
* Installment of Silent Generators to avoid noise pollution.

- Training of staff-To upgrade tourism management skills. Capacity building with local resource personals to run the Scuba-diving centers.
- Privatisation of facilities on stringent terms: Land lease rent, royalty and percentage of gross turnover.

Future Stock

The Lakshadweep administration has taken a holistic view of tourism development. The idea is to promote tourism as a composite package, developing all facilities and infrastructure required to promote eco-friendly tourism; not only provide accommodation but arrange transportation from and/to main land by ship/air, catering facilities, recreational facilities, water sports, scuba diving, boating, wind surfing etc.

It is slowly going in for privatisation of tourist infrastructure in a big way. Private investment is being encouraged, albeit on very cautious terms.

The facilities in two islands i.e. Bangaram and Agatti are being managed by private agencies. Private divers also run the scuba diving school at Kadmat. It is proposed to give facilities located in other islands, Minicoy and Kadmat, also to private entrepreneurs and encourage the local islanders to man the scuba diving schools.

The scope for water sports activities is also being exploited fully. It is proposed to develop Lakshadweep as a water sports destination, allowing only non-mechanised water sports. A water sports centre is being set up at Minicoy where a 20-bed tourist home has been constructed. Complementary to this, health club facilities are also being provided at Minicoy and Kadmat.

The thrust is on promoting ship-based tourism for Indian nationals at affordable rates. Besides ship, Indian Airlines has started six flights from Kochi to Agatti. There is also a proposal to start flights from Goa in the near future.

Two new ships have been ordered for local passengers. They will accommodate 150 passengers, so that more room is available for tourists in the two existing carriers, namely, MV Tipu Sultan and MV Bharat Seema.

New properties are also being developed, keeping in mind the carrying capacity of the islands and without adversely affecting the ecology. The resort at Minicoy and tent accommodation at Kadmat are the best examples.

Emphasis is also being laid on developing tours on glass bottom boats, wind surfing, sailing etc. at Kavaratti Minicoy, Kadmat and Bangaram. Glass bottom boats have been provided at Agatti, Kavaratti, Kadmat, Kalpeni and Minicoy besides Bangaram.

The important tourist islands are also being connected as circuits in a new tourism package. Additionally, a proposal is also being examined to include Goa as a tourist circuit and to acquire a dedicated cruise ship for tourists.

The High Power Committee constituted by the Government of India to study about the shipping requirements of Union Territories has recommended the acquisition of a dedicated cruise ship for tourists at a cost of Rs 50 crore.

The administration has already started taking action on this. In the Xth plan provision for acquisition of cruise ship has been included.

Some of the other plans for the Union Territory as listed by Dr M S Sayed Ismail Koya, director-Information, Publicity and Tourism are as follows:

- Setting up of dive centres in more islands since the Lakshadweep islands are one of the best diving spots in the world. At present, diving facilities are available at Bangaram, Kadmat and Kavaratti. Recently the administration of the Lakshadweep has decided to establish more dive centres at Agatti and Minicoy.

- Development of the islands of Cheriyam, Thinnkara and Suhali Validyakara for international tourism and opening of more islands of domestic tourism. At present, only four islands are opened for domestic tourism. They are Kavaratti, Kalpeni, Kadmat and Minicoy.
- Interested islanders are being trained in Scuba Diving for enabling them to contribute in maintaining the ecology of the islands and to work as watch and ward of this administration. One diving centre has been started at Kavaratti and more diving centres will be opened in the focal islands in the near future.

RAJASTHAN—THE DESERT ROSE

Rajasthan, a state replete with beauty and valour, is a land of marvelous havelis, magnificent forts, opulent palaces and exquisite handicraft. Heritage is the essence of the state.

Tourism has always been Rajasthan's mainstay. The state has retained its medieval flavours. Its cities are composed of variety of atractions. Ajmer is a major pilgrim centre for Hindus and Muslims, Bharatpur is a popular bird sanctuary, Bikaner is a citadel of culture and camels, Chittaurgarh is a city that echoes with tales of romance and valour, Jaipur is the pink city, Jaisalmer flaunts the glory of the golden fort, Mount Abu is a pleasant retreat set amidst lush forested hills while Udaipur is the lake city.

The government has also played a pivotal role in tourism promotion. Interrestingly the state has got publicity thorugh sheer luck. Despite low-key publicity campaign, word of mouth has been enough to give Rajasthan its renown.

Paving the Way for the Future

Rajasthan tourism's direction is toward making it a 'people's industry'. With the private sector's assistance, the growth rate of the tourism industry in the state has been phenomenal in the last few years. The annual rate of growth for domestic tourism has been seven per cent and international tourists registered a five per cent growth. Efforts are on to facilitate the flow of institutional finances for increasing hotel and tourism units in Rajasthan. NRIs are also being asked to take interest in the projects.

A special cell to facilitate and assist entrepreneurs willing to set up tourism-related projects in the state is the department of tourism's latest idea. A mechanism will be provided to process loan applications for the tourism sector at a single window at the Rajasthan Tourism Development Corporation (RTDC) level, where officers from banks, TFCI, RFC, RIICO will be available as and when required to assist those who are willing to establish their ventures. Besides, there will be a special cell in the Bureau of Industrial Promotion (BIP) to process and expedite the projects. RTDC will also associate itself in establishing tourism-related ventures in the 'assisted sector' by selective equity participation. At present, the state receives about 0.59 million of the 2.3 million foreign tourists, who visit India annually. Over 50 lakh domestic tourists, also visit the state annually. The world famous golden triangle has put Jaipur on the world tourism map, therefore, 60 per cent of international tourists visiting India, visit the state too.

A Palace on Air, on the lines of the Palace on Wheels train that takes tourists to eight destinations, is also being envisaged. By the scheme, a luxury chartered aircraft would take tourists to five-six destinations in the state. Though, it is still in its initial stages, a tie-up is planned with the domestic carrier, Indian Airlines.

Subsequently, in a significant move to protect tourists' interests, the Rajasthan government has planned to enact the Tourism Regulation and Promotion Act (TRPA). This Act was conceptualised to bolster the image of Rajasthan tourism which had been tarnished following unfair and misleading practices by some elements in the state's hospitality and travel trade. At present, TRPA is being framed and discussed at several forums. Once the TRPA comes into place, there would be a substantial reduction in the malpractices.

By this Act, it will be optional for hospitality and trade organisations to register with the department but only those who register will be granted official recognition. TRPA is the fallout of the new state tourism policy, which clearly states that a law must be enacted to protect tourists' interests. Analysts are optimistic that promulgation of TRPA will put an end to unethical practices and give a fillip to Rajasthan's reputation as a premier shopping destination.

One of the best things to happen to Rajasthan has been the much acclaimed Palace on Wheels concept. It is today the USP and 'cash cow' of RTDC. Despite the worldwide slump following the 9/11 attacks, Rajasthan Tourism Development Corporation (RTDC) managed to stem the tide and slashed the rates substantially to Rs 10,000 a night per person.

Revealed Mukesh Saxena, manager, RTDC: "Due to the social and political turmoil witnessed in India over the last few months, the Palace on Wheels, our principal tourism product, has been adversely hit, registering cancellations amounting to almost 50 per cent of its occupancy. Which is why, we decided to temporarily change our target market from inbound tourist to the domestic tourist."

Other plans include the continuation of a major marketing campaign across the country besides participating at all leading travel and tourism marts. In order to increase tourist inflow from South India, Indian Airlines has been asked to start direct flights from Trivandrum, Chennai and Hyderabad. It must be remembered that Rajasthan was also one of the first states to start the tourism police concept in the country. But it is at present limited to Jaipur. In order to give adequate protection to tourists, this facility is being planned to extend to two other destinations shortly. The next on line is the new train to be launched by RTDC. This tourist train, run in a joint collaboration with Indian Railways, will ply on the Delhi-Jaipur-Shekawati-Bikaner-Delhi sector, similar to the Palace on Wheels. Plans are also afoot to merge RTDC and RSHC, and form a single corporation.

Getting the Tourism Act Together

In a zealous commitment to enhance the development of tourism in Rajasthan and at the same time attract private participation, the Rajasthan government had conceptualised a new pragmatic policy taking into account the changing socio-economic and investment scenario in the state and the emerging trends in the tourism sector.

The tourism policy has been formulated to increase employment opportunities, especially in rural areas for unemployed rural youth. The highlights of the policy would include:

- Optimum utilisation of rich tourist resources of the state in order to attract maximum number of domestic and international tourists.
- To facilitate the growth of tourism in the states so that the private sector contributes significantly in the development of tourism in Rajasthan.
- Preservation of rich bio-diversity, natural, historical, architectural and cultural heritage of Rajasthan with special emphasis on conservation of historical monuments in Rajasthan.
- To develop a ready market for the rich and varied handicrafts and cottage industries of Rajasthan so as to ensure welfare of artisans/artists.
- To promote inter-cultural understanding through religious/pilgrim tourism and fairs and festivals.
- To promote socio-economic development of Rajasthan through tourism with special thrust on backward areas.
- To make tourism a 'people's industry' in the state.
- To open new vistas in tourism like adventure tourism, eco-tourism, camel/horse safaris, river and canal cruise, house boats in Rajasthan (Palace-On-Waves), educational tourism, caravan tourism and village tourism.

Other areas for develolment include rural tourism in order to generate employment opportunities in rural areas. For this purpose Paryatan Rozgar Yojana was launched along with the active participation of Panchayati Raj Institutions. It has also been decided to use electronic, print and cyber media for aggressive marketing of Rajasthan as a premiere tourism destination. It has also decided to establish a synergy between tourism and handicrafts and to market them through Haat Bazaar and Shilpgrams. Policy directions will be obtained through policy directions from the state tourism advisory board constituted under the chairmanship of the state's chief minster.

Infrastructure

With the announcement of the tourism policy, the government has recognised tourism infrastructure to be of prime importance. As per the policy, the government as well as the private sector will look at jointly helping in infrastructure development. While the state has to play a catalytic role in some sectors, there will be an endeavour to encourage private sector participation in developing tourism infrastructure. In order to develop infrastructure, the government will prepare an area-based master plan outlining the infrastructure necessary in each such area. Efforts will also be made to dovetail external assistance, central assistance, and state plan resources along with private investment to achieve goals set in the master plan The plan will be based on the potential of each destination for development of tourism. An investment plan will be evolved from this master plan which then be translated into an annual action plan.

The private sector would also be invited to participate in developing state-owned infrastructure. The government is also looking at enhancing tourism products in the form of promotion of handicrafts and cottage industries. Rajasthan has a rich and varied heritage of handicrafts, handlooms, and other products, which are appreciated and purchased by tourists visiting the state. Efforts will be made to improve direct access of tourists to artisans who produce these goods. To improve their marketing, RTDC will develop shopping arcades in their existing properties and provide space for artisans to display and market their products. Efforts will also be made to set-up Shilpgrams at various tourist destinations with the assistance of Development Commissioner (Handicrafts), Rajasthan Small Industries Corporation (RAJSICO) etc. A handicraft museum would also be set-up. Heritage tourism would be another focus in the policy since the state abounds with some of the best forts and palace in the country. The government will encourage the preservation, conservation and upkeep of such heritage properties and selectively open some of them for being developed into hotels/tourist complex.

The state will also encourage private investment in developing ancient buildings and heritage properties as tourist resorts. The corporate sector would also be invited to join hands with the government in conservation of heritage monuments in the state.

Subsequently, based on these policy guidelines various departments of the state government would formulate detailed action plans to implement the decisions and to achieve the objective of the tourism policy. Those departments which are directly associated with the tourism sector would also issue office orders in a time-bound manner to ensure compliance of the policy guidelines and decisions contained in the departmental action plan.

Scaling New Heights

With an already well-placed tourism policy that concentrates both on domestic as well as international tourists, Rajasthan is all set to take on the international arena with great gusto. The department is all geared up to present this magnificent state to the world at the upcoming World Travel Mart in London. Revealed the newly appointed Rajeeva Swarup, MD and commissioner of tourism, Rajasthan Tourism Development Corporation (RTDC), "Our plans for WTM is nothing spectacular. We plan to project every aspect of the state right from our USP, the Palace on Wheels, to our inherent strength, which is heritage tourism. Having taken a 30 square metre space at the exhibition, our main objective would be to also introduce our wild life packages and other packages as well."

Swarup disclosed his future plans: "My plans include making the best of the season, cashing in on the domestic tourist potential of the state and certainly introducing more affordable packages in future."

GOA

Goa exudes a very divine feel like no other place, there are churches practically in every corner. The most revered of the lot amongst Catholics is the Basilica of Bom Jesus, that is renowned the world-over. It is a World Heritage Monument. The reason for its popularity is the remains of St Francis Xavier, that is kept in a silver casket and enshrined in this particular church. It has been dedicated to the Infant Jesus.

This apart, the government and tourism department is now highlighting the temples of Goa like the Mahalasa, Mangueshi, Mahadev, Saptakoteshwar and Vithal Mandir.

Moving on to a topic close to my heart-food, Goan cuisine is as famous as their interest for poetry, painting and music. There is a lot of passion in every Goan art. Can one visit Goa and not try the Cashew and Feni, impossible. Goans have elevated cooking to a delicate art, thereby evolving a unique cuisine, so distinct to the state and people. However, the pride of place goes to the seafood with a host of fresh varieties on offer to travellers. Goan seafood satisfies the most discerning gourmet. There is another facet of Goa not to be missed-the Carnival-a three-day period of merry-making and revelry. Having witnessed a few, the Carnival, I can endorse, has the most enchanting views which includes the grand float parades and decorated traditional troupes performing on the roads. All said and done, Goa is by far a year round holiday destination worth a visit.

Looking Beyond the Beaches

The surf, sand and the sea, add a dash of Portuguese legacy, 'susegad' culture and lace it with 'booze' at dirt cheap prices, voila! you are guaranteed hordes of tourists. Goa's beaches have made a major impact on the world tourism scene and the state has certainly done a great job marketing itself so far. However, both the quantity and the quality of tourism in Goa is losing a little sheen and the reason is clear, for too many years they have put all their eggs in the beach basket. All that is changing.

One of the market leaders in the tourism industry in India, Goa has subtly reinvented itself as a destination. 'Go Goa 365 Days A Year' is the new innovative punch line for the state, part of the aggressive marketing campaign aimed at enhancing its brand image as the most versatile destination in the country.

A whole New Face

The hinterland of Goa is quite different from coastal Goa. Tourists world over have been attracted to the Portuguese-influenced customs and traditions of the coastal people of Goa.

This is Goa's USP and Goa Tourism Development Corporation (GTDC) is now using this image to attract tourists. The department of tourism has prepared a master plan for strategic development of tourism with Rs 13-14 crore utilised exclusively for marketing and promotional activities. This is besides the budgetary allocation.

The 2002-03 budgetary allocation which has increased to Rs 21.92 crore, is almost five times compared to the previous budget, has also provided the requisite fillip. Not only has the budget been increased multifold, but also industry status to all tourism-related ancillary and support services has been planned by the state.

The budget has also proposed to co-opt the private sector as associates in infrastructure development and marketing campaigns. Proposing a corpus fund for marketing, the government has announced its intent to contribute twice the amount of capital received from the private sector, subject to a ceiling of Rs five crore. In addition, the budget has also made special provision of Rs 50 crore for infrastructure like roads and other related developmental works, keeping requirements of the tourism industry in mind. This could thus really do away with several irritants of tourists like transport, water shortage or power shutdowns.

"In Goa, tourism has already been accorded industry status last year and with the new budget outlay, we plan to promote Goa as an ideal and safe tourist destination, through aggressive marketing and promotion. Besides beach tourism, Goa is making keen efforts to develop eco-tourism by making special budgetary provision and developing interior green spots like waterfalls, sanctuaries and lakes. Infrastructural development for adventure tourism along the coast as well as the equally magnificent interior hilly areas are also in the pipeline" says N Suryanarayan, the state tourism director.

According to Suryanarayan, the tourism department is entirely tuned towards promoting comprehensive development of tourism in the state. "We are making an all out effort to promote unconventional tourism products like backwaters, heritage houses, eco-tourism and a host of other innovative packages designed to lure in each and every strata of our target segment. Considering the kind of reputation we enjoy in the tourism sector, we will certainly be the first choice for every kind of tourist," he claimed.

The budget also makes tourists' stay and food much cheaper than earlier, rather than increasing taxation to generate revenue for the tourism sector. The luxury tax on accommodation has been reduced from 12 to 8 per cent, besides reduction of sales tax on cooked food and non-alcoholic beverages from 10 to 8 per cent and on LPG from 20 to 8 per cent.

"I may incur a loss of around Rs six crore annually due to this exercise, but ultimately it would accrue more income due to more business in more areas", stated Manohar Parikar, tourism minister for state. He also quoted figures of a 21 per cent rise in luxury tax collection last year due to such a tax reduction exercise.

Suryanarayan claims that the state contributed Rs 1,250 crore in the form of foreign exchange to the government of India in the year 1999-2000. This according to him is possibly going to increase substantially in the coming years owing to the overall improvement in the tourism infrastructure and the diverse products offered by Goa tourism. In order to attract up-market tourists, the state government will also be sprucing up their existing resources and adding five new deluxe luxury hotels, this year.

The other noteworthy and innovative scheme undertaken by the government of Goa at the behest of the Union Ministry of Tourism is to preserve/maintain the heritage houses that are over 200 years old. Through its 'Go Goa 365 Days A Year', the state government, is planning to exploit a previously untapped resource. The state plans to upgrade the heritage houses with modern amenities and open it for tourists, either for accommodation purposes or as a heritage site of archeological importance.

"Inbound tourism in Goa has gone down by 20 per cent since September last year, while domestic tourism has registered a growth of 18 per cent which is very positive. An increasing numbers of domestic tourists have urged us to reinvent Goa as a tourism product highlighting features with historical and architectural importance. With over a hundred heritage homes it only seems apt that we promote heritage tourism in Goa," says Suryanarayan.

The heritage house scheme has been take up by the Government of Goa at the behest of Government of India, Ministry of Tourism, to ensure that heritage houses of Goan architecture which are more than 200 years old are preserved and maintained. The state government has constituted an eight member committee headed by architect K D Sandhale and chairman Pereival Norohna.

According to Suryanarayan, fifteen houses have tentatively been identified while the scheme is still to be finalised. Ten of these houses have shown keen interest in renting out their homes to tourists. The average cost of restoration is reportedly approximately Rs 5 lakh per house and the modalities for funding this scheme is been worked out. The renovation programme is completely sponsored by the department of tourism, government of Goa. The draft scheme has already been submitted to Union Government with a request for central financial assistance.

It is also learnt that of the 15 properties, ten will be offered for accommodation while the others will be open sightseeing. The original tenants will continue to stay in these houses. In homes made available to tourists for accommodation, certain rooms will be offered to the tourists while the original tenants will occupy the rest of the house.

Hotels in Goa have seen an increase in demand during the period April to July 2002, according to hospitality research and consulting firm HVS International. Goa leads the pack among Mumbai and Bangalore with a 6.7 per cent growth in demand. Goa has emerged as a leading tourist destination for domestic tourists. Subsequent to a rise in demand, Goa has reported a 17 per cent increase in room revenues or revenues per available room (revpar). Goa has focused on the domestic leisure and conference segment which has led to a positive growth in troubled times.

In yet another initiative, to reduce if not eliminate problems faced by tourists on account of the untrained and unauthorized guides in Goa, the government of India tourist office (GOITO) of Goa is taking stringent measures to do away with any malpractices plaguing the tourism scenario in the state. "Untrained and unauthorised guides are not only a threat to the security of the tourists but also tend to misguide the tourists by concocting their own fictitious tales and stories" says Ronjon Lahiri, assistant director, GOITO, Panaji-Goa.

The Tourist Guide's Federation of India (Goa Chapter) has been duly formed and registered under the Societies Registration Act (1860) on 27th August 2002.

A formal body such as this is expected to regularise and discipline the guides besides eliminating touts posing as guides. The formation of the TGFI-Goa chapter will aid and assist guides in addressing issues which were otherwise left unattended.

Building Infrastructure

Taking cognisance of the substantial drop in domestic and international tourist arrivals in the wake of slowdown in the hospitality industry worldwide, the state government has provided a shot in the arm with an increased budgetary allocation and churning out a slew of marketing initiatives aimed at enhancing its brand image as the most versatile destination in the country.

The state plans to continue with its thrust on tourism. Says Suryanarayan: "It is absolutely imperative to continue in the same vein and impart a cutting edge to this sector which is facing stiff competition from other destinations in the country. Due to the initiatives taken and an aggressive marketing strategy in place, overall tourist traffic to the state increased almost by 9 per cent despite the events of September 11. Against all odds, this task was achieved due to focused marketing initiatives and brand building exercises.

Industry status has already been accorded to this sector. Improvement of road network in stretches of tourist importance, illumination of temples, mosques and churches and upgradation of GTDC hotels and tourist information centres have been completed on a large scale. The state tourism authority proposes to take up further improvement of roads and infrastructure facilities in the state to the tune of Rs 50 crore through the Goa State Infrastructure Development Corporation. A budgetary provision of Rs 3 crore has been made made towards payment of annuity to Goa State Infrastructure Development Corporation for this purpose. The projects of development of Nanda Lake at Curchorem, Alorna Fort and Harvalem waterfalls which have significant tourism value would also be taken up.

Beach safety arrangements have been substantially augmented by deployment of trained additional lifeguards who have undergone rigorous training at the National Institute of Water Sports. Synergy between information technology and tourism has been realised by undertaking initiatives like touchscreen kiosks and virtual walk-through CD Roms. The website for the tourism sector will impart a new thrust to IT-led tourism marketing and would showcase Goa in all its kaleidoscopic finery to the world. The Tourism Master Plan and the tourism policy spelt out by the Goa government are prominent signposts on the road to be traversed in making Goa the ultimate tourist destination.

Since tourism the world over is essentially a private sector activity, Goa has announced its intent to co-opt with the private sector as associates in infrastructure development and marketing campaigns.

For this purpose, a corpus fund for marketing has been set up, into which the government will contribute double the amount received from the private sector, subject to a ceiling of Rs 5 crore during the current year. The fund will be managed by the government with help from representatives of the tourism industry and utilised for the sole purpose of marketing the state. This would be in addition to the normal outlay of around Rs 6 crore for marketing activities which have been earmarked separately in the tourism budget.

A multilingual signage system and promotional material are also being made available for the convenience of foreign tourists. New and potentially promising source destinations like Russia and Scandinavian countries are being tapped for attracting tourists. "I also intend to focus on diversification of the tourism product by increasing the thrust on heritage and eco-tourism so as to increase the retention period and quality of tourism that the state has on offer" reveals Suryanarayan.

In order to create an appreciation of its composite heritage, Goa has also launched a 'heritage house' scheme, with the help of private participation. Training of various holders in the industry like tourist taxi drivers and strengthening of the regulatory mechanism to offer better services to tourists tops Suryanarayan's priorities.

In the recent budget 2002-03, all tourism related ancillary and support services have been accorded the status of industry. Extended facilities and incentives at par with the tourism industry including subsidies have been given to them. These measures are expected to increase cohesion and integration among all players in the industry and give them leeway to offer cost effective and attractive packages to the tourists.

The immense potential of Goa is being effectively tapped as it is being promoted as a brand name and prime destination for European and other foreign tourists thereby ensuring long term sustainability of the industry. "I firmly believe that cooperation, more than competition, is the need of the hour. We have already recognised this sentiment by entering into MoUs with Karnataka and Andhra Pradesh State Tourism Corporations for reciprocal marketing of products and services. All out efforts would be made to further these marketing synergies with other states and airlines during the current year," informs Suryanarayan. The Goa Tourism Development Corporation also aims to expand its ambit of activities by facilitating bookings for smaller hotels which are not in a position to incur marketing overheads. "Keeping in mind the thrust on this sector, Goa has increased the outlay for the tourism department to Rs 21.92 crore, which is almost four times the outlay three years ago" adds he.

Bullet Train: The Superfast to Goa

An increasing number of charters flying into Goa have catapulted the inbound tourism numbers as the state has registered a healthy surge in inbound traffic. With Konkan Railways endeavour at launching India's fastest train, Goa is now set to augment its domestic tourism numbers. "Konkan

Railways' recent venture, nicknamed 'The Bullet Train' plying at s speed of 150 kilometres per hour is expected to be India's fastest train. With Goa being an established and a much sought after leisure destination, this project is set to capture the weekend getaway market. Goa will be an ideal getaway for stressed-out business executives from Mumbai, and other places down the coastal belt, as the travelling time will now be reduced by more than half," revealed Baban Ghatge, manager, Public Relation & Protocol, Konkan Railway Corporation Ltd (KRCL), Goa. According to V C Sinha, Deputy Chief Commercial Manager, KRCL, "While the superfast train will not really be a 'bullet train' which generally plies at the speed of 250 kilometres per hour, this high speed train will still be India's fastest offering on rail. We are test running in December 2002, and expect to flag off the project come 2003." Despite the fare structure remaining to be decided, the travel community is agog with anticipation while the tourism authority waits with optimism.

MADHYA PRADESH

What comes to your mind when you think of Madhya Pradesh? The temples of Khajuraho, right. But there is more to the state. Madhya Pradesh is not called the 'heart of India' just because it is located in the centre of the country. It has been home to the cultural heritage of Hinduism, Buddhism, Jainism and Islam. Innumerable monuments, exquisitely carved temples, stupas, forts and palaces are dotted all over the state. The natural beauty of Madhya Pradesh is equally varied.

Bhopal, the capital of the state, combines scenic beauty, historicity and modern urban planning. The city presents a multi-faceted profile; the old city with its teeming market places, fine old mosques and palaces bearing the aristocratic imprint of former rulers, while the new city astonishes the visitor with its verdant, exquisitely laid out parks and gardens, broad avenues and streamlined modern edifices.

Another attraction of the state, Chitrakoot, the 'hill of many wonders', is nestled peacefully in the northern spurs of the Vindhyas. It is a perfect getaway with tranquil forest glades and blue rivers. Chitrakoot is also a pilgrim destination, blessed by the gods and sanctified by the faith of pilgrims. Moving on, when you touch Gwalior, the transition the place has made from a feudal kingdom to a vibrant, bustling city is immediately apparent. The city boasts the remnants of a multitude of reigning dynasties, of the great Rajput clans of Pratiharas, Kacchwahas and Tomars who have have left indelible etchings of their rule by way of palaces, temples and monuments. Then there is Indore, another major city which has derived its name from the 18th century Indreshwar temple. One-third of Madhya Pradesh is forested. The state offers a unique and exciting panorama of wildlife in sylvan surroundings. Spectacular mountain ranges, meandering rivers and miles and miles of dense forests are on offer for those who visit the state. Check it out.

Mystical, Magical and More

Can the land of Khajuraho be any less exotic than the famous temples? Madhya Pradesh (MP) is not called the 'heart of India' just because it is located in the centre of the country. The state has been home to the cultural heritage of four main religions viz Hinduism, Buddhism, Jainism and Islam. Innumerable monuments, exquisitely carved temples, stupas, forts and palaces are dotted all over the state. The natural beauty of MP is equally varied. Consisting largely of a plateau, the state has-spectacular mountain ranges, meandering rivers and an abundance of dense forests. In fact, one third of the state is forested, offering an incomparable and exhilarating panorama of wildlife in sylvan surroundings.

From being the first-ever state in the country to announce its exclusive heritage policy, to that of conducting the first road show in the Capital and other metropolises in India, Madhya Pradesh tourism has arrived with a bang. Marketing its product as `Mystic Madhya Pradesh' the state has firmly declared its presence on the tourism map of India. Consequently, the Madhya Pradesh State Tourism Development Corporation (MPSTDC), the official body and tourism facilitator of the state, in association with the local CII representation, with the support of the MP state government and other state tourism and hospitality bodies and associations have formulated concrete plans to position the state as a world class tourism destination in India.

Getting its Act Together

In a bid to expedite the development of tourism in Madhya Pradesh, the state government has announced a proactive tourism policy. The new tourism policy envisages creation of an environment conducive to attracting increased private investment in the tourism sector, and a more meaningful role for the government. The policy has also conceptualised the strategy for development, wherein the focus shall be on the following areas:

- Improvement and creation of adequate basic infrastructure.
- Upgradation and augmentation of accommodation, catering and recreational facilities.
- The stepping up of transport facilities.
- Marketing of destinations to ensure optimal use of infrastructure.
- Evolving suitable policies for increasing foreign exchange earnings.
- Promotion of traditional arts and crafts of the state.

Role of the State Government: The state government will confine its efforts to infrastructural development like ensuring uninterrupted electricity, water supply and provision of basic medical facilities. It will also be responsible for dissemination of information, organisation of festivals and interdepartmental co-ordination to create conditions for attracting private sector investment for the tourism sector. For this, it will provide fiscal incentives, assist in providing suitable sites and remove bottlenecks, especially those connected with infrastructural development.

MP Specials

A special package of incentives has been advocated for the tourism industry. These incentives will be available for private entrepreneurs for any of the following activities:

Hotels, Motels and Restaurants: The MP government ha amplified its tourism drive by attracting bids for developmen from private sector in the area of hospitality investment. Say

Ajay Singh, minister, panchayat and rural development, tourism and culture, government of MP: "Inviting the hospitality industry to invest in our state is one of the most important plan of action that MP tourism has identified. The state government has also shorted-listed locations that could attract hospitality investment."

The investment covers the hospitality segment would be in heritage hotels, health farms, recreation centres, rope-ways, golf courses, museums, amusement parks, craft villages, convention centres, and all other bonafide tourism-related activities recognised by the government.

Subsequently, hospitality giants of the country have also evinced interest in investing into the hotel sector of the state. Revealed Jamshed S Daboo, chairman, CII tourism sub-committee, western region, and chief operating officer-leisure hotels, Indian Hotels Company Limited (IHCL): "The state has got tremendous potential in the area of tourism, so IHCL would definitely look at investing in the region in the near future. The avenues, which the state has to offer for hospitality investment are worth exploring."

Highlighting the potentials and plans with respect to tourism and infrastructure development, the state has identified the hospitality industry as one of its prime movers in strengthening the tourism position of the region.

On the Anvil

Apart from announcing its heritage policy, and hosting various road shows across the country, the government of MP has put in place the state's eco and adventure tourism policy, declaring itself as a 'wildlife and adventure tourism state'.

The state aims to position itself as a 'wildlife' destination, especially as the 'Tiger State' both in the national and international arena.

Disclosed an official from the state tourism department: "Today's tourists are not content with cultural or religious tourism alone-what one looks for is some thrill, fun, adventure and something other than the routine. So, in keeping with this change of attitude in tourists, the state government has decided to actively promote eco-tourism and adventure tourism. Further, to popularise and develop these forms of tourism, the government is for the first time seeking participation of private investors. Adventure tourism provides tourists a special thrill whilst participating in sporting activities like river rafting, trekking etc. MP with its rich natural flora and fauna, unexploited so far, has immense potential for such sports."

Instead of depending on its limited resources, the state government has decided to open up this sector for private participation for optimum utilisation of these natural resources.

While on one hand, with these efforts, the government hopes to attract tourists in larger numbers, on the other hand, it is expected that it would help in generating greater demand for local products, and creating new employment avenues for local communities.

In order to attract private participation, the state government has finalised a set of simplified guidelines that are hassle free and would make it easy for entrepreneurs to conform with.

Gwalior: A multitude of reigning dynasties, of the great Rajput clans of the Pratiharas, Kacchwahas and Tomars have left indelible etchings of their rule in this city of palaces, temples and monuments. Gwalior's tradition as a royal capital continued until the formation of present day India, with the Scindias having their dynastic seat here. The magnificent mementoes of a glorious past have been preserved with care, giving Gwalior an appeal unique and timeless.

Orchha: Its grandeur has been captured in stone, frozen in time, a rich legacy to the ages.

Khajuraho: Famed worldwide for the erotic sculptures on its temples. These breathtaking sculptures capture life in every form and mood.

Bhopal: Bhopal, the capital of Madhya Pradesh, combines scenic beauty, historicity and modern urban planning. Bhopal today presents a multi-faceted profile; the old city with its teeming market places, fine old mosques and palaces still bear the aristocratic imprint of its former rulers.

Sanchi: The seat of Buddhist learning is famous for its stupas, monasteries, temples and pillars dating from the 3rd century BC to the 12th century AD.

Bhimbetka: Over 600 rock shelters belonging to the Neolithic age were recently discovered in this place of interest. Here, in vivid panoramic detail, paintings in over 500 caves depict the life of the pre-historic cave-dwellers making the Bhimbetka group an archeological treasure, an invaluable chronicle in the history of man.

Indore: The commercial centre of Madhya Pradesh, this bustling city has rare monuments built by the Holkar dynasty.

Ujjain: Ujjain is the site of the Kumbh mela, the largest religious congregation in the world. It is also known as the temple city. Modern Ujjain is situated on the banks of the river Shipra, regarded since times immemorial as sacred.

Omkareshwar: This place is a sacred island at the confluence of two rivers, shaped like the holiest of all Hindu symbols, Om. Here, at the confluence of the rivers Narmada and Kaveri, the devout gather to kneel before the Jyotirlinga (one of the twelve throughout India) at the temple of Shri Omkar Mandhata.

Narmada: This ancient city is also mentioned in the epics Ramayana and Mahabharata. It is renowned for its bathing ghats and the famous Maheshwari sarees.

Mandu: Each of Mandu's structures is an architectural gem; some are outstanding like the massive Jama Masjid and Hoshang Shah's tomb, which provided inspiration to the master builders of the Taj Mahal centuries later.

Amarkantak: Amarkantak is a great pilgrim centre for the Hindus, and is the source of the rivers Narmada and Sone.

Bhojpur: Founded by the legendary Parmar King of Dhar, Raja Bhoj and named after him, Bhojpur, is renowned for the remains of its magnificent Shiva temple and Cyclopean dam.

Chanderi: A crafts centre famous for its sarees and boracades. Chanderi was an important military outpost, prized by rulers with power or ambition.

Chitrakoot: Chitrakoot's spiritual legacy stretches back to legendary ages: it was in these deep forests that Rama and Sita spent eleven of their fourteen years of exile; here that the great sage Atri and Sati Anusuya meditated. A place with tranquil forests, rivers and streams.

Pachmarhi: This city is MP's most verdant jewel, a place where nature has found exquisite expression in myriad enchanting ways. Pachmarhi is also an archeological treasure-trove. In cave shelters in the Mahadeo Hills is an astonishing richness of rock paintings.

Shivpuri: This city is steeped in the royal legacy of its past, when it was the summer capital of the Scindia rulers of Gwalior. Thus, with an infinite number of heritage sites, coupled with extensive natural flora and fauna, MP easily works out be an adventure tourism and art and culture tourism destination. With wildlife being an essential element of the state, and around one-third of the state forested, the state has a lot to offer in wildlife tourism, which can be termed as the state's USP.

Promotion of Wildlife Tourism

The immediate jungle plan for the tiger country and other such attractions are part of the state's wildlife promotion drive include developing new areas in the state. The state is also serious about the future development of Kanha and Bandhavgarh National Parks, which can be arguably recognised MP's pride.

- *Bandhavgarh National Park:* One can be almost certain of seeing a tiger in this region. The density of the Tiger population at Bandhavgarh is the highest known in India. This is also White Tiger country.
- *Kanha National Park:* Kanha's sal and bamboo forests, rolling grasslands and meandering streams stretch over 940 sq km in dramatic natural splendour which form the core of the Kanha Tiger Reserve created in 1974 under Project Tiger. The park is the only habitat of the rare hard ground Barasingha (Cervus Duvaceli Branderi).

The Colourful Fairs and Festivals of MP

- *Bhagoria Haat, Jhabua:* This colourful festival of the Bhils and Bhilalas, particularly in the district of West Nimar and Jhabua, is actually in the nature of a mass svayamvara, a marriage market, usually held on the various market days falling before the Holi festival in March
- *Khajuraho Festival of Dances:* This festival draws the best classical dancers in the country who perform against the spectacular backdrop of the floodlit temples, every year in February/March. The finest exponents of different classical Indian styles are represented-Kathak, Bharatnatyam, Kuchipudi, Odissi, Manipuri, and many more.
- *Tansen Music Festival:* More than a monument, the Tansen Tomb is a part of Gwalior's living cultural heritage. It is the venue of the annual Indian classical festival held in November-December. Renowned classical singers of the land regale audiences through five mesmerising night-long sessions of the much-loved classical ragas.

KARNATAKA

The state is vibrant, rich in culture, a fact which is reflected in its people, architecture, monuments and cuisine. Let me start with Bangalore. It is a multifaceted happening city which is a capsule of contrast. One of the best things about it is the conducive weather and greenery.

But the tourism adventure starts beyond Bangalore, in places like Mysore, Hampi, Halebid, Belur, and their myriad attractions. Briefly, Mysore has the Mysore Palace and the much-acclaimed Vrindavan Gardens; Hampi and Halebid have their magnificent ruins with the former having acquired World Heritage Status.

Karnataka is also home to sandalwood. You can find a variety of sandalwood items in the state, be it carved tables, beads and pendants, dinner gongs and the best of the lot-tiny bookmarks which are a must-buy. With a profusion of monuments, Karnataka is also called the cradle of stone architecture besides being home to priceless flora, fauna and every kind of terrain except snow-clad mountains. Last but not the least is the cuisine. The state has an amazing variety. Try the spicy fish delicacy, Kane fry (lady fish) with rice; sannas (idli stuffed with toddy or yeast) or the neer dosa, an all-time favourite for most Mangloreans. To sum it up, touch down in the state and take your pick of the numerous offerings it has.

The Beginning of a New Era in Tourism

February, 14, 2002 marked the beginning of a new era in the history of Karnataka tourism. A first of its kind initiative, christened 'Connect', was launched to build a healthy, working relationship between the trade and the state tourism department. Now after a series of eye-catching promotional campaigns, branding and repositioning exercises coupled with back-to-back road shows in India and abroad termed 'Theatre of Inspiration', this southern Indian state is now a formidable force to reckon with in the global tourism arena.

A relatively new entrant in the world tourism circuit, Karnataka has already emerged as a contender for the global tourism pie. Thanks to the government's renewed commitment and active involvement of the private enterprise, the state is all set to position itself as a pre-eminent destination in South Asia. Already with limited efforts, the state has emerged as India's fourth most popular destination for domestic tourists, with 126 lakh arrivals, ahead of traditional rivals like Kerala, Maharashtra and Madhya Pradesh. In addition the state enjoys a 10 per cent share of international arrivals, totalling around 2.63 lakh arrivals for the year 1999-2000.

Says I M Vittalamurthy, commissioner of tourism, Karnataka and managing director, Karnataka State Tourism Development Corporation (KSTDC): "Tourism in Karnataka is ready for take-off. Our intention is to transform Karnataka into a major global destination. We intend to build Karnataka into a strong global brand. Karnataka is being positioned as 'Theatre of Inspiration', India's most dramatic and inspiring destination. A multimedia, multilingual advertising and communication campaign has already been finalised. We will certainly cash-in on the exceptional brand-equity of Bangalore as the Asian Silicon Valley. Karnataka has emerged as South Asia's 'Holiday Valley' for up-market tourists."

The new life that has been infused into the tourism sector is evident from the fact that Karnataka tourism department is already a partner state along with government of India in all major international travel and tourism fairs. The government along with the private sector has put its act together to woo tourists to this part of the world. Hoping to cash in on the state's core competencies and inherent strengths, the tourism department has evolved a strategy for promotion that is long-terms comprehensive and highly innovative.

Says Jose T Ramapuram, director-marketing, Trails: "The recent positive steps taken by the state government in promoting tourism has resulted in Karnataka being perceived as a dynamic pro-tourism state by the rest of the country. Destinations like Hampi, Belur, Halebeedu, Sravanabelegola, Mysore, Coorg, Kabini and Gokarna provide the right mix for success. Considering the capital-intensive character of the industry, the current marketing push provided by the government is expected to yield results only in the next four to five years. Karnataka is already on its way to becoming an alternative destination to the traditional Southern Kerala circuit."

After declaring tourism as an 'industry' and keeping in view the need for intensive development of the hospitality industry in the state, the Karnataka government's focus for several years now has more or less revolved around infrastructure development. In spite of being the first state in the country to come up with a comprehensive tourism policy, not much development took place until the late '90s. However, the dawn of the millennium witnessed a sea change in the Karnataka government's priorities, with chief minister S M Krishna donning the mantle of power. Intent on replicating the success of the Information Technology and Bio-Technology sectors, in which the state has made huge strides, the government came up with ground-breaking initiatives to prop up tourism infrastructure.

"Tourism infrastructure in the state is being strengthened in a big way. Highway tourism would be developed by creating rest and recreation centres along the highways. There is a plan to upgrade existing airstrips located all over the state. Already, the Karnataka State Highway Improvement Programme (KSHIP) has started up-gradation work. On the aviation front, the new Bangalore International Airport Project will be a reality now. Selection of joint venture partners for the airport project has been completed with signing of share-holders agreement with the consortium constituted by Siemens Project Ventures, Zurich Airport and L&T in January 2002," says Krishna.

Echoing his optimism, Dr C Manohar, secretary, Federation of Karnataka Chambers of Commerce and Industries (FKCCI), says: "There is a positive message in choosing tourism infrastructure as a key area of concentration, which is to restrict the government's role to that of a facilitator only. This certainly augurs well for the hospitality development and would gradually pave way for increased private investment in this sector. Though the state has taken giant strides in the last two years, the need of the hour is to adopt a cluster approach to infrastructure development and achieve synergies."

Marketing Strategy

In a bid to position Karnataka on the global tourist map, the state is busy brewing a slew of initiatives on the marketing front. In an endeavour to forge a strategic relationship with the travel and tourism fraternity, Karnataka tourism had earlier this year kicked off private-public integration exercises. This has had a major impact on the comprehensive development of the tourism sector in the state. Tour operators, travel agents and a host of industry professionals are involved in all matters related to tourism on a regular basis. This has helped synergise the department's efforts to promote the state nationally and globally. Aimed at reinforcing its marketing and promotional efforts, the state government has already enhanced its budgetary allocation for the tourism sector to Rs 18 crore, almost a 50 per cent increase over last year's outlay of Rs 12 crore.

The government has sought to spend its limited resources selectively and to work hand-in-hand with the private sector participation. Envisaging to streamline the functioning and to ensure better management, the budget has also proposed to transfer popular tourist destinations like Nandi Hills, Kemmanagundi, and world famous Brindavan Gardens near Mysore to the state tourism department.

The government in its bid to encourage more private sector participation has also announced a slew of concessions and benefits. Notable measures include tax concessions on aviation fuel to encourage domestic aviation industries, underwriting of certain number of tickets, so that industries would have assured revenue and many such sops.

A few years ago, Karnataka's participation at global tourism exhibitions and events was unimaginable. But now, Karnataka tourism is a regular and a major participant at all major events like ITB Berlin, Arabian Travel Mart (ATM), WTM London, etc. It has already created ripples in the tourism market worldwide with the successful launch of its punchline 'Theatre of Inspiration', which has been widely received and acclaimed by everyone.

However it was at the International Tourismus Borse (ITB-March 2002), the world's largest travel and trade fair in which Karnataka tourism really made it's presence felt. For the first time ever, Karnataka was India's partner state for ITB and in another first, the department of tourism networked with the tourism entrepreneurs in the state and ensured that Karnataka tourism was represented well in Berlin.

"Karnataka is undoubtedly the destination of tomorrow, especially for holiday-makers from the Arabian Gulf. Our product-mix comprising the joys of modern Bangalore, mixed with the splendour of Hampi's ruins, adventure camping, fishing at Kabini were big draws. While the trade response was gratifying, we realised the urgent need to open the skies into Bangalore and hence opened discussions with major airlines in the Gulf markets. Emirates and Qatar Airways have expressed their keen intent to connect the Arabian Gulf to Bangalore and we believe that our participation at the Arabian Travel Mart has opened several windows of opportunity for Karnataka's destination management companies and resorts. This was our first ever entry into the Arabian Gulf markets and we are most impressed with the response from private players from Karnataka," says Vittalamurthy.

Buoyed by the tremendous response at the ATM, a contingent of state tourism ministry reprresentatives including the travel-trade fraternity recently completed roadshows in Dubai, Abu Dhabi, Muscat and Bahrain. In addition to presenting the strengths of Karnataka as a destination, the investment potential in the state as well as the highlight of the new tourism policy were detailed out to a diverse audience.

"WTM is an important platform to showcase the amazing tourism potential of the state to a global audience. We will be participating at this event in a major way along with at least five to six leading private players. The department certainly hopes to catch on the frenzy that we have created through our participation in ITB, Berlin and ATM," he added.

On the home front in Bangalore, the department has initiated a major effort to promote tourism through Meetings, Incentives, Conventions and Exhibitions (MICE). In an attempt to woo corporate big wigs like Infosys, Intel, Sun Microsystems etc, the tourism department has undertaken a series of presentations regularly. Already efforts are on to get corporate firms to conduct meetings and conventions in Karnataka. The state-owned Jungle Lodges & Resorts is already working on hosting two international events this year to mark the international year of eco-tourism. This apart, the department has also kicked off a series of innovative cultural events christened 'Discover Karnataka'. The idea was conceptualised to bring in traditional and contemporary art forms to centre-stage by using them to highlight Karnataka's magnificent monuments, hill stations, wildlife sanctuaries, beaches etc.

Investment Opportunities

A number of private investors from middle-east countries, Australia and Germany have approached the Karnataka government with proposals to set up a variety of hospitality operations like beach-side resorts, entertainment and amusement projects, hotels etc. A high-level committee on industrial development constituted by the government of Karnataka, has cleared a mega tourism project involving a total investment of Rs 3,000 crore in the state. The high-profile project envisages the development of integrated resorts and tourism infrastructure in Mysore on the lines of Sun City in South Africa.

The project, which also involves the development of a major amusement park, is to be executed and financed by Mobius International P Ltd, in association with Ryder Hampton development team, a major global player in hotels, resorts and tourism related business. On the other hand several investors have evinced interest in investing in tourism hot spots like Hampi, Mysore, Kabini, Shimoga, Karwar, Mangalore and a host of other destinations in the state.

With Hampi hogging the limelight in recent times, a number of investors from India and Abroad are eyeing the prospects of conceptualising high profile luxury resorts in the vicinity. A number of hospitality majors like the Taj Group of Hotels, Hotel Leela Venture are in direct talks with the state tourism department for the last six months. The tourism department has gone all out to provide land at a subsidised rate to the prospective investors. This apart, a number of other smaller players are also planning to set up their properties.

Hampi-The New Global Hotspot

The decision of the Union Finance Ministry to accord special area status to world heritage site Hampi and subsequently to develop it into a viable international destination has set the stage for a whole new era of promoting high-end tourism in the state. Subsequently, in an attempt to supplement the Union tourism ministry's efforts, the Karnataka Government has already constituted a statutory body called 'Hampi Development Authority' to oversee tourism infrastructure in and around Hampi.

Union tourism and culture minister, Jagmohan has made his intentions clear on developing Hampi as a one of the major hotspots in the country. He has extensively toured the Hampi heritage complex and assured the state government of all possible help and assistance from the Union ministry of tourism.

"Hampi is top priority for us. We are moving the entire government machinery into an action mode. The direct involvement of the chief minister as well as union tourism minister will ensure that the restoration will move ahead with greater urgency, in a well-coordinated manner, deploying the required resources. At the end of the effort, we believe that Hampi will be a world-class destination on its own, with the same significance as the other great heritage sites of the world I would not be surprised if Hampi gains the stature of 'Angkor Vat'," Vittalamurthy said.

Beckoning a New Breed of Tourist

Mysore Circuit: Mysore is said to be the perfect destination for a tourist to unwind. Often referred to as the cultural capita of Karnataka, this ancient city boasts of magnificent palaces museums, gardens and wild life sanctuaries. The Mysore zoo St Philomena's church, Jayachamarajendra art gallery Chamundi hills and the Brindavan Gardens are some of the attractive tourist spots within the city area. Mysore is als famous for its Dassera festival celebrated lavishly every yea in the months of September and October. The nine day festiva reflects the rich and diverse ethnic culture of the state and i an attractive billing for tourists from all over the world.

Coastal Circuit: Encompassing one of the most exoti locales in the whole of South India, this place is renowned fo places like Karwar, Sirsi, Banawasi and Dandeli, Gokarna Dharmasthala, Mangalore etc. On the other hand Dandeli i a natural habitat for wildlife and is mostly frequented b adventure enthusiasts and nature lovers. The famous Dande Sanctuary houses some rare species like the Barking Dee Sloth Bear, Panther, Sambar, and Gaur. The importar destination is Gokarna, literally meaning Cow's ear, is a tow formed by the ear-shaped confluence of two rivers. Devotee throng to this place to have a glimpse of the legendar 'Atmalinga' in the ancient temple here.

Shimoga Circuit: This place is noted for a variety of exot locales like the world famous Jog Falls and Bhadra Wildli Sanctuary. Plans are also afoot to transform the Jog Falls in an all seasons destination by having regular water supply eve during the summer.

Belur and Halebid Circuit: It is known for th architectural splendour of the Chennakeshava temple built b the Hoysala dynasty. The temple with its exquisite architecture and stone carved statues remains one of the main attractions in the state. Halebid is located around 17 kms east of Belur and is one of the finest examples of stone sculpted architecture.

Hampi Circuit: Once the mighty capital of the erstwhile Vijayanagar empire, the Hampi ruins are now one of the global tourist destinations in the state. Hampi is unlike other ruins as a small fraction of it is still used by the local population. Hampi is abundant with palaces, temples and ruins of forts which bring alive memories of a vibrant civilisation which flourished in the 16th century. It is famous for its Virupaksha temple, stone chariot, Lotus Mahal, queen,s bath and huge stone statues of Narasimha and Ganesha.

Tourism Infrastructure and Regional Hospitality

The Karnataka Government has already secured necessary clearances for the Rs 2,000 crore Bangalore-Mysore Infrastructure Corridor Project (BMIC). The high profile four-lane expressway project between Bangalore and Mysore also envisages comprehensive development of recreational facilities, heritage centres and eco-tourism projects, commercial centres. While the heritage centres will encompass amenities like heritage crafts, arts, traditional treatments, and healing centres, the eco-tourism projects will have attractions like theme parks, cultural centres etc.

"The BMIC assumes significance with the Bangalore hospitality market almost reaching a saturation point. Currently, room supply is more than demand. It is definitely good that plans are underway to commence work on the project. This would encourage more hotel projects to come up on either side of the highway and would also help people to plan short break trips, thus giving hotels weekend travel business both in Mysore and Bangalore," says Veerendra Shadakshari, director, Ramanashree Group of Hotels.

The government, aware of the fact that Northern Karnataka is a veritable tourist paradise comprising among other attractions two world heritage sites, has taken up a proactive stand in developing a northern tourist circuit and for the purpose is providing more infrastructural facilities in this region.

Accordingly, it has commenced work on the Karnataka State Highways Improvement Program (KSHIP), under which nearly 2,269 kms of state highways and major district roads will be improved. In addition the state has also called upon the Union Government to declare at least six roads in the state as National Highways. This apart, the government has mooted a proposal to come up with another four lane national highway connecting Bangalore-Kolar-Chennai circuit costing an investment of Rs 243 crore.

Analysts opine that rapid progress on the road development front, will have far-reaching impact on the growth of tourism and hospitality sectors in the state. Another crucial factor to be considered is the recent recommendations of a cabinet sub-committee (CSC) on tourism. With a view to provide a fillip to hospitality projects all over the state, especially in strategic tourist locales and on highways, the CSC in its report has recommended government land to entrepreneurs at 50 fifty per cent of market value to establish resorts. In addition the report has called upon the government to create necessary infrastructure so that entrepreneurs can open resorts, hotels, amusement parks etc.

Says Gopinath Nair, CEO, Cruise & Travel P Ltd: "This is going to be a crucial driver of tourism on this segment. It has been seen in many parts of the world that faster road access fosters tourism and hospitality industries. The number of road users will increase, leading to greater use of facilities such as resorts, restaurants etc. Public-private partnership is crucial to development of tourism since the government cannot do everything on its own. Tourism development requires private participation to build and run hotels, resorts, supply quality transportation as well as to sell and market destinations to prospective customers. The role of the government should remain focused on providing the basic infrastructure to boost tourism."

This apart, to determine infrastructural development needs in various sectors and assist the government in developing viable infrastructure projects in the state in accordance with the infrastructure policies already announced, the Infrastructure Development Corporation Limited (iDeck) has been established in partnership with Infrastructure Development Finance

Company Limited (IDFC). The basic function of iDeck is to advise the state in developing sector strategies, assist in project development, selection, preparation, procurement and implementation of projects.

The winds of change finally seems to have caught up with the hospitality and tourism sectors. With a focussed aim on upgrading infrastructural facilities, the government is pulling out all stops. In keeping up with his promise of providing equal priority to tourism as that of other core sectors, S M Krishna has appointed D B Inamdar as the new minister for tourism, information technology and biotechnology. The move is clearly an indication of the state government's serious commitment toward comprehensive development of hospitality sector in the state.

There is an inherent synergy between tourism, IT and BT, which needs to be tapped to its fullest extent.

However, my immediate task will be to improve existing tourism infrastructure at all strategic locations in the state on a war footing," Inamdar disclosed. This apart, the tourism department has taken a proactive stand with regard to marketing and is also looking at major promotional activities abroad. It has already made its presence at the ITB and Dubai Travel Marts this year. Already several NRI's and entrepreneurs from Dubai have expressed keen desire to set hospitality projects in regions like Karwar, Shimoga, This clearly stands testimony to the growing prowess of Karnataka tourism. In addition, the government will stand guarantee for a Rs 125 crore loan to be raised by the tourism department from the HUDCO to create infrastructure like roads and airstrips. Though, it is a bit premature to comment on the future, tourism in Karnataka is clearly poised for a rapid growth in the coming years.

MAHARASHTRA

Racing on Tourism's Fast Track

Maharashtra has embarked upon a marketing blitzkrieg and initiatives to promote tourism in the state are on the roll. 'Maharashtra Unlimited,' the new slogan of Maharashtra Tourism Development Corporation (MTDC), symbolises the vast potential of the state to metamorphosise into a premier tourist destination.

When one thinks about tourism, Maharashtra may not surface as the classic example of a 'must-see' destination in the country. The state has always been recognised as India's most pro-business state and has firmly established itself as the country's powerhouse, with its capital-Mumbai-as the centre point of India's commerce. Tourism as an activity has rarely been associated with Maharashtra, but the state is now undergoing a strategic metamorphosis to evolve as a tourism product par excellence. Maharashtra is now getting serious about fun, realising the potential of tourism as an efficacious revenue raker for the state.

Along with Mumbai, the commercial capital and one of the gateways to India, Maharashtra has a wealth of tourist attractions ranging from forts, tribal art, caves, quaint hill stations, virgin beaches, pilgrimage centres, wildlife sanctuaries and much more making it a complete tourist destination. Tourism has now been placed high on the priority list of the state government, which has taken up ambitious plans to market Maharashtra as a premier global tourism destination. Apart from a few destinations, which have been high on the popularity charts to the extent of being over-exposed, there are several other interesting regions waiting in the wings to take centre stage.

New Tourism Policy in the Offing

In a bid to enhance the tourism potential of the state, the government of Maharashtra will soon be presenting a new tourism policy. Utpal Mukhopadhyay, principal secretary, tourism, government of Maharashtra, disclosed, "The new tourism policy will certainly encourage the sagging morale of tour operators and the hospitality industry. It will mainly look at improving existing infrastructure as well as creating an opportunity for developing new ones. To actively promote tourism, we need to market these places, as well as create the necessary infrastructure, thereby making it potentially viable."

Subsequently, the policy will also create a 'one-stop counter'-a single window clearance for tourism purposes such as licences for hotels, resorts, lodges, entertainment houses, leisure parks, etc. "We have divided the state into different zones, such as beaches, hill stations, grasslands, historical places and also plan to develop and market them. We plan to initiate development by helping private operators to open new hotels and resorts and market it to tourists," stated Mukhopadhyay. The policy also proposes to offer tax incentives to encourage development of new establishments.

Publicity, Promotion and Promulgation

According to Ashish Kumar Singh, managing director of MTDC, "We are working on an international marketing strategy to promote the theme of 'Maharashtra Unlimited' and have commenced a public relations exercise in Germany and the UK. We want to exploit the tourism potential of Maharashtra by promoting regional strengths. Some of the tourism products we are highlighting are eco-tourism in the Sahyadris, the sun, sand and sea experiences at virgin beaches like Tarkarli and Ganapatipule, wildlife in Vidarbha, heritage in Aurangabad, religious tours in North Maharashtra and the metro experience in Mumbai and Pune and Nashik."

The state has participated in tourism fairs at Berlin and London, where Maharashtra along with Kerala, West Bengal and Rajasthan have been identified as partners by the government of India. It has set up a high-level committee to clear all tourism-related projects in the state. Fort tourism and development of beach tourism by improving accessibility to the beach areas are being highlighted. Promoting the concept of coastal cuisine, especially Malwani cuisine, is under consideration. Land has been identified for tourism promotion for prospective buyers. A strategy is being evolved to increase the promotional budget for tourism. The present budget for tourism in Maharashtra is Rs one crore and the demand at present is to increase the budget to around Rs 15 crore, which is yet to be finalised.

Maharashtra is on the threshold of announcing its new tourism policy, where newer roles and dimensions have been planned for the Maharashtra Tourism Development Corporation (MTDC), as a facilitator for promoting tourism investment.

The Bollywood Connection

In an effort to promote Maharashtra as a world class destination and encashing on its status as the Bollywood hub in India, MTDC has announced its intent to organise a host of 'Bollywood shows' around the globe. Towards this end, Chhagan Bhujbal, who had taken a high powered delegation to the United Arab Emirates recently, has returned with agreements in principle from the UAE and is set to organise the first such Bollywood show in Dubai.

Commenting on the initiative, Bhujbal says: "I am aware of the fact that Dubai is an ardent fan of Hindi cinema and since the largest Indian film industry is in Maharashtra, the show could be arranged. The proposition has been mooted by Sheikh Ahmed, minister of civil aviation and chairman of Emirates who firmly believes that the proposition is very interesting. "We can definitely consider the possibility of organising a Bollywood show in the year 2003," he informed.

Neoteric Offerings

The state's 720 kms long coastline has remained relatively undiscovered and unexploited compared to states like Goa and Kerala. Sindhudurg district, which was declared by the Maharashtra government as the 'Tourism District', has some of the best beaches in the state and country. Kunkeshwar, Tarkarli, Deobagh, Vengurla, Mochemad, Shiroda are some of the scenic beaches dotting the coastline of the district.

Tarkarli has already evolved as a major destination in the district with MTDC setting up a beach front resort with Konkani style cottages. A new concept of 'houseboat' on the sands with two suites has been introduced. The famous sea fort of Sindhudurg, off the Malvan coast close-by, is the biggest attraction besides the casurina tree-lined Tarkarli beach. International cruise liners operating in Indian waters have included Tarkarli as a day-long excursion in their itinerary.

Ganpatipule with the swayambhoo Ganpati temple on the beach and Bhatye beach in Ratnagiri have also developed as major beach destinations. Others up north like Harihareshwar, Murud Janjira, Kihim, Alibag are already popular while there are a number of other beaches like Murud-Harnai, Velneshwar etc, which have remained relatively undiscovered due to lack of accommodation.

Lonar is undisputedly a virgin destination and Maharashtra's most recent offering as a tourism product. Situated on the outskirts of Lonar town in district Buldhana, Maharashtra, the crater is a bowl shaped depression formed 50,000 years ago by the impact of a huge meteor, which carved out a bowl roughly 1.8 km in diameter. The size and age make it the largest and oldest meteoric crater in the world, ante-dating its nearest rival, the Canyon-Diabolo of Arizona, United States by a clear 2.30 centuries. Research has shown that the stone mass, which struck the earth, was approximately 60 meters in diameter and weighing about a million tons. At the bottom, a beautiful lake has been formed over thousand of years by the perennial streams flowing into the crater. The water of the lake, however, is very salty, the pH being 10.7. Today, Lonar Lake is the third largest natural salt-water lake in the world. Tourists there can watch aquatic birds like the Flamingos, Indian Moorhen, Coot, Dabehick and so on. One can also hear and see many peacocks in the crater's forest. On the beach of the lake, there are a few temples, built in the 12th-13th century.

There are many other tourist attractions in and around the area. To promote tourism in this area, MTDC offers fine accommodation in its Crater View Tourist Complex which harbour 66 rooms.

PACKAGING ADVENTURE AND THE WILD WEST

The Sahyadri range stretching North to South separating the tiny Konkan coastal strip and the extensive Deccan hinterland, offer plenty of opportunity for trekking, hiking and rock climbing. Unfortunately neither MTDC nor the state government has promoted adventure sports. There are a number of interesting mountain-top forts, a window to the hey-day of the reign of the Marathas, which are part of the rich historical legacy of the state.

MTDC has however taken steps for the promotion of adventure and wildlife tourism in the state, especially in the

Nagpur belt. It has joined hands with the neighbouring Madhya Pradesh government towards the same. Madhya Pradesh (MP) is the leading state as far as wildlife tourism is concerned. Though Kanha and Bandhavgarh tiger sanctuaries in MP are world renowned, Maharashtra has Tadoba and Melghat which are bigger tiger sanctuaries but they have not been developed and marketed strongly. There are many other sanctuaries and pockets of thickly forested areas in the state which could be developed and promoted as adventure and wildlife tourism zones.

Scaling New Heights With Fort Tourism

MTDC has set out a plan to promote fort tourism in the state. Various forts, especially in the western Maharashtra region,which were built and used by Shivaji, have been identified as prospective areas of interest for tourism. The proposal of drafting a special fort itinerary which will be spread over a period of approximately 15 days is on the anvil. Provisions in the nature of professionals and experts with a specific guided plan along with identified accommodation area will be offered.

According to Ashish Kumar Singh, "It is important to build awareness of such regions where more people should take the initiative of visiting. Once there is an increase in visitors, infrastructural development of the area will be immediately follow. The main aim is in regards to the promotion of the places".

Exploring Greener Pastures with Eco-Tourism

In the recent past Vilasrao Deshmukh, chief minister, Maharashtra had expressed his desire to aggressively promote eco-tourism in the state. "In the coming year, I am going to promote Maharashtra as a popular destination, both commercial and tourist. The government is also looking at concentrating effectively on eco-tourism, heritage and convention centres. More so, the Maharashtra government is looking at inviting a lot of private participation from both domestic and foreign investors," he asserted.

In the same vein, the Forest Development Corporation of Maharashtra (FDCM) Ltd has appointed the Indian Society for

Environment, Art and Cultural Heritage (Indsearch) to conduct eco-tours in the vicinity of the forests in Maharashtra. There is excellent potential for eco-tourism since Maharashtra has a estimated forest cover of more than 103 square km. The FDCM along with the forest department of Maharashtra plans to utilise the existing available infrastructure for the development of eco-tourism along with Indsearch, who will conduct guided tours in various forests, sanctuaries and wildlife areas.

Eco-tourism is growing at a rate of 200 per cent globally, but in India it stands at a negligible 30 per cent, this can primarily be attributed to lack of correct and timely information meted out to tourists. Indsearch, in close association with FDCM, will also be conducting nature camps, rural tours, outdoor management development programmes for the corporate sector.

Propagating Pilgrimage Sites

Shirdi, recognised as the country's second largest religious centre in terms of visits after Tirupati, is a religious destination that is currently undergoing upgradation. The government in collaboration with the Shirdi Trust has charted out plans for further development. Shirdi falls under the 'Special Area Development Plan' of the Maharashtra government, where public policy management schemes have been planned to ameliorate the region. Measures have been adopted to augment the accommodation facilities in the form of dormitories besides setting up of new five-star properties.

Nashik with one of the 12 jyotir lings in the country is yet another major pilgrimage centre. Thousands flock to this city during Mahashivratri. With such a large influx of tourists, the scenic places around the city can be developed as tourist destinations. The ancient Shiva shrine at Bhimashankar is yet another example of a wonderful place without any proper infrastructure. A mountain-top shrine located in the most densely forested area of the state it is one of the most beautiful places.

Going Back in Time with Historical Tourism

Maharashtra is fast introducing the concept of historical tourism, where an insight will be provided into the state's culture. Famous for its Ajanta and Ellora caves, the state also has other Buddhist and non-Buddhist caves such as Karla, Elephanta and Kaneri. With the support of the Japanese Government, restoration work is under execution in phases at the Ajanta and Ellora caves. The first phase concentrated on infrastructural development, while the second phase of restoration, scheduled to commence from April 2002, will focus on monumental preservation and conservation. Flight connectivity from Aurangabad to New Delhi has been proposed to further boost tourism.

Non-Traditional Tourist Sectors

Non-traditional tourist sectors like the Pune-Nashik and Mumbai-Nashik region have been mapped out as potential areas for wine development and production. Special incentives and schemes, promotional policies and financial assistance form part of the development scheme in this region. Besides, wine tours will also be initiated in the region.

Presenting a Range of Unexplored Hill Stations

The state has some wonderful hill stations. Unfortunately only a few have been really developed and publicised while the rest are languishing in obscurity. Hill stations like Matheran, Mahabaleshwar, Lonavala though scenic are fast losing their charm to unplanned commercialisation and over-exposure. Amboli near Sawantwadi on the Goa border or Malshej ghat near Mumbai are relatively untouched and retain that idyllic feel. Jawahar, the seat of the Warli tribals in Dahanu district is a beautiful and quaint hill station, its tourism potential virtually untapped due to lack of infrastructure.

Merchandising Pune as 'City of Festivals'

Pune hoteliers have taken the responsibility of promoting Pune as a city of festivals, more so because Indian fairs and festivals hold much brand value in the international market. Work in the required direction has been initiated with the support of a non-governmental organisation (NGO) Pune Yaspeeth. Pune Vyaspeeth was set up to promote the city as a tourist destination, to attract a larger share of the domestic market and inbound tourists.

Mumbai-A Destination in Itself

The city of Mumbai has been identified as a promising destination in itself by the state tourism authorities. Efforts are being made to highlight the tourism dimensions of the city, over and above its fame as the commercial capital of the country. Apart from complete support from the private sector, organisations such as Western India Automobile Association (WIAA) will also help in highlighting traffic information for the benefit of the general public. The aim is to market Mumbai as a leisure destination, where the businessman who 'comes to' the city needs to 'get into' the city.

New Tourism Products

'The Great Mumbai Bazaar-2002', was a good innovative concept to promote Mumbai as a destination. An event chalked out on the lines of the Great Singapore Sale and the Dubai Shopping Festival, the idea failed to materialise on account of lack of government support. With perhaps the most happening night life and plethora of weekend getaways, the objective is to promote Mumbai as a leisure destination. The city can be easily identified as a high-potential convention destination. A number of attractions can be introduced in the city, such as walking plazas and artists' sections where art and culture can be displayed and performed at strategic locations in the city. Lighting up the city by night would also add to the charm of the place.

CHHATTISGARH

Chhattisgarh in fact has many such getaways. Endowed with a rich cultural heritage and attractive natural diversity, the newly-born state offers a plethora of attractions like ancient monuments, rare wildlife, exquisitely carved temples, Buddhist sites, palaces, waterfalls, caves, rock paintings and hill plateaus.

Enticingly, most sites in the state are untouched. Chhattisgarh is a veritable green carpet with 44 per cent area under forests. A sense of romance and adventure envelopes the atmosphere there. Three National Parks and 11 Wildlife Sanctuaries afford plenty of opportunities to view a wide range of wildlife, especially the endangered Wild Buffalo (Bubalis

bubalis) and the even more endangered Hill Myna (Graculis religiosa peninsularis).

Some of the must-see places in the state are Mainpat (Surguja), Keshkal Valley (Kanker), Chaiturgarh (Bilaspur), Bagicha (Jashpur), Kutumbsar caves, Kailash caves, Tirathgarh falls and Chitrakote falls (Bastar).

A predominantly tribal belt, Chhattisgarh is the best bet to experience and understand the mystique of aboriginal tribes. The state is setting up adventure camps with tree-top houses and typical tribal dwellings inside the jungle to offer an insight into the life of numerous tribes. The tribal ethno-medicine, which predates even Ayurveda, is being highlighted as a tourism attraction.

Comprising of small fiefdoms in the pre-independence era, Chhattisgarh is dotted with small but grand palaces, some of which have opened their doors to tourists, like Kawardha Palace, giving visitors a glimpse of the grandeur of a bygone era.

The state is also dotted with ancient monuments, some like the Bhoramdeo temple near Kawardha are exquisite works of art and worthy to be deemed as world heritage monuments. An ancient temple on the banks of a lake, Bhoramdeo, though smaller, matches the temples of Khajuraho in architectural design. Other prime sites for heritage tourism in Chhattisgarh are Rajim, Sirpur, Tala, Malhar and Sheorinarayan. All in all the state is a kaleidoscope of tourist attractions waiting to be discovered.

Young and Raring to Go

Metaphorically, Chhattisgarh represents India's centre of gravity being located at the heart of the country. This new-born state is as old as yesterday and as new as tomorrow. Within just two years of its statehood, Chhattisgarh has emerged as a complete destination with the right mix of infrastructure and opportunities. The state is generously endowed with a rich cultural heritage and attractive natural diversity. It is adorned with mesmerising waterfalls, enchanting monuments, breathtaking landscape and an assortment of wildlife comprising rare animal species, and what not. The state is indeed a colourful mosaic painted by the creator himself. However, the true USP of the state is that it is still undiscovered and unexplored. This green state has 44% of its area under forest cover, and is one of the richest bio-diverse areas in the country. Some of these areas have been developed by the Government into national parks and wildlife sanctuaries.

The potential of the state as a tourism product is so vast that it can easily beat established products such as Kerala and Rajasthan to the top slot. Surging forth with a synergistic approach to tourism from both public and private sector. On a proactive note, the government has announced its intent to double the budget outlay to Rs 1.5 crores in the year 2003-04. The recent success of the 'Bastar circuit' promotion drive followed by an even more effective 'Dassera festival' held at Bastar has kick started an already motivated tourism authority into making this decision.

Chhattisgarh, for the uninitiated, is home to abundant natural beauty, which includes unique flora and fauna, rare wildlife, waterfalls, caves and hill plateaus. In fact, the Chitrakote Falls, located on the River Indravati is one of the biggest falls in the country. Ancient caves such as the Kutumsar and Kailash Gufa still have the stalactite and stalagmite formations of yesteryears. A state, rich in its cultural heritage, Chhattisgarh houses several sites of archaeological and religious importance. Ancient monuments, Buddhist and Hindu temples and palaces like Kawardha and Kanker are an attraction for students of architecture and design.

Tourism has an Industry Status

Taking the initiative a step further and walking the talk, a proactive Chief Minister and head of the Chhattisgarh Tourism Board, Ajit Jogi, has accorded 'industry status' to tourism and will grant a 15 percent subsidy upto a maximum of 20 lakhs, for new hotels. Players will also be exempt from luxury tax for 10 years. The power-surplus state will also offer attractive power tariffs for investors and will encourage partnerships between the public and the private sectors. Fast emerging as a tourism product in the reckoning, the states road, rail network and general infrastructure is at par with the best in the country.

Charting the Course

One big impediment this newly formed state faces is the lack of education and awareness about its location, not only in the travel industry but also with the discerning traveller. According to Dr. A Jayathilak "The first issue that needs to be addressed on priority is the total lack of awareness about the state, its location and subsequently its resplendent beauty. In the first phase of our promotional exercise, we are therefore embarking on an aggressive education drive across the country. All facets of the state and what it has to offer as an all encompassing tourism product is what needs to be communicated to tour operators across the country who will in effect convey the same to their clientele."

Realising the true potential of tourism as a revenue raker for the state, the state has undertaken large-scale development and improvement of infrastructure to create a conducive investment climate. Accordingly, the State will take up Integrated Development of special tourism areas and share a constructive collaboration with the private sector. Tourism development will be primarily driven by the private sector with the role of Government being that of a facilitator and a catalyst. The State has set up a State Tourism Promotion Board as the nodal agency for translation of the policy into action for the sustained development of the sector. The state will be focussing on eco-tourism and ethno-tourism, while facilitating private sector initiatives. "We will promote a scientific approach to the planning, management and development of sustainable tourism products and activities in the region" asserts Jayathilak.

Dishing Up a Cultural Treat with Heritage and Ethno-Tourism

Viewing an increasing interest in the international tourist to explore and experience a rural or cultural experience, Chhattisgarh has identified and is developing earmarked villages to provide a cultural extravaganza. The private sector has been brought into the picture for proper maintenance and professional site management of important heritage sites and monuments. Bhoramdeo, Rajim, Sirpur, Tala, Malhar and Sheorinarayan are prime sites for heritage tourism. Festivals like Dassera at Bastar, Madai at Dantewada and Narainpur, Bhoramdeo, Raut Nacha, Chakradhar Samaroh and Rajim are being marketed for global exposure.

In order to showcase its rich heritage, the state will identify and develop villages and heritage properties ie. old palaces, havelis, baras as places of tourist interest. These will be integrated with eco-tourism circuits to ensure that tourism development across the state is focused. This product offering will also showcase local art and craft and provide a fillip to rural employment. The state will ensure proper maintenance and professional site management of important heritage sites/ monuments. Bhoramdev, Rajim, Sirpur, Tala, Malhar and Shivrinarayan are some of the archaeological sites that will be promoted as prime sites for heritage tourism. The state will also periodically organise fairs and festivals to promote its rich culture. An artisan village cum craft park ie. 'Urban Haat' will be set up at Raipur. Financial assistance and training will be given there to artisans and craftsmen to revive local art.

Going Green with Eco-Tourism

In order to position the state as a unique multi-attraction tourism destination, the state has identified the following potential areas for developing Eco-tourism.

The state will actively identify opportunities to promote nature-based tourism with increased local participation. Wildlife areas, camping grounds and trekking facilities will be some of the prime attractions. With 12% share of India's total forest cover, Chhattisgarh's three national parks and eleven wildlife sanctuaries are a principal attraction. Several protected areas such as Kanger Valley National Park, Barnawapara, Sitanadi, Udanti and Achanakmar Sanctuaries still remain unexplored. The endangered Wild Buffalo (Bubalis bubalis) and the even more endangered Hill Myna (Graculis religiosa peninsularis) are both found here.

The mystique of aboriginal tribal ethno-medicine, which predates even Ayurveda, has been preserved and practised over the millennia. Mainpat (Surguja), Keshkal valley (Kanker), Chaiturgarh (Bilaspur), Bagicha (Jashpur), Kutumbsar caves, Kailash caves, Tirathgarh falls, Chitrakote falls (Bastar) are all exhilarating destinations being promoted for nature and wildlife tourism. As part of its drive to promote eco-tourism, the state will leverage on its wealth of medicinal plants to encourage development of herbal gardens and natural health resorts.

Scaling New Heights with Adventure Tourism

The state will promote adventure sports such as trekking, rock climbing, canoeing, water rafting, bungee jumping etc. Mahanadi River, Gangrel Dam, Madamsilli Dam and Kodar Dam have been marked for this purpose. The state government shall make efforts to provide training to youth so that they are able to take up these activities on a commercial basis and ensure the enforcement of safety standards.

Promoting a Pilgrim's Paradise

The State has encouraged development of pilgrimage centres. Rajim, Champaranya, Dongargarh, Sheorinarayan, Girodhpuri, Dantewada, Ratanpur, Sirpur and others which are prime destinations for pilgrim tourism. Sirpur and Dongargarh would be part of the wider Buddhist tourist circuit. The state will also create necessary facilities like Dharamsalas. It will develop sites for Buddhist pilgrims and become part of the wider Buddha circuit.

Trapping the MICE

With a growing thrust on innovative conferencing in the corporate world, Chhattisgarh is laying great thrust on establishing convention centres of international calibre to promote the destination to both the leisure traveller and the MICE market.

The state has encouraged investments in establishment of business-cum-recreation centres to cater to the needs of business travellers. State-of-the-art convention centres, seminar halls etc for corporate events are in the pipe line. Investments for the entertainment needs of business tourists with high purchasing power, facilities such as hotels, entertainment and amusement parks, multiplexes, health spas, shopping malls and golf courses are being encouraged.

A Shot in the Arm for the Hospitality Industry

The growing hospitality industry within the state is to benefit from the step indoctrinated, as the government has implemented a relaxed tax structure for hotels and restaurants with added incentives and concessions offered to new projects and developments. "Through government's action, private entrepreneurs looking at investing into the hospitality and tourism sector will be positive and will be urged in its endeavour to intensify its venture in the state. With tourism being accorded the industry status, it will receive various tax holidays and monetary assistance," divulged Ajit Jogi.

To garner a considerable participation of the private sector in development of tourism related infrastructure, the State government has decided (in collaboration with the private sector) to take effective steps towards development and upgradation of basic infrastructure like air and rail connection, road access, water, electricity and communication facilities. The state government will not involve itself in the construction and management of hotels and restaurants. However, the government, on its part, will provide suitable land on lease basis and encourage private sector through incentives, such as five year tax holiday on expenditure tax and sales tax.

With leading hotels of international repute such as ITC and the Taj hotel chains looking at business prospects here, Chhattisgarh is positioned to grow and set to succeed. The state, as projected by the government, is looking at urbanising considerably only in certain areas, therefore the option of setting business hotels and boutique hotels could be also considered.

Special Tourism Circuits

The Chhattisgarh tourism board has partnered with the great India Tour Company to promote and showcase special tourism circuits. The company is currently promoting two special packages to Bastar, which has been accorded a lot of importance as a circuit. Other circuits such as Raipur-Kawardha-Kanker and Jagdalpur offer a royal tribal experience. While the government will be responsible for the development of attractive tourist circuits, the private sector's responsibility will be operations of these circuits. The circuits will be developed in consultation and coordination with private tour operators, travel agents and hospitality industry.

The circuit-New Delhi, Jabalpur, Kanha, Bhorandev, Raipur, Rajim, Bastar, and Araku Valley have been proposed to the government for approval. Heritage property owners will be encouraged to convert these buildings into heritage hotels to attract foreign tourists. Private sector will be encouraged to develop budget hotels and motels extensively.

Tourism Policy at a Glance

The State has taken a conscious decision to do away with past legacies and adopt a fresh approach to tourism Development. The tourism Policy is focussed on creating unique image for the state and to position it as an attractive destination for both domestic as well as foreign tourists".

The Government of Chhattisgarh is firmly committed to capitalise on its 'New State Advantage'. The tourism policy reflects these contemporary views of the Government of Chhattisgarh. It is not a modification of any earlier policy and has been developed based on a comprehensive analysis of best practices of other Indian States and countries in the region.

The Tourism Policy is focused on creating an unique image for the State and to position it as an attractive destination. It aims at promoting economically, culturally and ecologically sustainable tourism in the state.

Besides strengthening the quality and attractiveness of the tourism experience in Chhattisgarh, it strives to preserving, enriching and showcasing the rich and diverse cultural and ecological heritage of the State. Increasing the contribution of tourism to the economic development of interrelated sectors, encouraging and promoting private sector initiatives in developing tourism related infrastructure, transforming the role of Government to that facilitator, promoting new concepts in tourism such as time-share, eco-Tourism, village tourism and adventure tourism while respecting the intellectual integrity and rights of the local communities are some of the policies prima focus.

Efficacious Marketing

To project the state as a unique and desirable destination to visit, the government will implement a marketing strategy in collaboration with industry stakeholders and the local populace. It will identify and promote anchor projects to precipitate the emergence of local attractions and develop a tourism portal, touch screen information kiosks and multimedia CD-ROMS to disseminate tourism related information.

Market research will be carried out at regular intervals to monitor tourist trends. Marketing strategies will be adapted accordingly. Other tourist friendly initiatives to be implemented will be metered taxis, computer based information and reservation systems, setting up of a chain of exclusive shops for sale of souvenirs, distribution of brochures, leaflets and other local items at all important tourist places, organising fairs to promote local cuisine, art and craft, folk songs and dances, participating in national/international fairs, trade shows.

The state will also have tie-ups with the tourism development boards or corporations of other states and international bodies for reciprocal sales and marketing of each other's travel & tourism products. Monetary and non-monetary awards will also be given to promote excellence in tourism. Finally, to make the campaign a success, professional advertising agencies and public relations companies will be hired. The private sector will be involved in planning and executing the promotional campaign.

TAMIL NADU

The most famous item of Tamil Nadu cuisine are the idli and dosa which has been recognised as India's staple breakfast diet. But there is more to the state's food fare, like the Chettinad cuisine. If you plan to commence your journey from the state's capital, Chennai, don't miss out on the beautiful sarees which are a specialty of this city, formerly known as Madras. Locals still refer to the city by its old name.

If temples are not your calling and nature is your religion, Tamil Nadu still does not let you down. With world famous hill stations such as Ooty and Kodaikanal on its map, you have nature in all its glory. Soak your self in the beautiful waterfalls of the region, as they are pure music to the soul. If you like a dash of salt in your water, Tamil Nadu has the country's most spectacular beaches, thanks to the Bay of Bengal. Check out Mandapam beach.

Once in Tamil Nadu, not visiting Kanyakumari would be a crime. Located at the confluence of the three seas engulfing India, Kanyakumari is also called Triveni Sangam. Renowned for its Swami Vivekanada temple, the region has one of the best sunrise and sunset panorama to offer. Take time off to observe the journey of the majestic sun at the tip of India.

A Classical Amalgamation of Culture and Heritage

Tamil Nadu is fast, gaining the strong attention of tourists worldwide like never before and the state tourism department has taken efforts to provide for world class infrastructure. This has resulted in the administrative forces working together for a common cause, to promote tourism through vivid and interesting culture and heritage on which the state rides high. Tamil Nadu is located alongside the coastline of Bay of Bengal, and her western border is flanked by breathtaking sights of the western ghats which fulfils even the minute desires of nature and adventure lovers. This state is also a home to the rarest confluence of three oceans, namely Arabian Sea, Indian Ocean and Bay of Bengal where a memorial is dedicated to Swami Vivekananda. Apart from this the sunrise and sunset here is a joy of beauty that is beyond explanation, especially on full moon days. The state is highly industrialised and the metropolitan state capital, Chennai is now the best-sought destination in India for its state of the art health care units, IT, biotechnology and is also known as the automobile capital of the country. For tourists who have visited this state, Tamil Nadu is not just a state with pilgrimage centres, beach resorts, theme parks but a destination where the ancient past continues to shape a dynamic present.

Etched in the sands of time are the voluminous manuscripts dated several thousand years back, which proves the existence of culture and style from our ancestors which has not forgone any change even today. Tamil Nadu's vivid history spans more than 2000 years and there goes a saying the older it gets the finer it becomes and the legacy left behind in the form of sculptures, monuments, and art takes tourists into the virtual past. The state's boasts three monarch dynasties-Cheras, Cholas and Pandyan who have left indelible marks not only in influencing present day culture and tradition but also exposing to the world the grandeur of their marvellous creations. The Pandyan legend king Kulasekara founded the city of Madurai in 6th century BC in a place believed to be the spot where a few drops of nectar fell from Lord Siva's locks, when he came down there to bestow his blessings.

Pandyas are also associated with Madurai's older and perhaps more absorbing and enthralling legend of the mother goddess Menakshi, who was born to king Malayatwasan and queen Kachanamala of the Pandyan dynasty.

Tamil Nadu is renowned worldwide for its excellent temple architecture, thanks to the Chola dynasty (the longest by a dynasty in Indian history). Cholas are the greatest builders of temples in the state and this can be discerned by the architectural style adopted by them, especially at the Brahadeeshwar temple in Tanjore, which pioneered a startling perspective to temple conception. They also introduced Bharat Natyam (Tamil Nadu's traditional dance praising the mythological gods and goddess) as a temple dance and several martial dances viz Simhaattam, silambam, marpor, jalli kattu. The tourism department of Tamil Nadu is keeping that tradition alive by organising dance festivals from time to time in various temples which have emerged as strong pilgrimage destinations.

It was about 600 AD that the Pallavas gained a stronghold in the northern part of Tamil Nadu with Kancheepuram as their capital. They have also created world-renowned monuments in that region. The Pallavas are responsible for the construction of the famous Mahabalipuram in the 7th century AD. Mahabalipuram is filled with unique monuments including sculptural panels, monolithic panels, structural architecture and cave temples. The beauty of this place is that all the monuments were created out of rocks. These rock monuments are a blend of mythological episodes, epic battles, demons, men and animals. The most famous and elegant of them are the five chariots, the shore temple and Arjuna's penance. Another major attraction for temple lovers in Kancheepuram, the 'Golden City of Temples' once a proud capital of the Pallavas, Cholas, Vijayanagar kings, the Muslims and then the British. But Kancheepuram is not just a city with temples. Out of this place, comes one of the world's most elegant clothing-the Kancheepuram silk sari.

Kancheepuram is just one of the many places in Tamil Nadu that protects its heritage and culture to this day.

If the temples in Kancheepuram zap you, then Tanjore will hold you spellbound. It is another major heritage spot filled with temples. The place is also known for its exquisite handicrafts, pith models, South Indian musical instruments and above all its bronzes. Connoisseurs of art worldover revere the paintings in Tanjore. The Cholas who were responsible for the growth of Tanjore were great administrators and builders, not just of temples but of other public structures too. During their reign, metal casting and making of bronze figures developed to a speciality, an outstanding example of which is the beautiful sculpture of the Cosmic Dancer at Chidambaram. Tanjore is known for its bronze and other metal carvings even today-a remnant of the legacy that was left behind by the greatest dynasty that ruled the South.

Tamil Nadu's heritage is not just its temples and saris. It spans across education, culture and music as well. And these traits come from time immemorial. Though it is not possible to date the exact period when the great Tamil Sangams [groups] flourished, historians say that two Samgams were held well before the Christian era and the third between 100 and 250 AD. The Tamil Sangam is the a major source of knowledge about the administration, art, architecture and economic conditions that existed then. They mark the golden era of Tamil literature.

Tiruvalluvar's Thirukkural which has been translated into many Indian and foreign languages consists of 1330 couplets about morality in private and public life combined with some of life's greatest truths. It is one of Tamil Nadu's gift to the world of poetry. Other great works by Tamilians include those by the saint-poetess Avviayar; Pathupatu or Ten Idylls which is a compilation of the work of several authors on philosophy, intermingled with descriptions of the natural world; and Ettuthogai or the eight anthologies. Of these, the last is historically the most important as it contains a description of the daily life of the people. This collection of poems is the earliest of its kind recorded in the history of Tamil Nadu.

Later years saw other great poets like the Nayanmars, the Alwars and the poet Kamban who composed the Tamil version of Ramayana.

When it comes to art and culture, Tamil Nadu represents the quintessence of Dravidian culture. The state has been the home of Dravidianism across the ages except during the last 300 years, when the British added a 'continental tinge' to Tamil culture. As the Dravidian dynasties entrenched themselves, they nurtured temple music and art at places like Thanjavur, Tiruchirapalli and Madurai. Nataraja-The Dancing Shiva was conceived by Vira Chola Raja at Chidambaram (940 AD). Thyagraja who lived in the 17th century he initiated a new genre in music-Carnatic Music. He enriched the musical reservoir of Sama Veda with his own vision and aesthetics, thereby inaugurating a singularity of rhythm, note and scale that thrives even today.

The wonders of the bygone eras can be found today at the Art Gallery (Chennai); Museum (Chennai), Kalakshetra, the National Art Gallery, the Government Museum, Cholamandal Artists Village, Kapaleeswarar, Art Gallery (Ooty) and Saraswathi Mahal Library (Thanjavur).

Every district in Tamil Nadu is rich with its own heritage and culture. There are many other tourist attractions like age-old churches and temples of monumental dimensions, whose history and glory can be traced back to ancient periods. They are a constant reminder of the fact that this was a place where once great minds had worked for great causes.

The culture and heritage of Tamil Nadu has for long been a mystery. One of the main reasons for this is because unlike other places, the rulers of Tamil Nadu, often from opposing dynasties, far from destroying the cultures they overran, developed theirs over the foundation of the fallen empire giving birth to unique new cultures and heritage. The result is what we are reaping today-a land filled with the rich resources of the past, an art form passed from generation to generation that is in existence even today. Or it could be the glorious churches and temples that bring serene peace for all who visit them.

Cultural Extravaganza-Mamallapuram

Mahabalipuram, situated near Chennai, is full of unique monuments, comprising of sculptural panels, monolithic panels, and structural architecture and cave temples. It has been declared as a world heritage destination. The Pallavas are responsible for the construction of Mahabalipuram in 7th century AD. The beauty of this place is that all the monuments were created out of solid rocks. These rock monuments emphasise on mythological episodes, epic battles, demons, men and animals.

The most famous and elegant of them are the five chariots, the shore temple and Arjuna's penance. Mamallapuram is other name for Mahabalipuram. Looking at the increasing influx of domestic and inbound tourists, the tourism department in the state has created a golden triangle circuit that connects Mamallapuram with Senji and Kancheepuram and this has become an instant hit. The state tourism department has been organising a mega event-the Dance Festival of Mamallapuram-every year from December 25 to January 15 to highlight the culture and heritage of Tamil Nadu to the world. This cultural extravaganza is declared open normally on the eve of Christmas. The grand New Year's Eve and the famous Pongal [harvest festival] celebrations during this dance festival makes it the ultimate colourful event. The organising of the dance festival in the peak tourist season enables all the foreign tourists to witness and enjoy the cultural feast of India. It also gives them an insight about the various performing arts and heritage which has been carefully preserved even to this day.

Special arts and handicrafts fairs will also be unveiled for tourists to carry home an ever-lasting memcry of their visit to this unique destination. According to the tourism department in the state, Mamallapuram, recorded approximately 1,42,000 tourist arrivals during 2001 December-January alone.

The most important aspect of Tamil Nadu is the speciality cuisine, which has captured many hearts all over the world. The department of tourism will also be organising food fairs and food courts. Apart from this, special tour packages in and around Mamallapuram will be in the offing. The tourism department will also be finalising various tourism activities which will have a special bearing on the eve of the dance festival.

Rendezvous with Nature

There are 5 national parks and 17 wildlife sanctuaries in Tamil Nadu. It is blessed with the unique distinction of having the Nilgiris and Gulf of Mannar marine biosphere along with certain plant sanctuaries. The flora and fauna found in these forests and lands are spectacular and some are endangered species. In recent times, this tourism segment has gained immense popularity and is now turning out to be a perfect destination for educational and adventure tourism.

These forests can be explored by trekking, hang gliding and other adventure sports. Rolling meadows, lush green valleys, cascading water falls, salubrious climate, cloud capped peaks, whispering woods, undulating tea estates, coffee plantations, wild animals, chirping of birds are some of the attractions there. Amidst them is a sylvan trail taking you to a still more serene ambience. For adventure-loving tourists this is a place to explore a new relationship with nature. TamilNadu is also called The Land of Enduring Heritage.

The Bay of Bengal encompasses the state in southern peninsular India on the East, Western Ghat Mountains on the West, the Indian Ocean on the South and the Deccan Plateau on the North. The topography of Tamil Nadu is delightfully varied and diverse. Of the 1,30,058 sq km. Land area, 17.6 per cent is covered with forest area. These spreads over the plain and on mountain slopes. Dry lands are bestowed with dry deciduous forests, thorn forests, scrubs and mangroves making it a perfect paradise for trekking and the tourism department is facilitating for various adventure sporting activities in chosen places. The Western Ghats and a few cooler regions are endowed with moist deciduous, wet evergreen forests, sholas and grasslands. Some of the favourite wildlife sanctuaries, which attract lot of tourists, are listed below.

Indira Gandhi WildLife Sanctuary

Spread over 958 sq kms, this sanctuary can be reached through Topslip in Anamalai Hills on the Western Ghats. An ecological paradise, this sanctuary encompasses a National Part with an area of 108 sq km. Abutting Kerala on the West, this hill forest boasts of thick growth of trees, folds of terrains with evergreen sholas. About 800 species out of 2000 South Indian flora are distributed here.

Mudumalai Wildlife Sanctuary National Park

This sanctuary is located where the Nilgiri Hills, the offshoot of the Western Ghats meet the Eastern Ghats. The Mudumalai Wildlife sanctuary has varied mixture of flat land, undulating parkland, open grassland, swamp, valleys and nullas. The Mayyar River in this region forms a series of spectacular cascades on its way. 65 kms. Away from Udhagamandalam [Ooty] and situated along the Udhaga-mandalam-Mysore highway, this sacntuary could be reached from Mysore as well.

This 321 sq kms Wide sanctuary encompasses a National Park measuring an area of 103 sq kms The vegetation is varied. Primarily moist deciduous. It becomes dry deciduous towards Bandhipur, mainly mixed forests with Bamboos (Bambusa arundinacea (, Natural teak (tectona greandis), Anogeissus-lafifolia, Terminalia, Crenulata / Teminalia tomontasa, Grewia, and blooming trees like Indian labumusum, Aredesia, Solanancea are some of the flora. The fauna include Elephants, Gaur, Bonnet Macaque, Common langur, tigers and leopards, chital, dhole panther, Sloth Bear, Python, barking deer, Four-Horned Antelope, Crocodiles (mugger), giant flying squirrel, Sambar, Hyena, Wild Dog, Wild Boar, Mouse Deer, Spotted Deer, Jackal Hare, Porcupine and Mongoose.

This Birds listed in this sanctuary are peacock-our national bird, grey jungle fowl, the red spur fowl, the grey partridge quails, goggle eyed power, Malabar whistling thrush, large racket-tailed dronge, the shama, the magpie-robin, spotted babbler, snall green barbet, green pigeons, little prey, eagles, hawks, buzzards, harriers, falcons and king vulture are predominant, berides some migratory water birds, From Udhagamandalam you can (Base camp at Parson's valley) trek to this sanctuary and the Mukkurthi National Park.

Mukkurthi National Park

Located on the high altitudes of the Nilgiris, comprising rolling downs interspersed with temperate shalas, this park is also a part of Nilgiri Biosphere reserve and situated 40 kms from Udhagamandalam. It contains a viable population of Nilgiri Thar (Hamitragus-hilocrius), Sambar, Barking deer, Nilgiri marten and ofter, Jungle cat, Jackal, etc. Avifauna consists of hillbirds viz Laughing and whistling thrushes, woodcock, wild pigeon and black eagle. Butterflies with Himalayan affinity like the Blue Admiral, Indian Red Admiral, Indian Fritillary, Indian Cabbage white, Hedge blues and rainbow trouts can also be seen.

Trekking routes exist from Parsan valley, portimund, pykara etc. Trout fishing is recommended in the rivers and lakes of Mukurthi. Permission from Asst. Director, Fisheries Department, Udhagai must be obtained in advance for fishing.

Kalakkadu Wildlifc Sanctuary and Mundanthurai wild like Sanctuary

These are situated in an extensive preserve declared as a "Project Tiger Reserve"

Kalakkadu

Kalakkadu Wild Life Sanctuary is situated in an area of 223 sq kms in the Tirunelveli District, including the foothills of Western Ghats and the adjoining area. The flora ranges from forests of tropical wet evergreen green to Tropical dry deciduous and thorn forest at down hills. Lion tailed Macaque, Nilgiri, Langur, Bonnet Macaque and Common Langur, Nilgiri Tahr Sambar, Sloth Bear, Gaur, Elephant, Tiger, Flying Squirrel, Panther, Wild dog, Pangoline are some of the wild life seen in the sanctuary. Besides, a wide range of birds and reptiles could be seen. Trekking can be done with prior permission from the Forest (Wildlife) Department.

Tamil Nadu Welcomes you to the SKAL World Congress

SKAL Club is a professional organisation of tourism leaders around the world promoting global tourism and friendship. India has been associated with SKAL since 1954 with about 10 active units. SKAL India will be celebrating its Golden Jubilee in the year 2003\2004.

SKAL Chennai will be 40 years in existence then. For the first time in 60 years, India has bid to host the SKAL International World Congress and won it for the year 2003\2004.

Chennai was conferred with the opportunity to host the World Congress despite stiff competition at the Malta World Congress in November 2000. The Tamil Nadu Tourism Development Corporation, tourism ministry and SKAL CLUB India is welcoming all delegates and tourists to attend the Congress. A variety of activities and packages including leisure and interactive tourism itinerary will be unveiled soon. Efforts are on to make the event as colourful as possible as there will be more stress on the rich traditional and cultural heritage of Tamil Nadu through various performing arts, handicrafts, history, shopping etc. We once again welcome you all with open hands to attend this grand event and make it a grand success. We assure you that you will return with memorable experiences of Indian hospitality, especially that of Tamil Nadu.

KERALA

The state has carved a niche for itself in three main areas-Ayurveda, Backwaters and Culture. It used to be an untapped virgin destination unknown to commercialisation until the concept of God's Own Country took the country by storm.

To its guests, Kerala offers beaches, cuisine, culture, tradition, festivals, the much-acclaimed backwaters, ayurveda and lots lots more. The first-timer will immediately be awed by the ubiquitousness of lush green paddy fields, the colourful people and of course the placid waters of the lagoons. There are certain must-dos in the state. First, the Ayurvedic therapies. These herbal massages and Ayurvedic treatments provide a complete rejuvenation of the body, mind and soul. The best time to undergo these treatments are during the monsoons.

Second on the priority list are the backwater tours conducted on kettuvallams (houseboats). These houseboats are eco-friendly and redesigned to fit in with modern day requirements. A trip through these backwaters with swaying green palm trees on either side offer complete tranquillity. It is a feeling I am yet to experience anywhere else. The next best thing to explore in Kerala are the bullock-cart village tours which relives the magic of a bygone age as the cart traverses from one village to another. The seven-day trip from Kochi to Quilon (better known as Kollam nowadays) is not to be missed. The sojourn takes you through 13 different backwater destinations. En route is Alleppey, better known as the Venice of the East.

In conclusion, I can only repeat that no state comes anywhere near in comparison with the abundant beauty that Kerala possesses. God's Own Country is precisely that-God's Own Country.

Pioneering the Green Revolution

Kerala or should we say 'God's Own Country' has been a success story from inception. The state with a landmass of 38,863 square kilometres and a positioning at the edge of India, has been recognised by many travellers, both national and international, as a masterpiece destination. Whether, it is focussed marketing initiatives, or proactive contribution from the state government and tourism department of Kerala or for that matter, the destination in itself, the result has been simply amazing. The accomplishments have been many.

It is one of the most sought after destinations of India, especially in the international arena. It has also been acclaimed as the destination of the millennium due to its increasing popularity amongst the national circuit.

Attractions such as backwaters, beaches, hill stations, monuments, waterfalls, wildlife and the most prominent of them all, Ayurveda, has been successfully presented and projected, in India and the worldover. Kerala is a sheer example of success attained through aggressive marketing, perfect packaging and dedicated team work from both the private and public sector. The department of tourism is working non-stop to introduce new attractions and offers, to maintain its status of being an 'evergreen' destination. Upgrading its prime product and attraction, 'Ayurveda', by introducing innovative packages and offers is one of the important formulas for success identified by the state. Having secured a steady increase in inbound tourist influx in the recent years, the department of tourism, government of Kerala, has chalked out extensive and concrete plans and strategies for further development and progress.

Says T Balakrishnan, secretary, DoT, government of Kerala: "The state has a wealth of products to offer and we would not like to rest on our laurels. Strengthening our position as the most popular tourist destination of India, is of top most priority of the entire team at Kerala tourism." At a recently held meeting in New Delhi, K V Thomas, minister of tourism, government of Kerala, spoke about the importance of tourism as the primary revenue generator of the state, along with highlighting the importance of bringing in more international travellers to the country.

Future Prospects

Kerala is all geared up to develop new circuits and attractions, for which the entire tourism department, along with the chief minister of the state has identified 'tourism' as priority area. Speaking with regards to the development of tourism infrastructure of Kerala, Thomas added: "Various financial institutions should provide loans with terms that are not rigid and the Central government should be willing to bear a percentage of the interest charged for these loans."

- The Kerala Travel Mart (KTM) 2002 which was held at Kochi in October, was termed as a highly successful travel meet, gaining participation from all other southern states for the first time. Keeping in view the achievements met at this year's Mart, the government aims to take KTM at the international level in the future. KTM also proved to be the ideal platform for Kerala tourism to showcase its developmental aspects and present offerings in a comprehensive manner.
- Following the success of KTM, the state also organised the first National Boat Show in Kochi, which functioned as a venue for manufacturers and dealers of

boats, water sports equipment, and life saving devices. The boat show also received central aid of Rs 2.5 million.

- Fort Kochi has recently received attention from the central government, where the minister for tourism, government of India, Jagmohan has identified Fort Kochi to be one of the places that would be developed as one of the tourism and cultural hubs in the country. Apart from the region's development, annual dance festivals will be held at the venue with an aim of encouraging local art forms.
- As part of Kaladi-Malayattoor sector tourism development, the Muthalapadi area will get Central government financial assistance worth Rs 5 lakh for its beautification programme.
- The master plan for a project worth Rs 290 crore, envisaged to transform Varkala into a prominent tourist destination in India has been prepared by the NATPAC for the District Tourism Promotion Council (DTPC). The implementation area of the project will cover some of the picturesque stretches that include the Municipality of Varkala, the Panchayats of Edava, Vettur and the backwaters of Kappil and Nadayara. The master plan aims to address issues, which warrant immediate development like tourist infrastructure facilities for beach and backwater-based tourism; to enhance the basic amenities at pilgrim centres, practice of Naturopathy, Ayurveda, Yoga, Meditation; to increase the rail, road and water transportation services; wastage processing; distribution of quality drinking water; boarding facilities; enhanced commercial activities and others in a mega scale. The project also intends to bring additional attractions at the Papanasam beach, Varkala Janardhana Swami Temple and the Sivagiri Mat from a tourism point of view.
- The government has sanctioned a sum of Rs 1.1 million for modernising the boat club at Neyyar Dam, that attracts innumerable tourists including international visitors. The District Tourism Promotion Council will be

responsible for the whole project and orders have been issued to complete the project within by the year end.

- The Department of Tourism has drafted a project called Zero Waste Kovalam worth Rs 7.1 million, intended to make the international tourist destination Kovalam into a waste-free zone. The proposed project will be implemented under the initiative of two non-government organisations panchayats viz Venganoor and Vizhinjam along with Kerala Hotel and Restaurant Association (KH&RA). Out of the total cost, the department of tourism will meet expenses estimated at Rs 3.5 crore and the government has granted the approval for the same.
- The prospects of joint tourism marketing with Sri Lanka travel trade are also being explored by the state tourism department. The state heads have had interactions with representatives of Sri Lankan travel trade in Colombo to formulate a strategy for developing a tourism zone consisting of Kerala, Sri Lanka and Maldives.
- As part of the Dubai Airport Expo, Kerala will have its representation in the Arabian Travel Market slated to be held from May 6-9, 2003. The event will have a Kerala pavilion to highlight the tourism potential and facilities.
- The states of Maharashtra and Kerala will join hands to devise a project for bringing tourists, both domestic and foreign to their respective states and also for active propaganda and campaigning at overseas venues. A decision to this effect was taken at a meeting held in Mumbai, in which talks were held between the minister for tourism K V Thomas and the deputy chief minister of Maharashtra, Chaggan Bhujbal. The ministers also focussed on tapping the increasing number of tourists from the Gulf region arriving in India for treatment purposes. Kerala is a favoured destination for Ayurveda treatment and plans are in the pipeline for setting up Ayurveda resorts and treatment centres in Mumbai and other parts of Maharashtra.

- The tourism department has also set base to promote Thenmala as an eco-tourism destination. The Thenmala Eco-tourism Promotion Society (TEPS) has been formed to implement the eco-tourism project at investment of Rs 8 crore.

Vision 2025

The main aim of Tourism Vision 2025 is to serve as a guiding force which will provide a clear direction to optimise the tourism potential of the state. The state has also done a SWOT analysis about its product.

Heritage tourism, eco-friendly tourism, health tourism and pilgrimage tourism are the other tourism elements which the state aims to promote and position in the future. The department of tourism is seeking investment in the region from both India and abroad. It is planned to capture the high spending, up-market tourist.

Targets

The state has identified some key target areas which are as follows:

- To increase earnings from tourism at the rate of 10 per cent annually.
- To achieve an annual rate of growth of 7 per cent in foreign tourist arrivals and 9 per cent in domestic tourists.
- To create 10000 employment opportunities every year.
- To add hotel rooms proportionate to demand in star categories every year, in both popular and upcoming destinations.
- To innovate and promote at least one new tourism product or destination every year and to constantly offer the world untapped elements of the state.

The state aims to make tourism the main vehicle for economic and employment growth; a vehicle for physical, social and economic development.

It also aims to promote sustainable tourism development with a focus on conservation and preservation of heritage. The participation of Panchayathi Raj Institutions, development of infrastructure through private sector and private-public partnership, promotion of sale of souvenirs, handicrafts, artifacts and other products are the strategies identified.

Public-Private Synergy

Kerala tourism has also taken serious initiative to encourage hospitality investment in Malabar region, with the help of Malabar region supporters. With public private synergy being the most accepted policy adopted by states across the country, Kerala tourism and the department of tourism, Kerala, has taken up the lead yet again in this direction. Special facilities and schemes are being planned for speeding up hospitality investments in the Malabar region, which has been targeted by the department as a promising tourism hub of Kerala.

- The state government is also encouraging private investment in developing houseboat facilities for the further promotion of the state. Houseboats holidays are unique to the state, which also proves to be a highly promising tourism attraction.
- Kerala will also host the Global Investor Meet, in January 15-19, 2003, to exploit the investment potential in the state, of which tourism would hold a prominent position. In a nutshell, with the state's Vision 2025 and the Tourism Act in perfect place, there is in fact no looking back for Kerala.

GUJARAT

Gujarat is a very colourful state: be it the locals, fairs and festivals, artifacts and even the destinations. Even the Gujarati people are very practical, pragmatic and enterprising. Religion plays a very important role in regulating people's lives there. It's ironical that the two most commonly used words in Gujarati-Kem Cho?-has so much in meaning besides the ordinary-how are you? It is a sign of welcome; one can break the ice with these two words; kem cho is also a sign of help and friendship.

One of my most memorable experiences of the state was going on the Royal Orient train that departs from Delhi and provides a complete window to many colourful destinations. Commencing with Chittaurgarh, the ride includes exquisite island palaces, grand buildings, 18th century gardens with fountains. The train moves on to Udaipur and Mehsana and then to Ahmedabad, the commercial capital of Gujarat. Sasan Gir and the awesome Lion Safari in Gir Forest follows. We then move on to Delwada visiting Diu and then depart for Palitana, the temple town. The other destinations en route are Sarkhej, Rankapur, Jaipur and finally back to Delhi. This trip is worth a try, at least once in your lifetime. In conclusion, I will add that to briefly write about Gujarat would not be doing justice to it.There is a lot to the state. Besides, I forgot to add that Gujarat is also the land of Gandhi. It is from here that Gandhiji undertook the Salt March at Dandi. Gujarat is also the land of khadi. These are just some of the facets of the state. There's much much more to it.

On the Tourism Highway

Billed as the 'Jewel of the West,' Gujarat is a state with myriad faces, a destination offering something for everyone. One of the country's most industrialised and progressive states, Gujarat showcases a perfect blend of the modern milieu and age old traditions.

A journey through Gujarat unfolds a religious, cultural and historical panorama. A veritable land of temples dotted with important pilgrimage centres like Dwarka, Somnath, Palitana, Pavaghad, Ambaji, Modhera Sun Temple etc, Gujarat is also steeped in history.

Besides being the birth place of Gandhiji and an important theatre of our freedom struggle, excavation sites like Lothal and Dholavira, provide a window to our ancient civilization. Comprising of a number of feudal states in pre-independence days, a number of palaces have been converted into heritage hotels offering tourists a glimpse and experience of a bygone era.

Gujarat could well be termed as the land of 'Festivals and Fairs' with almost 3,500 of them being celebrated in different parts of the state every year. Fairs like 'Tarnetar No Melo,' a match-making fair, the 'Kutch Utsav' are perfect ground to witness age old traditions in this day and age of satellite television. The state has also preserved its rich tradition of song, dance and drama of which Ras and Garba along with the Bhavaia form of folk drama, are the most famous.

Blessed with a variety of habitats Gujarat plays host to some rare wildlife species like the great Indian bustard, the wild ass, the blackbuck, flamingoes, the octopus, sea hare and 200 species of molluscs. Gir National Park is the only and last refuge of the Asiatic Lion. While the coastline of Gujarat may not be so famous for its beaches, there are a number of picturesque ones like Mandvi, Ahmedpur-Mandvi, Tithal are excellent for a sun and sand holiday.

Kutch, clubbed as the gateway to a timeless existence, is the biggest district in India and a fascinating destination. The sweeping vista of the great Rann of Kutch from Kaladungar or the Banni grasslands/marshlands, only known breeding ground for flamingoes in India and the Dhand marshes, the plains of Lakhpat and the mangrove swamps of Koteshwar, the Gulf of Kachchh with its coral reef make up for an unforgettable experience. It is also the hub of the most wonderful craft tradition, a colourful expression of the life of hardy tribals inhabiting a harsh desert landscape. Kutchi crafts range from Bandhni work (block printing on textiles), exquisite bead work, Sodha embridoery, patch work of Bhirandiyara, leather creations, silver work, wood and lacquer work.

Government's Role and Infrastructure

In spite of possessing a host of tourist attractions, Gujarat has not really been able to tap its vast tourism potential compared to other states. A combination of factors such as lack of effective policies, inadequate infrastructure, ineffective marketing and lack of decent facilities for tourists are believed to have led to this state of affairs. A series of calamities, natural and man-made, in the last couple of years has further compounded the situation.

However, according to P K Laheri, managing director, Tourism Corporation of Gujarat Limited (TCGL), "The worst is over and Gujarat is looking foward to an accelerated growth on all fronts including tourism. While the state government is in the midst of finalising a new tourism policy, the existing one gave a new impetus to tourism in the state with a policy of offering incentives for a variety of tourism projects."

During the ninth five year plan, the state attracted an unprecedented investment of Rs 1,350 crore in 230 tourism projects and this has helped the TCGL, the nodal agency to implement the incentive policy, earn surplus revenue for past three years. The main strategy adopted by TCGL is to coordinate its efforts with India Tourism Development Corporation as well as other state tourism corporations to augment tourist inflow and provide reliable and cost effective service.

The current tourism policy was drawn up with the objective of undertaking intensive development of tourism and increasing employment opportunities. As part of this larger objective, the policy focused on identifying and developing tourist destinations and related activities, diversification of tourism products in order to attract more tourists through a varied consumer choice, comprehensive development of pilgrimage centres as tourist destinations, creating facilities for budget tourists, strengthening the existing infrastructure and developing of new ones, creation of tourism infrastructure to preserve handicrafts, folk arts and culture to attract more tourists.

The state has already accorded industry status to tourism and the concurring benefits are available to tourism projects. The government is also emphasising on strengthening of infrastructure, particularly in special tourism areas. The state is also looking to set up effective mechanism to build meaningful coordination with the various state government agencies, local self government bodies, NGOs and the central government for promotion of tourism. It has also worked upon building effective linkages with relevant economic agents and agencies such as the national and international tour operators, travel agents, hotel chains and global tourism institutions like WTO.

State financial institutions which have made an important contribution in creating a conducive environment for industrial enterprenuers have been called upon to do the same for tourism enterprenuers. Lending by state financial institutions, so far largely confined to hotels, will be enlarged to encompass activities for tourism projects like wayside facilities on state highways, amusement parks and water sports, handicraft village complexes, fairs and festivals, camps and adventure facilities, sea/river cruise projects, sound and light shows, ropeways, safari projects, golf courses etc.

As the tourism policy focused on market-led developments, the state government had proposed to make commercial services available entirely through private sector or in association with it. As part of its role of upgrading and developing infrastructure, reputed consultants have been roped in by the state to prepare area development master plans/feasibility studies for important tourist destinations and potential ones like Sardar Sarovar Project Area, Kutch, beach sites and areas covering Porbandar, Gir forest, Verawal, Somnath, Ahmedpur-Mandvi, Saputara, Modhera etc.

The state has also gone in for privatisation of all commercial and competitive activities of TCGL except where no entreprenuer is coming foward to meet the existing need. The privatisation is aimed at helping the financial position of the corporation and also help provide quality services to the tourists. In addition to its existing offices in Mumbai, Delhi and Chennai, TCGL is slated to open offices in all major cities of India for wider publicity and dissemenation of information of tourism in Gujarat and to market its products. The government has also gone in for a single window clearance system for speedy clearance of various permissions, approvals required so that prospective investors do not suffer protracted and complex administrative processes.

The current tourism policy also envisaged the TCGL and Directorate of Tourism playing an active role to attract investors from outside the state as well as other countries, including non-resident Indians, to invest in tourism on a large scale. The tourism policy also planned the formation of a high powered committee under the chairmanship of chief secretary with the director of tourism as the member secretary with the objective of securing effective co-ordination among various government department, agencies as also to speed up decision making process. The committee, which is required to meet regularly, would enjoy full powers of government, provided the approval of the chief minister and council of ministers is obtained whenever required.

Planning and Development of Products and Circuits

Gujarat government has gone in for a prespective plan for tourism development in consultation with experts focusing on bolstering and creating new products in the following segments:

Religious and Archaeological Tourism: Gujarat has a preponderance of pilgrimage centers. Somnath and Dwarka, two of the ancient Hindu temples, are situated in the state. Temple architecture reached its heights of excellence in Gujarat's Jain temples at Shetrunji, Girnar and Taranga. The temple of Ambaji situated in Aravalli range in North Gujarat is an important religious centre for devotees in the country. Dakor, Pavagadh, Bahucharaji, Shamlaji, Narayan Sarovar, Sudamas Porbandar, Kabirvad Shuklatirth, Kayavarohan, Bhadrakali Temple in Ahmedabad and Tankara, Maharshi Dayanand Saraswati's birth place, are also important pilgrimage destinations which have kept alive the religious sentiments of the people.

These places are visited not only by devotees from all over thc country but also by non-resident Indians and travellers, especially from the eastern part of the world. The state government is focusing on creating and augmenting the necessary facilities and related services at these sites. For ensuring orderly and planned development of pilgrimage centres, the state government has constituted the Pavitra Dham Vikas Board chaired by the Chief Minister. The Board will prepare and implement plans to provide necessary facilities to the devotees and also ensure conservation of a cultural atmosphere consistent with the sentiments of visiting devotees.

Shamlaji is an ancient site for Buddhists. The excavated relics of the Buddhist period at the site are now kept in a museum at Baroda. There are a number of places of archaeological importance such as the temple-town of Palitana, Modhera with its Sun temple, the historical Ranki Vav at Patan with relics of an ancient capital, the Girnar Hills with Hindu and Jain temples, Junagadh with a historical fort, Dabhoi,

Champaner, Pavagadh, Gandhi Ashram, Siddi Sayed Jali etc. These are being marketed aggressively by the government and can be developed by providing necessary infrastructural facilities to be marketed as tourist destinations.

Heritage Tourism: The state is cluttered with a number of old palaces, havelis, darbargadhs. While a few of these historical buildings have been converted into hotels, restaurants or museums by providing suitable incentives to owners the state is working to increase their numbers. The government is also planning to create wildlife and pilgrimage circuits linking these heritage properties as development of this sub-sector will not only attract foreign tourists but also provide encouragement and support to local art and craft. Besides the government private enterprenuers have also taken the initiative in promoting heritage tourism in the state. Gopi Group, a leading heritage hotel management group of Gujarat, has created a whole new circuit connecting their properties. It is perhaps for the first time that a hotel group in Gujarat has created an exclusive circuit to promote their properties.

Besides Balaram Palace Resort, their flagship heritage property near Palanpur, Gopi Group recently added the Old Bell Guest House at Salya, Garden Palace (the Nawab's Palace) at Balasinor, Wakaner Palace and Rann Riders at Dasada. They have created four different packages ranging from 6 nights/7 days to 12 nights/13 days, which include a few or all their properties in the itinerary along with places of tourist interest closeby. The packages are not only aimed at augmenting revenues for all the properties but also boosting tourism in the state.

According to Dilip Thakkar, managing director, Gopi Group, "The success of Balaram Palace, which was conferred the SATTE Award by Indian National Trust for Art and Culture Heritage (INTACH) on the occassion of World Heritage Day, in April this year, prompted the Group to acquire other palaces and heritage properties to design a circuit to showcase the rich heritage of the state. Priced at Rs 2,000 per person per day (approximately), inclusive of transportation, food and accomodation, the packages are designed for foreigners and domestic tourist during Diwali and summer holidays."

Wildlife Tourism

There is substantial scope for development of wildlife tourism in the state. Gir Forest of Gujarat is the last stronghold of Asiatic Lions. The Bear Sanctuary at Ratan Mahal (district Panchmahal), Black Buch Sanctuary at Velavadar (Bhavnagar), Bird Sanctuary at Nalsarovar (Ahmedabad), Wild Ass Sanctuary (Kutch) etc. can be effectively developed into tourist destinations by providing infrastructural facilities. In order to facilitate visitors to these areas the government is working in coordination with various other agencies.

Coastal and Beach Tourism

Gujarat has the longest coastline among maritime states of the country. The state has identified stretches of coastline for tourism development and is working on providing accomodation and other facilities including water sports. Various tourist destinations, easily accessible from the coast, will be linked through coastal shipping circuits.

Tourism based on Fairs-Festivals and Arts-Crafts

Banni in Kutch, Khambhat, Junagadh etc. are known for their craftsmanship. Similarly, there are hundreds of fairs that are celebrated throughout the year and are showcases of the rich cultural heritage of the state. Kutch Utsav in Bhuj, Tarnetar Fair in Surendranagar district, Chitra Vichitra Fair at Poshina (Sabarkantha district), Kanwat Fair at Chhota Udepur (Panchmahals District), Dang Darbar in Dang. Bhavnath Fair of Junagadh, Vautha Fair of Ahmedabad etc. have immense tourism value and have been promoted aggressively by the state with great success. By developing accommodation, transport and other facilities, these fairs and festivals have become international events. The government has created circuits including places of importance, arts and crafts and other interests revolving around fairs and festivals offering tourists packages for a composite experience.

Corporate Tourism

The conferencing market is huge and realising its potential the state government is actively wooing the participation of the private sector to build state-of-the-art convention centres, seminar halls etc. Participants of corporate events like seminars, workshops and annual general meetings generally have high purchasing power and the government envisages a boost to the local economy with the boom in corporate tourism.

Adventure Tourism

This is also a territory with possibility of development as a sub-sector. The government is examining the promotion of new activities like camel safari in Kutch, horse-riding in the Aravalli Hill ranges, parachuting in Saputara, trekking in Dang, Pavagadh, Palitana. Such activities though targeting a niche market will help create large scale employment opportunities for guides, coolies, traders who hire tents and equipments etc. and will also encourage paying guest accommodation in such areas. Government is encouraging private entrepreneurs and institutions to develop such facilities.

Highway Tourism

Gujarat is among the leading states of India which have a good network of state and national highways. In the absence of adequate rail network most travellers prefer a road journey which due to the geographical expanse of the state, tends to be quite long and boridng. The state has realised the need for creating facilities like hotels, restaurants, picnic spots, water parks etc. along the highways at suitable intervals for the highway travellers to relax. In fact, travellers can be induced to follow certain traffic routes if such facilities are better developed.

Highway facilities and wayside amenities are so well developed in some states that this has become the mainstay of tourism. The state is encouraging private investors to create such facilities on highways.

Royal Orient: A Ride in Time

One of the world's most exotic trains, the Royal Orient takes you back in time to the days of Maharajas.The ride is a memorable week-long kalideoscopic journey through the prime attractions of Rajasthan and Gujarat. A joint venture of the

Tourism Corporation of Gujarat Limited and the Indian Railways, the Royal Orient is one of Gujarat's prized tourism products.

The train's thirteen salons have five star ammenities, a multi-cuisine restaurant, a well stocked bar called The Watering Hole and a library to make the experience akin to travelling in a new plane. Chugging out from Delhi, Royal Orient takes you on a journey through the historical and cultural mosaic of Rajasthan and Gujarat.

The train's route includes Udaipur with its romantic palaces, the pink city of Jaipur and Chittorgarh in Rajasthan. Sightseeing stops in Gujarat include Palitana, famous for its cluster of 863 Jain temples atop Shertrunjaya mountain; Somnath, housing one of the twelve holiest Shiva temples which was razed 17 times by Mughal invaders; Sasan Gir, the last and only refuge of Asiatic lions in the country; Ahmedpur Mandvi with scenic beaches and Diu island, the former Portuguese colony.

A week on board though pegged at tariff ranging from approximately US $ 50-350 per day will recapture the resplendence of the days of kings and queens and make you feel like royalty. All in all, a magical journey that you will cherish for a lifetime.

UTTARANCHAL

Scenic, divine, pure and peaceful are a few adjectives that immediately come to my mind the moment I think of Uttaranchal. As soon as you step in the state, the pure mountain air starts its cleansing therapy on you. You don't have to travel far to experience the specialties that nature has to offer in the state. Nature is there walking by your side every moment, every step.

An all-season destination, Uttaranchal has the country's most popular summer getaways, with Mussourie and Nainital being the all time favourites. Don't miss the tranquillising boat trips in the Naini Lake. The feeling it generates is nothing but sheer bliss. If you are in the mood for a spiritual sojourn, the Char Dham experience will get you nearer to that search for truth.

And for those who have a streak of the explorer in them, the state has snow capped hills and mountains waiting to be explored. Skiing is a sport which is very popular in winters and there are destinations such as Auli which is a treat for adventure sports lovers. For the nature lover, the state has rich flora and fauna. It is a destination meant for eco-tourism. Check out the Pahadi food of this region, which is made of special spices and herbs that have therapeutic values. The mountains of the Garhwal and Kumaon are destinations in their own right.

Carving a Niche in Indian Tourism

In this age of increasing globalisation, with the spread of Internet, the world has come closer. Travel, as S K Misra, vice-president, Intach puts it, "has become much easier on one hand. On the other, the core experience of travel-discovery and exploration of the unknown-has become elusive. Those areas of the world, which can offer richness and variety of experience are, thus, natural magnets for contemporary tourists." The newly formed state of Uttaranchal is fast emerging as such a magnetic attraction. Richly endowed with natural splendour, this picturesque state with a breathtaking panoramic view of the Himalayas promises tourists a visit full of unforgettable moments. The magnificent glaciers stretching like sheets of silver, the majestic snow-clad mountains, the gigantic peaks, the mighty, gurgling rivers meandering through lush valleys, the valley of flowers, skiing slopes and dense forests-the sublime beauty of this natural mosaic fills one with an ecstatic feeling, an invigorating experience that revels you every time the beauty flashes on your inner eye, teasing the travel bug within to come back again and again.

Putting the Best Foot Forward

That a planned, coordinated strategy coupled with adequate private sector participation and capital investment in infrastructure is needed to enable the tourism engine move on fast track was realised by the Uttaranchal government right from the beginning. The cash-strapped state earmarked tourism to give it the breather in the revenue mobilisation effort. Currently, the state is on a high. The government of India has awarded the National Tourism Award in the category of Special

Award for Efforts in the Development and Promotion of Tourism to the state. No mean achievement for a two-year-old new kid on the block. The award speaks volume about the state bureaucracy's mindset toward tourism.

The state government, from the moment of its birth (November 2000), has taken some concrete steps to emerge as a tourism force to reckon with. A forward-looking Tourism Policy, which clearly recognises the strengths, weaknesses and potential of tourism in the state, was announced in April, 2001 and put forth a definite action plan. However, as one's experience shows in India, many a gap exists between the intention and implementation. For a change however, one noticed that the state government has lost no time in taking important steps towards the implementation of the action plan.

The first and foremost step, with far reaching implications, has been the establishment of the Uttaranchal State Tourism Development Board (USTDB), abolishing the tourism directorate. Drifting away from the bureaucracy norm, the board incorporated five non-government members, including private sector representatives, who will also be a part of the administrative setup. "The participation of S K Misra, vice-chairman Intach, M P Bezbaruah, former secretary tourism, Jehangir Katgara, president, TAAI (Travel Agents Association of India), Maharaj I S Wahi, president, IATO (Indian Association of Tour Operators) and B K Gupta, former president, FHRAI (Federation of Hotels and Restaurants Association of India) who have been included in the board, will help us take the right decisions. Also, the idea is to gain leverage with TAAI, IATO and other associations to reach out to tour operators and hoteliers," said N N Prasad, secretary tourism, government of Uttaranchal.

"The board will have enough financial and administrative autonomy in order to provide a new thrust and direction to the development of tourism in the state. The budget allocated by the centre and the state will be handled directly by the board, instead of coming through the Planning Commission and other financial institutions. Soon, there will be a director each, appointed from the private sector for finance and investment, marketing and publicity and project formulation," said Prasad.

The state government is also adopting the master plan approach for development of 14 areas, such as wayside amenities, new tourist destinations, development of Tehri Dam area as a tourist spot et al. A sum of Rs 1.20 crore has been earmarked for it. While special emphasis is being accorded to promote cultural tourism and wildlife tourism, efforts are also on to develop the souvenir industry. The Tourism Board has empanelled 100 consultants including Tata Consultancy Services, AF Ferguson, PKF Consultants and JTCI Consultants, in 18 different categories ranging from landscape architects to agencies and has entrusted them with the job of preparing the master plan and identifying potential tourism areas that can be developed. The consultants will present their draft proposal at the investors' meet to be held in February 2003 in conjunction with CII at Mussoorie.

Getting the Basics Right

A strong base is essentially the first step of building a mammoth structure. And accordingly, the state is going ahead with a massive infrastructure development programme. Enhancing connectivity to augment tourist inflow tops Prasad's priority list. "The civil aviation ministry has sanctioned Rs 80 crore for creation of a national level airport at Dehradun. In addition, four new airstrips, one each in Chamoli, Pithoragarh, Chinialisor and Gaucher will be made operational in the next three months for small Dornier aircraft. We have also approached the civil aviation ministry to introduce heli services to the pilgrimage sites," Prasad stated.

Besides the proposal of a four-lane superhighway connecting New Delhi, the main domestic market for the state, the state is also lobbying for an exclusive train to Corbett National Park. The infrastructure development in the city of Haridwar, which will serve as a gateway to Uttaranchal, building new rope-ways are the other ambitious plans. Focused, planned and time-bound development of trek routes, yatra routes and adventure sports such as river rafting, paragliding, skiing, mountaineering are also on the cards, pointed out Prasad. On the flip side, no five-star hotels are being built in the state. However, at least 30 tourist lodges and guest houses would be built by the Garhwal

Mandal Vikas Nigam and the Kumaon Mandal Vikas Nigam. Accordingly, the number of beds in the government tourist lodges and guest houses, currently 7,500, would increase by another 3,000. Apart from upgrading the existing tourist lodges, the government is also promoting camp tourism, while a number of moderate hotels and paying guest accommodations are coming up under private participation. Most importantly, the state government has gone a step ahead by allocating funds for cleanliness. "This is the first state where the state government is spending money on keeping tourist attractions clean. Various tourist spots have been cleaned and beautified. We have roped in some NGOs for the work and have totally banned plastic bags." The tone of pride in Prasad's voice was not to be missed.

Wooing Investors

"We are looking at 100 per cent private investment and the state will act as a catalyst." This remark of Prasad outlines the state's viewpoint on public-private synergy. The state government is already in the process creating a Tourism Fund for tourism development activities. Arrangements will be made to mobilise finances for this fund through voluntary contributions from travel trade representatives, industrialists and other establishments connected with tourism. For this, a separate set of rules will also be framed. Besides, it has entered into an MoU with the Infrastructure Development Finance Company to ensure private sector participation in major tourism projects and for leasing out of tourism properties in the state. Under the new Uttaranchal Tourism Development Scheme, the state promises up to 20 per cent assistance for projects up to Rs 10 lakh. The projects could range from fast food joints, handicraft outlets and amusement parks to transportation and accommodation facilities.

What's important, the new amusement parks and rope-ways installed will be exempted from payment of entertainment tax for the first five years. The new tourism units will also be allowed rebate/deferment facility in the payment of luxury tax for a period of five years from the date of commencement. Further, norms and procedures for determining luxury tax on hotels will be modified and simplified. No doubt, a good opportunity to take a plunge in the splurge!

New Products and Circuits

If the first year, after gaining a separate state status, was mainly focused on making its presence felt in the market, the second year witnessed activities to showcase the state's diverse attractions. "In the first phase, we did a consistent campaign to create our identity. In the second phase, we are promoting specific products, such as adventure tourism, spiritual tourism, pilgrimage tourism, wellness, heritage and eco-tourism," noted Prasad. Winter months in Uttaranchal, marked by clear blue skies and bright sunshine, are particularly pleasant. Yet tourism here has been mainly confined to summer months. "To augment year-round tourism our special focus is on adventure tourism. Development of aero-sports and winter sports will give a big boost to adventure tourism in the state, which is already popular as a trekking destination. Development of Auli, Munsyari, Pauri and Pithoragarh as winter resorts and the creation of several new destinations such as Khirsu, Chamba, Dhaunolty, Binsar, Jageshwar, Patal Bhuvneshwar, Panchprayag etc tops our agenda. A new ski resort at Dayara Bugyal is being developed," he observed.

Domestic tourism, according to lieutenant general (retd) Tejpal Singh Rawat, minister of tourism, Uttaranchal, is the main focus market for the state, which aims to promote itself as a one-stop destination for spiritual, health, adventure and eco-tourism. USTDB is creating attractive tour packages to sell the Golden Triangle of Dehradun-Haridwar-Rishikesh, besides Char Dham (the four most sacred and revered Hindu temples namely, Badrinath, Kedarnath, Gangotri and Yamunotri nestled in the mighty mountains), and exotic hill stations like Mussoorie and Nainital. Two new circuits are also on the anvil to promote new destinations. The packages to be promoted with the help of tour operators will include air/rail/road travel, accommodation, excursions and sightseeing etc.

Marketing Strategy

Flaunting every saleable feature is the success mantra in tourism. And the Uttaranchal Tourism Board has adopted a multimedia approach to promote the myriad attractions the state possesses. "As for marketing, we have adopted a focused and well-structured approach to promote our products across the country and abroad. We have already partnered events like CII International Conference on Tourism & Heritage in 2001 and have been chosen the theme state at Surajkund in 2002. Further, Uttaranchal has actively participated in several events, namely the Travel and Trade Fair in Kolkata and the largest International Tourism Fair, ITB-2002 at Berlin in March, 2002," said Prasad. In fact, a high level delegation, headed by the tourism minister and comprising senior representatives of both government as well as the private sector was in Berlin. Significantly, Uttaranchal was also the partner state for the Indian pavilion during this fair. Apart from promoting the tourism potential of the state, a shelf of investment projects in the tourism sector was also offered to potential investors during the fair.

Looking homeward, New Delhi happens to be the main business-generating region for the state. "A full-fledged tourism office will shortly be opened in Delhi. We also aim to spread our presence in other potential states such as Andhra Pradesh, Tamil Nadu, Kerala and prime cities such as Mumbai and Kolkata. We have already signed an MoU with West Bengal Tourism department and hope to sign MoUs with other states as well," he added. That's not all. In order to give wide publicity to the exotic locales, efforts are being made to promote film shooting in the region. The board is toying with the idea of establishing a Film City in the region, which will provide the necessary infrastructure for film shooting.

A Peek into Some Tourist Attractions

Pilgrim Tourism: Pilgrimage has traditionally been the major attraction in Uttaranchal. The majestic Garhwal Himalayas that adorn the state is a rejuvenating spiritual experience for the devout. One would also find the four most holy pilgrimages of India-Yamunotri, Gangotri, Kedarnath and Badrinath, collectively referred to as the Char Dham. Traditionally, the yatra is done from the west to the east-starting from Yamunotri, then proceeding to Gangotri and finally to Kedarnath and Badrinath.

This state houses many other shrines and places of pilgrimage among which some of the best known ones are

Haridwar, Hrishikesh, Hemkund Sahib, Punyagiri, Nanakmatta, Meetha-Reetha Sahib and Piran Kaliyar. Many important religious yatras also take place in the state, of which Kailash Mansarovar Yatra, Nanda Devi and Raj Jat are the most popular.

Adventure Tourism: The sheer variety ranging from mountaineering (Bhagirathi, Chowkhamba, Nanda Devi, Kamet, Pindari Sahastrataal, Milam, Kafni, Khatling, Gaumukh), trekking, skiing (Auli, Dayara Bugyal, Munsyari, Mundali), water sports (like white water river rafting, kayaking and boating) to aero sports like hang gliding, paragliding (Pithoragarh, Jolly Grant, Pauri) and skating make the state a paradise for adventure sports lovers.

Nature Tourism: Untouched by the pollution and rigmarole of urban life, the hill stations of the state waits to open vistas of nature in their pristine glory. The rare diversity of flora and fauna, makes it an ideal setting for trekking on mountain and forest trails, nature walks, catch and release angling and jungle safaris. The hill stations, Musoorie, Nainital, Kausani, Pauri, Ranikhet Almora Pithragarh are some of places where Mother Nature has generously sprinkled its bounties.

Wildlife Tourism: Corbett is regarded as one of the true bird parks of the world. Out of the 2,060 species and subspecies of birds recorded in the Indian subcontinent, over 600 species/ subspecies of birds have been recorded from Corbett at one time or another. Apart from Corbett, other destinations are the Rajaji National Park, Govind Pashu Vihar, Asan Barrage, Chilla and Saptarishi Ashram. While the stress and pressures of the jet-age catch up with every city-dweller, Uttaranchal with its clean, fresh and invigorating environment, is a wonderful world to physically unwind and spiritually rejuvenate. The national award will, no doubt, serve as an encouragement for making all out efforts to establish Uttaranchal as a global tourist destination.

3

TRAILS AND TOURISM

The growth of the tourism industry has been one of the success stories of the post war world. International arrivals across the world have grown over 20 fold in the last fifty years. Globally, tourism now provides 10% of world employment, 12% of GDP, and is predicted to provide up to 100 million new jobs by 2010. Within that growth picture tourism is changing rapidly. There is an expansion in special interest tourism, in city based cultural tourism, in activity holidays and in rural tourism. The purpose built traditional resort is now paralleled by the concept of the world as a whole as a living resort.

> *"In Europe, tourism is increasingly seen as a possible partner for trail development and maintenance activities."*

The pattern of holidays is changing, with more holidays being taken, more out of main season holidays and more short breaks. The environmental impacts of tourism are increasingly recognised, and the concept of sustainable tourism (sometimes called ecotourism in the US) has been developed. Part of sustainable tourism's philosophy is to use tourism as a tool for regional and rural development, and for the conservation of human and natural heritage. It also proposes to cut the fuel burn involved in the tourism transaction by encouraging walking, cycling, rail and other fuel sparing holiday modes.

In Europe, tourism is increasingly seen as a possible partner for trail development and maintenance activities. Trails can benefit from financial and political support from tourism and local / regional development agencies. Tourism benefits from additional product, from new market opportunities and from image building. The economic benefits of well managed trails are now well documented: for the UK see Cope's 1998 paper in Journal of Sustainable Tourism: for the US see the 1998 publication by Roger Moore for the US Dept. of the Interior. This paper looks at how trail development has progressed in Europe, and why, from the 1980s onwards, trails and tourism development have begun to come together. It examines the key elements necessary for a successful relationship, and looks at issues for the future.

TRAIL DEVELOPMENT: THE 2 STAGES

1930-1980

This period was characterised by the planning and realisation by pressure groups and state agencies of a series of long distance trails-typically in excess of 60 miles-a length which requires more than a long weekend's walking. There are now 12 National Trails in Britain, with a total length of 2,000 miles administered by the Countryside Agency, a fusion of the conservation body, the Countryside Commission, and the Rural Development Commission: the new Agency began work on 1st April 1999. Many other European countries have similar systems.

These trails were never designed as tourist routes. They were essentially utopian creations designed to allow access across the countryside as a grand political gesture. They are challenge routes, used by a walking elite, typically middle aged professional men. They are not effectively marketed, few luggage transfer facilities are available, packaging of trail holidays does not go on. There is no agency responsible for increasing their use to boost tourism revenues to the areas they traverse. And the routes were not designed to be interesting, or easy to use. Long distance usage is small: they are symbols of freedom and hope rather than living usership reality. They are almost exclusively walking routes.

1980-2000

This period has seen a boom in trail development, and in the whole concept of the trail. Growing demand for outdoor recreation and rural tourism has coincided with a period where

European Union, national, regional and local public sector agencies have become active in creating new trails. The motives of those agencies have been many but include job creation, rural diversification, urban regeneration, and tourism development and management. Many of the new trails are short distance trails, and some of them are effective in tourism terms. But new types of long distance trails are also being created. Some of these long distance trails have captured the market's mood and its dreams and have become successful tourism products. Examples include Austria's Danube Trail, Britain's coast to coast C2C Trail, and Spain's revived Santiago de Compostela Pilgrimage Trail. In Britain, a national charity, Sustrans, is developing an 8,000 miles national cycle trail. Its free market, company sponsored counterpart, the National Byway, is developing a 3,000 mile route.

Trails have become multi-user and multi-purpose concepts-covering a range of purposes, not just "simple" recreation. And thebasic concept of a simple linear trail has changed. The 1980s saw the growing popularity of the circular trail, allowing users to return to their car or public transport. That concept was taken further by Tarka Trail in Devon, and Kingfisher Trail in Ireland to cover the Figure Eight Trail-able to link two trails at once in a unity. Trails which use multi-modes-part train, part foot for example-have emerged. And the speciality themed trail has become a common place. Throughout there has been the strong idea of using trails as a tool: one of those key tools has been for tourism development. And behind that idea is that trails should be economically productive if at all possible. Only then can the public sector back trails with resources and political good will.

Tourism is a key to the economic productivity of trails. Walking as a leisure activity was estimated to comprise no less than 850 million trips in UK in 1996, generating visitor expenditure in rural areas of £2 billion. Utilitarian walking is declining: leisure walking is increasing. Cycling is also a fast rising activity newly in fashion, with cycle sales outstripping car sales in most northern European countries in the early 1990s. Whole shelves full of new leisure activity magazines, speciality TV travel shows and travel channels, and bigger newspaper travel pages both reflect and spur this market.

TYPES OF TRAIL FOR TOURISM

The increasing expertise in the trail / tourism interface has led to the emergence of many new types of trail. These include:

- The Recreation Trail
- The Heritage / Commemoration Trail
- The Arts Trail / The Crafts Trail
- The Educational Trail
- The Nature Trail
- The Health and Fitness Trail
- The Youth Challenge Trail
- The Tourism Management Trail
- The Trail as a Tool for Local and Regional Development
- Trails as a Marketing Device and Niche Market Access Tool
- Trails for Grant Gaining
- Trails for Partnership and Reconciliation between countries, regions and peoples
- Trails for the re-cycling and conservation of routeways
- Speciality Food Trails
- River Trails
- Combination Trails

Although trails are increasingly seen as an essential part of the tourism infrastructure, many mistakes have been made in developing that infrastructure and many lessons are being slowly learned. Traditionally, trails were planned by trail enthusiasts, keen walkers and cyclists, often with powerful political ideals and skills. They were inspired people, inspired by the finite nature of the trail idea, coupled with its sense of movement and freedom within nature. The route, and the achievement of that route, dominated the trail making process. But to make trails work for tourism new skills are required.

DESIGN SKILLS

The key to success as a tourism product lies in the early planning stages of any trail. It must be designed to be attractive to its potential markets. That means (see below) that market assessments must be made at the design stage. The basic route should take account of prevailing winds and types of gradient, and the issue of stage lengths must be considered according to the types of market involved. Overnight accommodation, refreshment and toilet facilities should be brought into the design equation. And the route should be planned to be interesting-even exciting-to the market: tourism is essentially escapism, not a chore.

MARKET ASSESSMENT

An assessment of the likely markets for the trail can help the design process discussed above. That assessment should be based on the location of the trail, its potential characteristics, its likely marketing resources and partners, and the experience of other trails. It should note that speciality niche markets are likely to be involved, and consider the requirements of those niche markets.

Marketing

Tourism is an industry which is highly competitive and very dependent on marketing and promotion activity. Successful trails require effective marketing, and that is a complex issue. Tourism is a fashion product, an idea new to trails promoters. Success in trails marketing has come from effective co-ordination with existing local promotion, with effective use of promotions in the media, the integration of programmes of events, and in some cases with the development of Friends of Trails, user groups, and groups of people who help maintain the trails. The message for success is again that the trails must be what the market requires, and that above all the trail must create a fashionable image. Trails which are worthy but boring, or ill conceived, do not succeed.

Very few trails have their own marketing budgets or plans. The new trails consortium, Walking in West Cornwall, featuring specialist press advertising, the distribution of CD ROM's, and a web site is a pointer to future developments. The creation of marketing partnerships and involvement with the private sector is recommended. In Somerset, the River Parrett trail has developed a web site, first class guide book, integration with local area marketing, and a range of merchandise including CDs, and other goods.

Private Sector Involvement

Tourism is usually a private sector activity. Trail development is typically a public sector or non-profit agency activity. To be successful trails need to learn from the private sector, and to work with the private sector.

Market response and responsiveness is an area where the private operator can provide good practice examples.

For instance, the UK's cycle holiday and hire company, Country Lanes, is a splendid example of good practice, aiming at niche markets, using a range of electronic, print and media contact marketing approaches, and understanding the need for quality and fashion appeal. It maintains data bases on customers and customer enquiries, evaluates customer satisfaction and has a range of quality merchandise.

Working with the private sector can involve informing local providers of accommodation and meals about the needs of trail users, and introducing them to ideas which have worked successfully in other places.

In Switzerland for example, accommodations which provide special facilities for trail users are certified nationally according to two grades of facility. Grade awards depend on the availability of drying rooms, safe overnight cycle storage, basic cycle repair facilities, provision of packed lunches, luggage transfer etc. In return graded accommodations receive special promotion.

PRODUCT DEVELOPMENT

One of the areas where the private sector can play a key part is in product development, making the most of the opportunities that a trail provides. Product development opportunities can include:

- Introducing cycle hire
- Introducing speciality cycle hire

- Interpreting the trail to provide a fuller experience and valorize local interests
- Offering basic, middle range and de-luxe accommodation packages with luggage transfer
- Developing and marketing public transport access to trails
- Introducing events and festivals to the trail
- Encouraging retail promotions based on the trail
- Developing trail based books, CDs and tapes, calendars, mugs, T-shirts etc.
- Introducing new themes to the trail
- Working with tour operators to bring in long distance visitors

Partnership Approaches

One of the classic mechanisms to introduce successful integration of the public, private and non profit sectors is to develop a Trail Partnership. Partnerships can be used a fund raiser, a training agency, a marketing organisation, a lobbying group and a think tank. But while partnerships are relatively easy to create, they can be difficult to operate effectively. Much depends on the skills of the partnership manager, and the recognition by partnership members of varying agendas and abilities to deliver.

ISSUES FOR THE FUTURE

- Many mistakes have been made in developing trails for tourism purposes. Many opportunities have been lost. How can the future scenario be improved ? The following ideas are suggested for discussion:
- *A Handbook:* Tourism and Trails: a guide to making the link. This would be a full practical guide to design, market assessment procedures, marketing, product development, partnership operation and related issues for trail managers, and for local and state tourism interests.

- A national conference and / or regional conferences on making the link between tourism and trails
- A distance learning short course on how to develop linkages between tourism and trails
- A Diploma Course in Trail Management, incorporating tourism issues, available as a one year conventional course or a two year distance learning course
- Research into best practice in tourism and trails to back many of the above ideas
- A Register of tourism trails consultancies
- Development of data bases on organisations, tour operators, media outlets and individuals interested in trails tourism
- Networking between trails to discuss issues in tourism development
- A specialised tour operation(s) for US trails tourism ?

4

Tourism Marketing Strategic Approaches

- Marketing policy as a central component of overall tourism development & operational policy and the need for a strategic marketing planning approach
- The characteristics of tourism that affect marketing strategy:
  - — fragmentation of supply,
  - — interdependence & complementarity of tourist services,
  - — rigidity of supply,
  - — fixed in time & space,
  - — intangible-"expectation-experience-memory",
  - — price elasticity of demand,
  - — seasonality,
  - — consumer part of the product, and
  - — the importance of intermediaries.
- Strategic marketing planning based on differentiation and resource:market matching: Translating the situation analysis into product selection & development based on market demand & trends and leveraging factors such as: natural endowments, acquired endowments/public goods/externalities, risk mitigation. economic prowess. Need for ongoing research to adjust to, and/or take advantage of, market trends & exogenous factors

- Strategic marketing planning taking account of the different priorities of different stakeholders: NTOs, RTOs, state/province TOs, the national private sector and the foreign private sector (specifically foreign carriers, source market tour operators and international hotel groups)
- Marketing tools and techniques to achieve responsible tourism development & operation: Outline of the marketing mix to be elaborated in later sessions

To fully appreciate the role of marketing in tourism destination policy, strategy and planning, it is necessary to consider the several ways in which the tourism sector differs from other economic sectors.

TOURIST DESTINATION

A tourism destination has many different characteristics. It:

- is one product but also many,
- involves many stakeholders with differing objectives and requirements,
- is both a physical entity and a socio-cultural one,
- is a mental concept for potential tourists,
- is subject to the influence of current events, natural disasters, terrorism, health scares etc
- is subject to historical, real and fictitious events,
- is evaluated subjectively in respect of its value-for-money (based on reality compared with expectations), and
- differs in size, physical attractions, infrastructure, benefits offered to visitors and degree of dependence on tourism-in fact no two tourism destinations can be treated the same.

IMPACT OF TOURISM

Tourism has a far wider range of direct and indirect impacts than other economic sectors. At its simplest tourism can be seen to be a temporary addition to the population of a given location, with tourists having all the needs and impacts that the permanent population does, plus a few more besides. Government planning, regulation etc is therefore needed; yet tourism is an economic sector executed by the private sector. Tourism activity involves direct contact with the local population. Tourism, then, involves a triumvirate of destination interests-state, private sector and community. As such, tourism planning for development and marketing is unlike any other economic sector and requires special approaches, procedures and institutions.

PERCEPTION AND REALITY

How a destination, or commercial tourism organisation, promotes its products and/or services is a key factor in the realisation of developmental or economic/financial objectives. In an activity like tourism where the customer is "remote" from the place he/she is considering to visit, or from the tourism products and service he/she is thinking to buy, tourism marketing is a central component of tourism. Two of the adages of tourism marketing arising from this situation are that:

"you cannot test drive a holiday" and

"in tourism, the perception is the reality".

From the perspective of these three factors alone, it can be seen that:

1. Tourism is an industrial sector requiring a different policy and planning approach to others; and
2. Marketing policy is central to a destination's tourism development since it is the vehicle which will determine whether the destination succeeds in its economic and other objectives for the sector.

Government intervention in the form of tourism planning is justified in market-driven economies by one or more of market failure, market imperfection and public/social concerns about market outcomes. Market failure takes many forms: inadequate protection of the environment where tourism can exploit common resources ("tragedy of the commons"), exploitation of local populations, erosion of indigenous culture, and weak infrastructure provision-with high dependence on governments to act as the main providers-being the principal examples.

CHARACTERISTICS OF TOURISM WITH IMPLICATIONS FOR MARKETING

Before we can consider how marketing policy and strategy might be incorporated in a destination's overall tourism development approach, we need to consider those basic characteristics of tourism that have implications for the marketing function.

Fragmentation of Supply

The tourist product is a composite one, a combination of attractions, transport, accommodation, entertainment and other services. In most countries, there are many separate suppliers of these various components-airlines, hotel companies, tour excursion organisers etc. It is an important feature of tourism that, though an individual supplier of tourist services may serve more than one market, rarely, if ever, does a single supplier provide the entire range of products/services required by a tourist on a visit to a destination. Whether sold as a package or assembled by the tourist himself or by a travel agent, the tourist product is in practice a composite one. It is apparent, then, that given the fragmented nature of supply on one hand, and the demand for a combined set of products on the other, a fundamental challenge for a destination is to achieve coordination and integration of all components across all sub-sectors of the tourism industry-that is, of supply.

Interdependence and Complementarity of Tourist Services

It follows from the fact that tourism demand is for a composite product that the various tourist products and services are interdependent and complementary. The supply of one (for example international air transport to/from a destination) depends on the supply of another (such as hotel accommodation) and they complement each other. A destination's reputation can be set by the weakest link in the tourist product chain. This leads to the marketing policies and actions of one enterprise directly influencing other enterprises. A country with a liberal charter policy and/or an airline with an aggressive pricing policy may result in the attraction of low budget tourists, something that could damage the high quality image central to the marketing of a five-star hotel chain in the destination. There is again then the need for coordination and cooperation in order to enhance the effectiveness of individual marketing and promotional efforts of the various tourism suppliers.

Rigidity of Supply

Much tourism demand cannot be easily and quickly be adjusted in the short term to variation in demand. A hotel, for example, cannot add or remove rooms in line with demand. This relative lack of flexibility has obvious operational and economic implications. When demand falls below capacity, waste of resources occurs; when it exceeds capacity, the tourism industry fails to maximise its revenue. This "short term" can extend to years if the rigidity is caused by lack of airport or hotel capacity, given the extensive lead-time to construct a new airport or hotel.

Fixed in Time and Space

The composite tourism product cannot be stored-it is perishable-so a hotel room on a particular night or a seat on a given flight is available only once, and if not utilised, the sales opportunity is lost. Similarly, it cannot be transported. The need is to bring the consumer to the tourist product. The importance of ensuring, through marketing, as high a level of utilisation as possible is particularly marked because of the high fixed costs of many tourist operations. A hotel has to meet its fixed costs whether it has 5 guests or 200. The non-transportability of tourism products means there is no physical distribution in the strict sense in tourism marketing. Similarly, there are limited opportunities for merchandising activities, in consequence of the fact that the tourist product, unlike consumer goods, cannot be displayed at points of sale other than via proxy representations.

Intangible-"Expectation-Experience-Memory"

Tourist products, except items like souvenirs, are services rather than goods. As such they are intangible. The tourism product is subjectively perceived-each destination or individual tourist operation is a mental concept for each individual prospective tourist encompassing both physical characteristics and other abstract attributes. The subjective nature of perception involves an emotional and also an irrational element. In consequence, the tourist has to be offered psychological benefits. Clearly, this has important implications for advertising and promotion in tourism and generally on how a tourist product is presented to consumer groups.

In consequence of the intangibility of tourist products, when a supplier of a tourist services considers the potential market, the essential thought process should be: expectations-experiences-memories. This is the same whether the supplier is a destination promotion authority seeking to attract tourists to a specific country or location within that country, or the operator of a fixed-site facility like a hotel, restaurant or attraction, or a provider of tour excursion. Each tourist is a set of expectations. The tourism product cannot be test driven or known about with certainty in advance of being consumed. The tourist therefore builds mental images of the destination and of the facilities and other components of the tourism product of that destination. He/she has a set of expectations about the place to be visited. Experiences because the intangibility of tourism products means that the tourist engages in a series of activities-typically, for example, riding on transport, visiting attractions, staying in some form of accommodation, eating, drinking, recreating, interacting with other people-none of which produce a final physical product to take home. Each tourist trip, therefore, is a combination of various experiences.

At then end of the trip the tourist is left with nothing more than memories-the derivation of the word souvenirs-and proxies of the trip-such as photos or videos. The key for the marketer is that the expectations created achieve the fine balance between attracting the tourist while not promising more than can be delivered. The experiences are assessed by the tourist against his/her pre-trip expectations. A major determinant of success is how well the experiences match or exceed these expectations. This assessment has relative as well absolute dimensions. A destination may have a perception in the marketplace of being expensive or offering poor service, something which will limit its drawing power. If the tourist finds it is not so costly or that service is better than expected, his/her level of satisfaction will be higher. Of course, the reverse can also be the case with more damaging consequences for the destination. The intangibility of the tourist product and the consequent need for the marketer to address the potential market's perceptions of the tourist product has two dimensions: first, the need to offer psychological benefits to the prospective tourist; and, second, to recognise that the perception is the reality-with each tourist having sovereign power over his/her destination decision making-and that marketing activities should be designed to alter the market's prevailing images in line with the marketer's desired position.

Price Elasticity of Demand

Most forms of tourism demand involve the use of what economists call personal discretionary disposable income and free time. Holidaymakers or vacation travellers need both money and time to engage in tourism. They have freedom of choice as to how to use their money and time for tourism purposes, affecting decisions such as how much to spend, how long to go for, where to go, when to go etc. As a result, tourists are highly sensitive to price, and generally their demand for tourist services exhibits a significant degree of price elasticity.

The marketing implication of these demand characteristics is that the travelling public is susceptible to price inducements and to other marketing efforts in respect of choices relating to destination, place and type of accommodation, and timing of the trip. The price elasticity factor is growing in significance because of two interlinked factors, namely increased pressure on free time and greater ease of international travel ie more frequent services to more destinations at fares rising below prevailing rates of inflation. This will increasingly lead to a pattern of shorter but more frequent holidays.

Seasonality

It is a characteristic of most tourism markets that demand fluctuates over the course of the year. The principal determinant is climatic-either in the destination or the tourist generating markets. Residents of northern parts of the European and North American continents tend mostly to take domestic or intra-regional holidays in the summer months of June-September whereas they take long haul, inter-regional holidays more in the winter when the climate at home is generally cold and wet. As a result, tourist operators have periods when demand is near capacity and others when the level of utilisation can be 30 percent or even less, with the remaining months-the shoulder season-falling in between these two extremes.

These demand variations are all the more acute because of the fact that any tourism product cannot be stored-the perishability factor-and the concern of marketers is to generate as much demand in the trough periods as possible since the fixed cost element of any tourism operation do not change between seasons. The marketing response to seasonality can range from the reduction of prices in order to induce people to travel in periods other than would be their normal preference to targeting geographic markets with different seasonal patterns of travel so that the demand for the destination from one group complements that of the other group.

Other Tourists as Part of the Tourism Product

It follows from the fact that the production and consumption of tourism products and services are simultaneous-and that they cannot be made in advance and stored-that the producers/ distributors of such products and services are part of the tourist experience-hence the importance of vocational training programmes. It is also the fact that other tourists in the vicinity of the tourist when he/she is receiving tourist products/services constitute part of the experience. In tourism the customer is part of the product. This applies not only to hotels and restaurants, and tourist attractions or excursions, but to the whole destination. The type, quality, volume and other characteristics of restaurant customers, hotel guests or visitors to a destination influence the overall perception of that restaurant, hotel or destination by other potential customers, guests or visitors-that is, the market. Therefore, in marketing it is vitally important to identify and target the most appropriate market mix and ensure compatibility of the different target market segments. It would be unwise for a hotel to accept block bookings from two tour operators that specialise in older generation tourists and young tourists because the interests of these two groups are likely to be quite different and the behaviour of one an irritant to the other.

Importance of Intermediaries

A distinguishing characteristic of tourism is the relatively dominant role played by travel intermediaries. Tour operators or wholesalers and travel agents are all traditionally important in product design, pricing, distribution and promotion. In international tourism marketing the influence of travel intermediaries has its origin both in historical factors and in the physical distance between the generating tourist source markets and the destinations (or tourist receiving countries). This latter factor leads to the necessity for a special distribution channel. At the same time, the fragmentation of supply creates the need for the coordinating and facilitating role of the travel intermediary. Further, the relative lack of marketing expertise and capital resources on the part of individual destination-based suppliers of tourism products or services makes them dependent on travel intermediaries for the distribution and sale of their individual offerings. This often gives rise to the need for destination tourism operators to promote and supply at two levels through tour operators and travel agents (intermediaries) and direct to the ultimate consumer/tourist. The advent of sophisticated electronic technology has changed the balance of power, making it easier for destination operators-even relatively small ones-to communicate direct and at low cost with consumer. Nonetheless, the travel intermediary remains a major player in tourism distribution.

THE MARKETING RESPONSE

The distinctive characteristics of all service industries-identified by Middleton and Clarke (2001) as inseparability and intangibility, perishability based on fixed capacity in the short run and inability to create stocks, seasonality, high fixed costs and interdependence-coupled with those other aspects detailed above specifically related to travel and tourism strongly influence the attitudes and decisions of management in all sectors of the travel and tourism industry as they seek to respond to, and influence, prospective customers' demand for their products and services-the marketing response.

The role of marketing in the travel and tourism industry is to manage or manipulate sales-customer purchasing behaviour-on an orderly, continuous, regular basis, in order to utilise the maximum level of available, inseparable capacity, and to generate extra or marginal sales that contributes revenue at minimal additional cost.

While the principles of the body of knowledge about marketing, and its main theoretical elements, can be applied in all industries, the special characteristics of travel and tourism are so dominant in their implications, that standard marketing principles must be considerably adapted to be successfully utilisation in travel and tourism applications.

Middleton and Clarke (2001) identify three propositions about marketing in travel and tourism that are relevant to all the forms it takes:

1. In the context of opportunities and constraints arising from the business environment of a major global market, products in tourism are designed, adapted and promoted to meet the long-run needs, expectations and interests of prospective customers. This is the common ground with all forms of consumer marketing, and the cornerstone of all marketing theory;
2. Service products generally have particular characteristics of inseparability and perishability, which call for a different application of the traditional marketing mix variables. This is the common ground with the developing theory of services marketing as distinct from marketing goods; and
3. Marketing in travel and tourism is shaped and determined by the nature of the demand for tourism and the operating characteristics of supplying industries. The forms of promotion and distribution used for travel and tourism products have their own particular characteristics, which distinguish their use in comparison with other industries. These characteristics form the common ground on which marketing for travel and tourism is based.

5

THE PROCESS OF MARKETING PLANNING

INTRODUCTION

A marketing plan is essentially the means by which an organisation-whether a commercial company, a not-for-profit organisation or a government agency or authority-realises its goals in respect of its "market". It is a navigational chart and as such a tool for implementation, guiding the specific activities designed to influence the behaviour of the market and enabling the effectiveness of such activities to be assessed. The development of a marketing plan may not require intensive scholarly work; it is an attitude that will govern and influence the directions an organisation intends to go.

Drawing on Gartrell (1994), marketing plans typically include the following sections:

1. *Executive Summary*: the objective is to give a clear understanding of what the marketing plan is about without going into detail. Though presented at the beginning it is usually completed after the whole plan has been prepared.
2. *Situation Analysis (or what Kotler et al 2002 term "place audit")*: This assessment explores the structure, characteristics and performance of the sector, the community, the travel product, the economic environment, and the present and potential market. For tourism place marketing, some of the following questions should be examined:
   a. What is present demand for tourism attractions and activities in your area?

b. What resources and facilities do you have to market to visitors?

c. What is your community known for? What kind of image does it have among outsiders? And to local residents?

d. What are your strengths and weaknesses, and how do they impact your tourism markets?

e. What changes do you anticipate over the next five years-taking account of market and competitor trends-and how will they impact your ability to attract visitors to your destination?

f. What other developments and trends might impact your community/destination?

g. How responsive is your community to having visitors?

Developing a situation analysis is fundamental to better understand the capabilities, potential and interest that may exist for visitors within a destination.

3. *Objectives and Goals*: it is important in developing a marketing plan to establish measurable goals. This requires careful consideration of the demand and supply potential of visitors to the destination. Questions that address this issue are:

   a. What kind of goals should be established? ie short or long term? Is there a sound baseline against which such goals can be set?

   b. What kinds of tourism markets should be targeted, and what goals should be set for each target segment?

   c. How will the organisation assess the attainment of these goals?

   d. Are the goals realistic in terms of the organisation's resources, timetables and travel products?

4. *Market Segments*: The third essential element in a marketing plan is that of identifying and selecting the target markets-market segmentation, a topic that is

dealt with in a later session. No organisation has the financial resources to cover the whole of the market: it is necessary to identify and select those sub-groups with most interest in the products being offered. There are many means of segmenting the market.

5. *Marketing Strategies*: once the segments to be targeted are identified, the marketing strategies likely to produce the maximum penetration and benefit to the organisation are defined and specified. In selecting the most appropriate marketing approaches and deciding on the product's positioning, the organisation will need to ask itself the following questions:
   a. Which selected marketing strategies will be the most effective for an identified market segment?
   b. What are the strengths and weaknesses of a strategy?
   c. Who is affected by a selected strategy?
   d. What combination of strategies might be most productive in reaching a selected market segment?
6. *Marketing Mix*: how the product will be marketed to the targeted segments? Arriving at the most appropriate marketing mix will be determined by answering the four key questions:
   a. How will the product be offered to prospective tourist customers?
   b. What should be the pricing structure for the product?
   c. How should the product's positioning and image be communicated to its target market segments?
   d. How will the product be distributed-made available-to tourists?
7. *Resources*: an organisation needs to allocate its resources adequately to support the programmes outlined for attaining the desired goals. Without funding and personnel, programmes will not be productive. The following questions need to be addressed:
   a. To what extent will personnel and money be dedicated for a specific programme?

b. Will the allocation be sufficient to reach the desired programme goal?

c. Does the organisation have other community resources that might be employed towards a specific programme to ensure its success?

This section should also have a clear and transparent marketing budget.

8. *Implementation*: scheduling and timing are key determinants of the success of a marketing plan. These affect the placement of advertising and its impact on the targeted market segment. Questions that might direct the implementation of a plan include:

a. When is the best time to launch a specific marketing strategy for a specific market segment?

b. What kind of lead times applicable to various market segments would impact goal achievement?

c. In what sequence should various marketing elements be implemented? Does one strategy need to follow another to maximise impact?

d. Who is doing what? When? How? and with whom? In implementing a programme, is it coordinated for maximum efficiency?

9. *Assessment*: being able to evaluate a marketing effort is imperative. The questions to be posed include:

a. What kinds of results are being sought in a specific marketing effort? Are the results quantified?

b. What kinds of criteria have been established against which to assess a marketing programme?

c. What kinds of contingencies have been developed for a programme that may prove less effective than intended?

Terms of Reference (ToR6) for tourism marketing strategic plans vary in detail. The marketing plan is often prepared as part of an overall tourism strategic development plans; while at the other end of the scale a plan may be called for to address a particular marketing-related issue (eg brand image development) within an already-established marketing strategy. A number of examples of ToRs relating to typical tourism destination marketing policy and planning studies are included in the resource disk. As a general rule, these are drafted on the understanding that those undertaking the planning exercise will already be aware of the research and other tasks necessary to produce an appropriate plan. Emphasis tends to be on the liaison and reporting procedures so that the "client" organisation is kept fully informed about and is integrated within the planning process.

STRATEGY BASED ON DIFFERENTIATION AND "MATCHING"

What products do countries offer and market and how are they tailored to the needs of specific market segments? In a marketing mix, the first and foremost element is the product. No amount of creative marketing and promotion can disguise the shortcomings of an inferior offering. Yet, in tourism, it can be argued that the role of marketing precedes the development of the product. The marketer gathers information regarding the expectations of the target market (the customers). In the case of a country, its clients are its citizens, investors (both foreign and domestic), tourists, export destinations, multilateral organizations (the international community), non-governmental organizations (NGOs), and neighbouring states.

The marketer communicates to statal decision-makers what features and benefits each of these disparate groups desire and suggests how to reconcile their competing and often contradictory needs, interests, preferences, priorities, and wishes. The marketer or brand manager then proceeds to participate in the design of the country's "products": its branding and public relations campaigns both within and without its borders, its investment laws and regulations, the development and presentation of its tourist attractions, the trumpeting of the competitive or unique qualities of its export products, the tailoring and monitoring of its mutually-beneficial relationships with neighbours, NGOs, and international organizations.

In designing its "products"-and not just tourism products but the destination's total offering to the outside world-a country makes use of, and leverages, several factors. The way in which this manipulation is done produces a brand name and image/ perception among foreign groups (ie tourists, investors, trading partners). The factors include:

1. *Natural Endowments:* The country's history, geographical location, tourism sites, climate, national "mentality" (hard working, forward looking, amicable, peaceful, etc.)
2. *Acquired Endowments, Public Goods, and Externalities:* Level of education, knowledge of foreign languages, quality of infrastructure, the court, banking, and public health systems
3. *Risk Mitigation:* International standing and the resolution of extant conflicts (political risk), the country's laws, regulations, and favourable international treaties, its credit history, insurance available to investors and exporters
4. *Economic Prowess:* Growth promoting policies, monetary stability, access to international credit, the emergence of new industries.

Governments can influence many of these factors. While there is little they can do about the country's past history or climate, other factors can be shaped. Aided by input from its brand managers and marketers, a country can educate its population to meet the requirements of investors and exporters. It can improve infrastructure, reform the court system, pass growth-promoting laws, cut down red tape, support monetary stability, resolve conflicts with the international community and so on.

It is important to understand that the "products" and brand name of a country are not fixed and unalterable. They can and should be tailored to optimise the results of the marketing and branding campaigns. Maintaining the country's brand name and promoting its products are ongoing tasks-not one off assignments. They require a constant infusion of financial and human resources to conduct research and development to evaluate the shifting sentiments of the country's clients. States and regions are no different to corporate entities. They, too, must gauge and study their markets and customers at every turn and respond with alacrity.

STRATEGIC MARKETING PLANNING

For marketing purposes, strategic planning is the process by which an organisation: first, analyses its strengths and weaknesses in its current and prospective markets-"where are we now?"; second, identifies its aims and the opportunities it seeks to develop-"where do we want to get to?"; and, third, defines the strategies and costed programmes of activity to achieve these aims-"how do we get there?". Strategic decisions are always focused on the longer run, normally beyond three years.

Marketing strategy identifies and is designed to produce future sales revenue through the specification of market segments to be targeted, products to be developed and focussed on, and associated action programmes to realise the potential identified in these targeted product:market segments. Business strategy is not only about marketing, but all strategy for commercial organisations depends on its ability to persuade sufficient customers to buy enough of its products to secure a surplus of revenue over costs in the long run and to produce customer satisfaction. The key components of marketing strategy are:

- *Goals and Objectives:* The position or place in its chosen markets that an organisation seeks to occupy in a future period, defined in terms of sectors of business, target market segments, sales volume, product range, market shares and levels of profit.
- *Images, Positioning and Branding:* Where the organisation wants to be in terms of the market's (trade and consumer) perceptions of its products and values, including image and branding in relation to competitors.
- *Strategies and Programmes:* The specification of actions, including product development and investment, needed to achieve the goals and objectives set.
- *Budget:* what resources-human, technical and financial-are required to realise the goals.

- Review and evaluation: procedures and systems permitting the appraisal of the extent to which goals were met in the context of overall market conditions (including competitors' activities) and external factors.

As Middleton and Clarke (2001) state: "strategy is essentially proactive in the sense that it defines and wills the future shape of the organisation as well as responding to changing industry patters, technology, market conditions and consumer needs."

TACTICAL MARKETING PLANNING

Tactical decisions are always focused on the short run-from a few weeks to a maximum of one to one-and-a-half years-in which specific marketing campaigns are planned, implemented and evaluated. Tactics respond to market conditions and particularly to competitors' activities. Tactical, or operational, marketing plans include:

- *Objectives and Targets:* Specified, quantified, volume and sales revenue targets and other specific marketing objectives to be achieved.
- *Mix and Budget:* Decisions on the marketing mix (product, price, promotion, place) and marketing budget.
- *Action Programmes:* The implementation of marketing programmes and coordination of promotional activity to achieve specified targets.
- *Monitoring and Control:* An effective system of monitoring the results of the marketing and the application of control procedures related to the agreed targets.

The Strategic Market-planning Process

Kotler, Hamlin, Rein & Haider (2002) define the strategic market-planning process for destinations as going through five stages that answer the following questions:

1. *Place Audit*: What is the current state of the community of the destination, and how does it compare to places in similar situations? What are the community's strengths/weaknesses, opportunities/threats? ie what is

commonly termed the SWOT (strengths, weaknesses, opportunities, threats) analysis.

2. *Vision and Goals*: What do the community's businesses and residents want the community to be?
3. *Strategy Formulation*: What broad strategies will help achieve these goals?
4. *Action Plan*: What specific actions must be undertaken to carry out the strategies?
5. *Implementation and Control*: What must the community do to ensure successful implementation?

The Place Audit establishes what a destination is like and why. What Kotler et al cal "hard" and "soft" attraction factors are assessed in a comparative context. Sorting these factors into a SWOT analysis creates the basis for visions and goals. Economic and demographic factors are the basics but innovative and sensitive interpretation is needed.

For most destinations successful positioning and targeting takes account not only of tourist market trends but also the needs and desires of the resident population. Even finding a good fit with the local and tourist markets is not enough-the destination's competitors must be identified and assessed, with such assessment being made for each market segment. Kotler et al quote the example of Dubai-"the desert's most exciting city". In the early period of its build up to spectacular success-tourist arrivals doubled between 1999 and 2003 to close to 5mn-its marketing message was:

> *"It has spectacular beaches but is not Australia; it is one of the most secure cities but is not Singapore; it has opulent city hotels and superb beachside resorts but is neither Jakarta nor Bali. It has world-class shopping but is not Hong Kong."*

Called the sunshine destination, Dubai offers tourists a unique holiday adventure with five star leisure facilities, beautiful beaches, Arabian hospitality plus the modernity of a fast track, bustling metropolis. It may not accord to what many would term a "responsible" destination but it has pursued a highly successful tourism development and marketing policy and strategy in fulfilment of the objectives established by its government.

Relative to other destinations, a place can be better, broadly the same or weaker. If a destination is assessed to be a superior competitor, it needs to protect its position, though if it is outstandingly attractive this may lead to excessive demand growth possibly eroding its competitive advantage through overcrowding.

Where a destination is assessed to be a peer competitor, strategic options are for intensified competition or cooperation. This latter approach-termed co-opetition-can be a means of sharing the market between two destinations and reducing the costs of competitive marketing. A weak competitor will need to establish a new strategy and positioning.

Strategic planning is a long-term process so a clear understanding of likely future trends and developments that will impact the destination is needed. In considering Asian destinations, Kotler et al draw particular attention to the following: funding for regional and community programmes, globalisation, reducing financial resources, environmental forces and regulations, information technology and demographic changes (eg lifestyle changes, rise in the elderly population, decentralisation from national to local levels, integration between Southeast Asian nations).

In assessing a destination's competitive position, an "outsider-in" approach is needed in order to identify which of its characteristics represent:

— a major strength

— a minor strength

— a neutral factor

— a minor weakness

— a major weakness

Competitive positions are determined both by outside factors beyond local/regional influence and location characteristics that specific local actions can influence. The destination's long-term strategic approach should be seek to maximise the leverage of its major strengths and to improve its notable weaknesses. The "hard" and "soft" factors assessed in the strengths and weaknesses assessment can be presented in matrix form according to the five-scale degree of importance noted earlier in this paragraph. It may be necessary to develop such an analysis and matrix separately for each major segment being evaluated since not all the attraction factors will have the same meaning for each group. It will then be necessary to choose the factors of central significance to each segment and allocate importance values to these individual factors. In this way a performance:importance matrix can be developed per the model adopted from Kotler et al (2002) below.

For each factor, a rating should be assessed and entered in the matrix, based on, say, a numerical score from 1 (low) to 10 (high) for each of the perfomance and importance axes. When ratings are combined, four possibilities emerge. Where performance is lacking but the factors are important for the target market (cell A), critical improvements are indicated; where both performance and target market importance are strong (cell B) the need is to continue the value-adding process. Cell C indicates areas where the destination is performing poorly but which are not of high importance to target customers, so low priority is given for any action. In cell D, the destination is doing well but the factors of low importance so care should be taken not to over-invest.

Figure 1: Performance-Importance Matrix

Performance >> Importance V V	Low 1 2 3 4 5	High 6 7 8 9 10
High 10 9 8 7 6	*A. Concentrate here*	*B. Keep up the good work*
Low 5 4 3 2 1	*C. Low priority*	*D. Possible overkill*

Source: After Kotler, Hamlin, Rein and Haider (2002)

Even if a destination has a major strength, its value in strategy is whether it represents a comparative advantage to the destination over a competitor in respect of the target market segment. What is important is for the destination to have greater relative strength for factors considered important by the selected target segment. A place does not need to correct all its weaknesses or promote all its strengths, because factors vary in importance to different target markets. The destination should fully understand which strengths and weaknesses most affect the perceptions and behaviour of its targets. The resulting analysis becomes a major basis for developing destination marketing plans.

The next step is to identify a destination's opportunities and threats. An opportunity is where the destination has "a fairly good chance to achieve a competitive advantage" (Kotler et al, 2002) while threats come from unfavourable trends or developments in the environment that would erode its competitiveness. Each opportunity and threat has to be evaluated according to the probability of occurrence and the degree of advantage/harm its occurrence would have for the destination. By assembling a picture of the major opportunities and threats facing a specific destination, its overall attractiveness can be assessed:

Ideal: High in opportunities and low in threats,

Speculative: High in both major opportunities and threats,

Mature: Low in major opportunities and threats,

Troubled: Low in opportunities and high in threats.

Again, a helpful way to conduct this type of analysis is to use a grid with opportunities and threats on the axes and numerical ratings given from 1 to 10 for minor to major.

Carrying out the SWOT analysis and an examination of the key issues facing the destination enables strategic planners to develop a clear and full picture of the situation. However while many types of development and marketing action may be indicated from these analyses, they need to be consistent with a coherent overall vision so that these possible actions can be prioritised. Vision development calls for planners to solicit input from the destination's residents as to how they want their community to be in 10 or 20 years time-possibly through the circulation for comment of two or more possible scenarios (Kotler et al, 2002). A crude example might consider zero growth through a moratorium on new tourism development, managed quality growth based on a strict development approvals process permitting only specific types of development, to unrestricted growth encouraging all types of tourism development. Kotler et al (2002) also point out that the development of a vision should go further than simple distinguishing between potential growth paths by factoring in issues such as:

- which unique combinations of attraction factors should be targeted?
- which are the destination's target markets?
- what are the short-and long-term goals?
- what are the vision's operative prerequisites?

Once the "players" in the destination agree on a vision, it needs to be translated into specific objectives and goals ie clear statements about what the destination is aiming to achieve, and specific magnitudes and timescales for their achievement. Once the destination planning team has defined the vision, objectives and goals, it can translate these into strategies for accomplishing the goals.

Even in instances where a destination is found to have no obvious strengths, a strategy can be devised to create a competitive advantage. Kotler et al (2002) cite the examples of Varanasi and Sepang. The former has built international interest around events associated with the city's ancient and religious heritage-its 2,000-year-old history of knowledge and culture; while the latter has created a major event through the development of a world-class Formula One motor racing circuit, which attracts large international crowds for a small number of events BUT which is also serving to draw into Sepang other developments.

Strategy needs to be converted into an action plan with clear implementation responsibilities allocated-easier to do in small destinations than in larger ones! The action plan should list each action along with details of: who is responsible; how the action is to be implemented; what budget will be needed; and over what time frame will the actions be undertaken. A short-term horizon is needed for a tourism marketing action plan because of the need to be able to respond to the many influences on, and determinants of, a destination's tourism sector which cannot be anticipated when the initial pan is drawn up.

Strategy and implementation are the most important dimensions for a destination seeking to create a changed, relevant and strong tourism sector. The ability of a destination to succeed in these two dimensions varies and leads to what Kotler et al identify as four basic environments, as summarised in the following matrix.

Figure 2: Four Abilities matrix

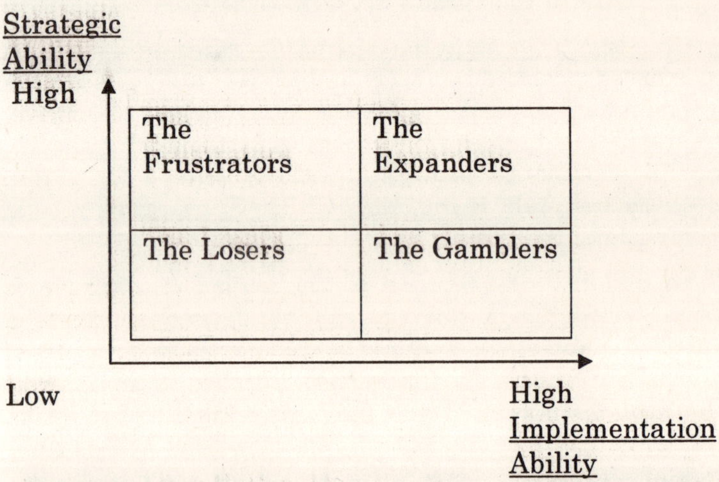

Source: After Kotler, Hamlin, Rein and Haider (2002)

"Losers" are those destinations with inadequate capacity to take action in either the strategic or implementation dimension. Communities demand subsidy and compensation arguing on the basis of "justice" or "need". "Frustrators" possess strategic thinking capability but not the necessary implementation skills. The planners end up being frustrated. "Gamblers" have weak strategic ability but strong implementation capability. Success comes-unpredictably and only occasionally-from luck and hard work. Targeted marketing is rare because the strategic targeting of the appropriate segments has not been made. "Expanders" are destinations where both the strategic and implementation capabilities are well-developed. The norm in such destinations is for leadership prepared to support long-term strategies and stimulate sub-strategies and action plans.

DISTINGUISHING BETWEEN STRATEGY AND TACTICS

Middleton and Clarke (2001) identify three strategic concepts to assist in distinguishing between strategy and tactics: strategic business units (SBUs) and business portfolio analysis; product-market growth models; and corporate and product positioning. Many large travel and tourism companies have a portfolio of businesses or SBUs, with separate management structures, profit and loss accounts and plans for the future. Within any such portfolio, performance and prospects will vary. Continuous analysis is conducted according to, inter alia:

- Share of market
- Market size, growth and stage of product life cycle
- Cash flow generation
- Return on investment
- Strength of competition

The Boston Consulting group matrix plots the first two of these factors. The vertical axis shows the rate of growth of the market in which the product is sold, while the horizontal one represents the market share of the product compared with its major competitor. The matrix is divided into four cells.

Corporate portfolios will comprise a mixture of:

- Relatively new product-market groupings with good shares of growth markets (stars)
- Profitable products with well-established shares of mature markets (cash cows)
- Products with weak presence in emerging high growth markets (problem children)
- Products with low shares of declining markets and poor profitability (dogs)

The marketing strategic response is to increase/maintain marketing support for stars (since the company may be forced to defend itself against competitors seeking a higher share of a lucrative market) and problem children (in order to gain a higher share of an attractive market), diverting funds from cash cows (where the low market growth makes it unattractive for competitors to target), and ignoring or terminating involvement with dogs.

Figure 3: The Boston Consulting Group Matrix

Product-market Growth (%)	*Market share – actual or relative* (%) High	Low
High	**Star** (maintain marketing investment)	**Problem child** (increase marketing support)
Low	**Cash cow** (divert profits to marketing for stars and problem children)	**Dog** (no marketing support; consider withdrawing product)

Source: After Kotler, Bowen & Makens (2003)

PRODUCT-MARKET GROWTH MODELS

Market conditions are constantly changing. Profitable product-market portfolios will usually be under constant competitive pressure, and it will be necessary to update and augment products continuously to match changing customer needs and market conditions. The options for strategic growth are incorporated in a four-box model devised by Ansoff (1987).

Figure 4: The Ansoff Matrix

Product	*Market* Existing	New
New	**Product development** (introduce new product to present market)	**Diversification** (launch new product to new market)
Existing	**Penetration** (modification and intensive promotion of existing product to present market)	**Market development** (reposition and target present product at new markets)

Source: Ansoff (1987)

Middleton and Clarke (2001) cite examples from travel and tourism for each of the four strategies of the Ansoff model:

1. *Penetration*-a hotel catering for the corporate traveller market decides to undertake an aggressive marketing campaign targeted at existing customer groups to increase market share.
2. *Product development*-a tour operator develops a new tour programme range which it markets to its existing market segments.
3. *Market development*-a Dutch holiday village operator sets up villages in new geographic markets (Center Parcs in the UK in the late 1980s).
4. *Diversification*-an airline company decides to buy and brand a railway operating company, stepping outside its existing product-market portfolio (for example, Virgin Atlantic acquiring the rail operation it branded as Virgin Rail)

Corporate and Product Positioning

The third concept is focused on securing competitive advantage through the creation of a perception in the marketplace designed to differentiate a company or its products from its competitors. Positioning thus underpins product/market growth through creating and sustaining a long-term favourable image among prospective customers. This topic is explored in detail in a later session.

COMMUNICATING WITH THE TOURIST

The marketing mix is the way in which the chosen marketing strategy is implemented.

It is commonly represented in marketing text books as a combination of a set of Ps-normally four (product, promotion, place-or means of distributing the product, and price) though Middleton and Clarke (2001) add people, process of delivery, and physical evidence arguing they are particularly useful in travel and tourism, which is typically a high contact service (the people component), an extended and complex service (the process component) and a service that can only be evaluated by the consumer as they experience the delivery (which incorporate the physical evidence component). The production-orientation of the four Ps can be converted into consumer orientation through converting these to Cs ie product = customer value, price = cost, place = convenience of access and promotion = communications. An analogy for the marketing mix is driving a car insofar as the individual elements-ie clutch, steering wheel, accelerator and brake in the case of the car-cannot be deployed with effect independent of each other.

The marketing mix will be dealt with in a specific session later in the programme.

6

E-MARKETING AND E-COMMERCE IN TOURISM

Information and communication technology (ICT) developments are permeating every aspect of tourism marketing. This paper proposes a methodological framework, which will enable tourism businesses to develop and implement their electronic marketing and commerce activities.

The paper initially reviews the e-business models literature. In the second section ICT implications in marketing and tourism are discussed. Then it presents the e-tourism business models and subsequently proposes a framework contributing to the planning and implementation of e-commerce initiatives. This methodological framework might also be used to analyse electronic applications in tourism.

It is suggested that a comprehensive strategic approach could allow travel and tourism businesses to overcome the challenges and exploit the opportunities presented by ICT.

INTRODUCTION

The rapid advancement of information technology, notably the Internet and the World Wide Web, has created challenges and opportunities for the tourism industry. ICT has considerably changed the role of each player in the value-creation process of the industry. Evidence indicates that effective use of information technology is crucial for tourism businesses' competitiveness and prosperity, as it influences their ability to differentiate their offerings as well as their production and delivery costs.

Barnett & Standing (2001) argue that a rapidly changing business environment, largely brought about by the Internet, requires companies to quickly implement new business methods, develop new networks and alliances, and be creative in their marketing. ICT stimulates radical changes in the operation, distribution and structure of the tourism industry (Buhalis, 2000). Structural changes in the tourism industry involve the necessity to elaborate an appropriate response to communication and transaction needs within a given nexus of market forces and opportunities. Therefore, there is an imperative need for tourism businesses to actively select between business models or frameworks that can best support an effective online strategy.

From a marketing perspective, the Web gives rise to a new and very effective tool and changes the way marketers define marketing mix variables (Kotler, 2003; Siegel, 2003). A plethora of tourism products and services are easily available over the Web. However, tourism is a highly competitive industry and consumers have many choices as to how and where they allocate time and money to their preferences.

This paper initially reviews the e-business models literature. In the second section ICT influences in marketing and tourism are discussed. Then it presents the e-tourism business models and subsequently suggests a framework, which will enable tourism businesses to plan and implement effective electronic marketing and commerce activities.

ELECTRONIC BUSINESS MODELS

Internet commerce has changed traditional business models and has given rise to new kinds of business models. However, there is no commonly acceptable definition of the business model's concept. Business models have been defined and categorized in many different ways. The probably best known definition and classification of electronic models is the one of Timmers (1998). According to him, a business model is an architecture for the product, service and information flows, a description of the various business actors and of their roles, as well as a description of the potential benefits of these actors and finally a description of the sources of revenue. In addition, he acknowledges the necessity of providing a marketing strategy, in order to accomplish a business mission. Timmers classifies the eleven generic e-business models he outlines, according to their degree of innovation and their functional integration.

For Rappa (2001) a business model spells out how a company makes money by specifying where it is positioned in the value chain. His taxonomy consists of nine generic e-business models, which classify companies among the nature of their value proposition or their mode of generating revenues. A very interesting framework is described by Rayport & Jaworski (2001). They divide an e-business model into four main pillars, which are the value cluster, the marketspace offering, the resource system and the financial model.

Osterwalder & Pigneur (2002) approached a business model as the conceptual and architectural implementation of a business strategy and as the foundation for the implementation of business processes. Three elements make up a business model: Revenue and product aspects; business actor and network aspects; and marketing specific aspects.

Obviously, the e-business models are implemented in a variety of ways and continue to evolve. Moreover, a company may combine different models as part of its overall Internet business strategy.

It would seem that a framework is more useful than a definition in contributing to the analysis of a business model's structure and in determining the critical success factors in e-commerce. Osterwalder & Pigneur (2002) formulated and proposed an e-business model ontology (e.g. rigorous framework) that highlights the relevant e-business issues and elements firms have to consider in order to operate successfully.

This framework is founded on four main pillars, which are product innovation, customer relationship, infrastructure management and financial aspects, as presented briefly in Table 1. According to these authors, a business model is nothing else than the value a company offers to one or several segments of customers and the firm's architecture and network of partners for creating, marketing and delivering this value and relationship capital, in order to generate sustainable revenue streams.

Table 1. The pillars of an e-business model

Pillars	Content & Components
1. *Product Innovation*	The products and services a firm offers, representing a substantial value to the customer and for which he is willing to pay. The main elements are the value proposition a firm wants to offer to specific target customer segments and the capabilities that a firm has to obtain in order to deliver this value.
2. *Infrastructure Management*	This element describes the value system configuration that is necessary to deliver the value proposition. This comprises the activities to create and deliver value, the relationship between them, the in-house resources and the firm's partner network.
3. *Customer Relationship*	Through the use of ICT firms can redefine the notion of customer relationship. The relationship capital the firm creates and maintains with the customer, in order to satisfy him and generate sustainable revenue.
4. *Financial Aspect*	It is transversal because all other pillars influence it. This element is composed of the revenue model and its cost structure. The revenue model determines the firm's profit model and therefore its ability to survive in competition.

Source: Adapted from Osterwalder & Pigneur, 2002

It is obvious that the four pillars are interrelated and mutually supported. As for the business strategy, it is worth stressing that e-commerce initiative is not an activity that might or should be developed and implemented independently and separately. It has been suggested (Porter, 2001; Strauss & Frost, 2002) that it is necessary to have a strategic approach to e-commerce as a medium to accomplish the business aims. Therefore, marketing in the electronic era requires innovative strategies.

Developments in ICT influence all marketing functions and the electronic marketplace brings new ways of marketing. It is obvious that ICT slashes marketing cost, removes intermediaries, and redefines marketing relationships (Rayport & Jaworski, 2001). The potential benefits resulting from e-commerce can be grouped into two categories:

- Improved effectiveness of current activities
- Broaden opportunities and new activities.

E-commerce has been defined as being "every kind of commercial contact or transaction between two or more parties, being done with electronic means and network, and having as direct or indirect aim to sell products and services" (Demetriades & Baltas, 2003: 40). It seems that this definition encompasses all marketing activities.

Rayport & Jaworski (2001) suggest that in order to compete in the electronic era, businesses must be prepared to use technology-mediated channels, create internal and external value, formulate technology convergent strategies, and organise resources around knowledge and relationships. On the marketing side, communication and customisation are among the new demands of the knowledge economy, whereby mass markets are a phenomenon of the past and interactive markets are the future (Wind & Mahajan, 2001).

ICT INFLUENCES ON MARKETING MIX

Evidence shows that ICT influences nearly every aspect of services marketing and the main stages in the marketing mix (Middleton, 2001). Kotler has restated the "Ps" (Product, Price, Promotion and Place) as "Cs" to reflect the consumer orientation that is central to modern services marketing thinking in an era of growing competition (Kotler & Armstrong, 1999). Product means Customer value; Price means Cost to the consumer; Promotion means Communication; and Place means Distribution, access or Convenience.

Moreover, the original four variables have been expanded to encompass People, Process (of service delivery) and Physical Evidence or design. These new marketing orientations are particularly relevant in the tourism field (Law, 2002a).

ICT has various influences in the fields of tourism and marketing. The Internet constitutes a medium of interactive communication and offers multiple uses for marketing purposes. Technological developments enable customers and businesses alike to change the way that they conduct exchange transactions, which are the core of all marketing (Hanson, 2000; Middleton, 2001).

The main implications of ICT on the principal processes in marketing include:

- Market research and marketing information systems.
- *Customer Relationship Marketing (CRM)*: The Internet has a catalyst role in CRM applications. The e-CRM tools contribute to the implementation of various marketing activities (Demetriades & Baltas, 2003; Vlachopoulou, 2003).
- *Strategic Planning and Networking*: Virtual marketing companies provide distribution and marketing services. They facilitate and provide a platform for the exchange of information and for e-commerce transactions for a wide range of products. The Internet also allows the creation of virtual enterprises in which ICT provides the linkages-especially networks for micro-businesses.
- *Advertising and Public Relations*: The Internet provides a completely new medium to communicate to targeted customer groups.
- *Information Materials*: The commercial developments of Web sites made the Internet an excellent and relatively low-cost medium for creating customer awareness using multimedia methods.
- *Sales Promotion and Pricing*: The Internet is an ideal medium for communicating prices, special offers and late availability of product. Through connectivity between databases and yield management programmes, sales promotions can now be customized to individuals.
- *Distribution and Access*: ICT has come to dominate the industry's way of thinking regarding the role and costs of distributing travel products. As a new channel for direct marketing communications, the Internet is also

reinventing distribution. Distribution channels are the new forums for product innovation and development; they establish the parameters for pricing against competitors and are becoming the most important tool for sales promotion and merchandising.

- *Consumer Behaviour*: The Internet-as a communication and promotional tool-is important, not only because customers buy products and services via electronic channels, but also due to its extensive use as an information medium (Turban et al., 2000).

Tourism is an important user of ICT and the industry is singularly well placed to benefit because of its special characteristics. Table 2 shows the main influences of the Internet in the tourism market.

Table 2. Consumption behaviour and Internet's influences in the tourism industry

Information search	Evaluation of alternative options	Purchase / transaction	Comments
- High information asymmetry - Mainly operational value - Satisfactory value	- Personal preference -High informative content -Low direct opportunity	- No particular contract requested -Simple payment -Simple delivery -High informative content -Purchase mainly for the result	-Frequent search is translated into frequent purchases -Low potential for consultative intermediary (preference market) -No prior assessment of the quality
Already in high degree on-line	Already in high degree on-line	Already in high degree on-line	Fast development in the Internet

Source: Adapted from Zeng & Reinartz, 2003, pp.125-130.

In the first decade of the twenty-first century, travel and tourism is one of the world's largest and most refined information based industries (Middleton, 2001: 218-219). Access to the Internet as a marketing tool provides a completely new means of bringing the two dimensions together by integrating promotion and distribution. The power of Web sites is that they can simultaneously advertise, inform, display, promote special offers, make a sale and provide instant booking and confirmation in customers' homes or offices.

E-TOURISM BUSINESS MODELS

Because tourism is an information-based industry it is one of the natural leading industries on the Internet (Anchi et al., 2003). It is anticipated that most, if not all, sectors in the travel and tourism industry throughout the world will have sites on the Internet; showing the suitable marriage of two of the world's fastest growing industries: information technology and tourism.

That is why e-travel is the leading and fastest growing category of e-commerce (Law & Leung, 2002; Demetriades & Baltas, 2003). In order to exploit these opportunities in the market environment, tourism businesses have developed and implemented several business models. Table 3 shows the most frequently used models in the tourism industry.

Table 3. Business models used in the tourism and travel industry

Type of Model	Description and Forms
Brokerage	Brokers are market makers; they bring buyers and sellers together and facilitate transactions (Law & Huang, 2003). Brokerage models include the following forms:
	Marketplace Exchange: offers a full range of services covering the transaction process, from market assessment to negotiation and fulfillment.
	Demand Collection System: it is the "name-your-price" model pioneered by Priceline.com. Prospective buyer makes a final (binding) bid for a specified good or service, and the broker arranges fulfillment.
	Auction Broker: conducts auctions for sellers. Broker charges the seller a listing fee and commission scaled with the value of the transaction.
Advertising Model	The web-advertising model is a Portal; usually a search engine that may include varied content or services. A high volume of user traffic makes advertising profitable and permits further diversification of site services. A personalized portal allows customization of the interface and content to the user.

Contd...

Type of Model	Description and Forms
Infomediary Model	Firms function as infomediaries (information intermediaries) assisting buyers and/or sellers understand a given market. Travel infomediaries are globally branded 'virtual businesses' on the Internet that collect and sell information about a specific sector of a market and create a convenient platform (Cyber marketplace) on which buyers and sellers can gain information and do business (examples: Expedia; Travelocity; BargainHolidays and Travelselect).
E-tailing	Business operating exclusively in electronic retailing. This model might take three forms (Turban et al., 2000; Kleindl, 2001): • *E-store*: a single tourism shop • *E-mail*: consisting of many electronic stores • *E-broker*: simply provides aid to customers searching for products and business. It gains a commission from the businesses.

R. Law (2001) provides valuable insights into the Priceline.com model. It offers products for sale in two categories: a travel service that offers airline tickets, hotel rooms, rental cars, packaged vacations and cruises; and a personal finance service that offers home mortgages, refinancing and home equity loans through an independent licensee. Priceline.com has pioneered a unique new type of e-commerce known as a "demand collection system" that enables consumers to use the Internet to save money on a wide range of products and services while enabling sellers to generate incremental revenue. Priceline.com is the world's first buying service through which consumers name the price they are willing to pay. Priceline.com licenses its business model to independent licensees.

Orbitz.com has implemented the Marketplace Exchange model. It is a leading online travel company that enables travellers to search for and purchase a broad array of travel products, including airline tickets, accommodation, rental cars, cruises and vacation packages.

A FRAMEWORK TO DEVELOP AND IMPLEMENT E-TOURISM BUSINESS INITIATIVES

This section examines the factors that are critical to the success of an e-tourism business initiative and subsequently proposes a framework to plan and implement related activities.

Researchers have attempted to approach and analyse the critical success factors in electronic tourism business initiatives (Bindiganavale et al., 2002; Demetriades & Baltas, 2003). Evidence indicates that these factors include Value/ Product; Marketing Uses; Supporting Systems; Service Provision; ICT Infrastructure. Apparently, the most important factor for a successful Web site is its ability to focus on customer needs.

The key is how to satisfy travelers' individual needs precisely and conveniently. (Anchi et al., 2003; Sigala, 2004). Additionally, the Web presence must be used efficiently; that is to say for marketing purposes. Web sites have to be dynamic interactive relationship marketing tools rather than electronic brochures (Morrison et al., 1999). Law & Leung (2002) have proposed an e-travel business framework to assess airfare reservation services in travel Web sites. This framework consists of information quality, system use, system quality, service quality, and customer loyalty. Rodríguez (2003) suggested a methodology for designing and deploying electronic enterprises-a step beyond intuitive or rule-based approaches and provided a framework for guiding the e-business development process.

Demetriades & Baltas (2003: 212-213) have summarized the various elements and have suggested five constituting dimensions of an e-business model / framework. These dimensions are:

- Value Proposition to customers and other business actors (products, services). This is the main corporate marketing decision.
- Revenue Model: Choose the potential sources of revenues (sales, advertising, subscription, and affiliation).
- Organisation Structure and Cost Structure: operational structure, business processes, and management information system.

- Positioning to the Market Value Chain: strategic positioning and business relationships.
- Networks: alliances and partnerships.

It is clear that every company might determine its own business model, a mix of the above five dimensions. Hence, adapting Osterwalder & Pigneur (2002) ontology and taking into account the factors proposed by the related research, we suggest the e-tourism business framework which consists of five elements shown in Figure 1. Its right side could be considered as managerial and the left one as being marketing-oriented. Therefore, the proposed framework takes into consideration the two important pillars of tourism business operations, namely management and marketing; the emphasis being placed on the latter.

Figure 1. Framework to develop and implement e-commerce initiatives in the tourism industry

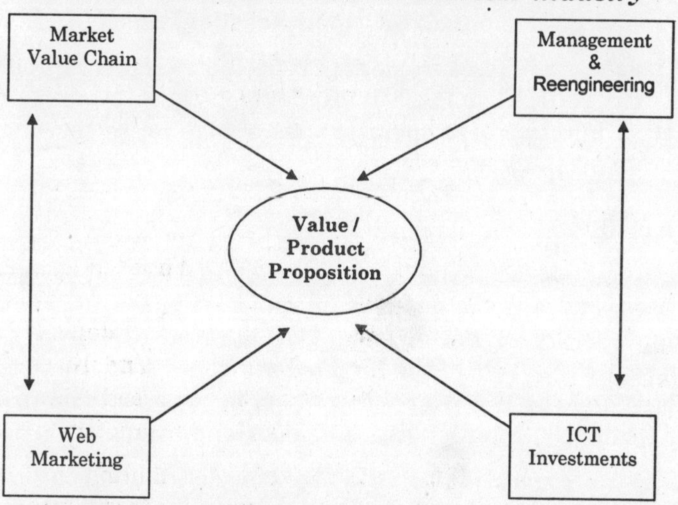

It should be noted that these factors-briefly described below-are interdependent and interlinked.

1. *Value / Product Proposition*: The customer's purchase should be approached as a search of "solution" for its needs, a solution that gives a benefit and involves a cost (Kotler, 2003). Select the appropriate marketing strategy.

2. *Market Value Chain*: Build up the appropriate network and alliances in regional / destination level. Recognize that business processes will change; for example, through new linkages and partnerships with portals and other e-commerce operators.
3. *Web Marketing*: Aiming at customer attractiveness and interactive marketing relationship. Create a meta market offering the whole package of travel services in order to support the customer experience's customization.
4. *Management & Reengineering: Resources and assets management*: This element encompasses the financial aspects (costs and revenues). Reengineering services processes producing and delivering the service offered (Tinnilä, 2002).
5. *ICT investments*: Necessary information technology investments; the electronic media and tools to be planned and implemented; and their adequate uses.

The above-proposed framework reflects a strategic approach (Christian, 2001; Kleindl, 2001) in order to integrate e-commerce initiative into business operations as a medium to serve the corporate strategy and aims.

CONCLUSIONS

Information technology leads to flexible and market-oriented business, and success depends on quick response to rapidly changing customer needs, using ICT in order to deliver the appropriate products to the targeted segments. The use of the Internet and the WWW enable tourism businesses to improve their flexibility, interactivity, efficiency and competitiveness.

The new economy is radically changing distribution patterns and traditional customer behaviour. A key issue for all tourism business is how to evolve their companies from an old economy to a new economy business. Undoubtedly, the Internet, both as a channel and technology, has created a disruptive change in the tourism and travel industry. It has been suggested (Soteriades, 2002; Siegel, 2003) that only a strategic marketing approach can allow the tourism industry to take advantage of ICT.

Tourism businesses have to consider and approach the Internet as a form of technology offering strong potential, a set of tools that can be used in almost every market and business. The crucial point is not whether a company should use it or not, but the way it should be exploited in order to create value (Porter, 2001). To take full advantage of the Internet; a company has to take into account the informative content of the product / service, the whole value proposition, contact and the interactive relationship that can be developed with its customers. In addition, it is important to point out that the "conventional" (off-line) and electronic (on-line) activities and applications must be complementarily planned and implemented.

We believe that the above-proposed framework contributes, on the one hand, to the development and implementation of effective and successful e-commerce initiatives; and on the other, constitutes a basis to evaluate the use of a commercial Web site as a marketing tool. We believe that it is worth stressing the following points:

- There is an imperative need for an integrated planning and implementation of e-commerce initiatives and Web presence.
- Beyond the strategy's formulation and organizational planning, the development of an Internet business presence involves some particular and specific actions in order to ensure its quality, thereby, contributing to the general marketing strategy's effectiveness.
- Evidence indicates that failing to introduce innovations, such as ICT, is due either to the lack of strategic planning or to the non-acceptance and implementation of the strategy in-house (Porter, 2001; Demetriades & Baltas, 2003). Therefore, the integration of e-commerce activities into business operations should be considered as a 'top-down process', which must be supported by general management.
- Finally, the e-commerce operation is not an aim per se, neither an activity that might be developed independently and implemented separately. It should be incorporated as a new media that serves current or future corporate general strategy and aims.

7

The Marketing Mix

- Matching, packaging, distributing & selling products for target markets using the marketing mix: product, promotion, place & price
- Mainstream (resort, general interest) vs. special interest (thematic tourism, niche products)
- Routes and route development based on clusters of tourist attractions/facilities taking account of transport access
- Public-private partnerships in product packaging. AMPM model-improving a destination's attractiveness (A), marketing (M), productivity (P), management of its tourism system (M). Product development consistent with overall tourism policy & strategic development goals. Public-private-community partnership in natural resource management.
- Promotional basket: advertising/public relations (developing positive response to products); sales promotion, merchandising (for immediate sales)
- The components of marketing communications and how they interact with each other. AIDA-awareness, interest, desire, action. Objectives of marketing communications-informing, persuading, reinforcing. Stimulus-response model of buyer behaviour. Personal & non-personal communications.
- The importance of public:private partnerships in tourism marketing. NTO facilitation processes. Reconciling the contrasting-sometimes conflicting-attitudes of local and foreign tourism operators towards the destination.

Creating a path for mutual benefit. Collaborative marketing schemes eg La Maison de la France. Methods of financing. Key success factors.

- Preparing a marketing communications programme to achieve given goals and strategies. Relating the power & method of influence of the different marketing tools to market & segment objectives & goals. Determining the extent and form of public:private collaboration possible. Budgetary & skills considerations.
- Responsible tourism vs ecosell. Increasing marketing's role in responsible tourism
- Promoting tourism investment opportunities. Development of tourism investment portfolios in fulfilment of tourism development policy, objectives and plans, and consistent with foreign investment regulations. Attracting investment into a high capital cost sector-role of incentives.
- Pricing in the marketing mix: the perception and reality of value-for-money.
- The role of intermediaries: relationship between retailers, wholesalers, inbound brokers, etc.: the different distribution models: direct or via intermediaries.
- The role of the DMO in tourism distribution and pricing: representing the destination in tourist source markets. Own network of overseas offices vs. marketing representation company.
- The role and impact of electronic technology. Impact on distribution-on-line reservations systems, spread of consumer usership for destination research and travel arrangement booking. Impact on destination communications-portals, gateways, one-to-one marketing. Opportunity for reducing the inequalities between local producers-even small ones-and foreign operators.

PRODUCT-CUSTOMER VALUE

The unique characteristics of the tourism product-and demand for it-and the wide range of determinants of this demand make it essential for all elements of the marketing mix to be right. At the same time it is necessary to remember that tourism is developed in the underdeveloped world for the benefit of the people of the destination. In developed societies it is a social activity with economic consequences, while in developing nations it is an economic activity with social-and other-impacts. In planning the tourism product of a destination, therefore, it is necessary to create maximum benefit for local society while giving maximum satisfaction to the tourist customers.

There are two possible approaches to strategic product planning:

Market approach: "what do we have that can be developed in a way to attract and satisfy tourists?"

Destination approach: "what are we prepared to develop that tourists might be interested in?"

In practice few destinations adopt either of these extremes but rather choose an approach somewhere towards the centre of the continuum, either to the "market" or "destination" side of it.

It is imperative to select the right package of product offerings for the most attractive market segments-in terms of reward for the destination. Then the destination positioning and branding to promote the product:market mix needs to be determined to ensure that maximum benefits are realised. The complexity of the task is increased by the fast-changing and evermore competitive marketplace. A place's ability to secure a unique position and positive image in the marketplace is a crucial part of strategic place marketing. Each place must formulate a combination of offerings and benefits that can meet the expectations of a broad number of possible investors and new businesses as well as visitors.

Kotler et al (2002) define place marketing as having four core activities:

- developing a strong and attractive positioning and image for the community;
- setting attractive incentives for current and potential buyers and users of good and services;

- delivering a place's products and services in an efficient, accessible way; and
- promoting a place's attractiveness and benefits in such a way as to ensure that potential users are fully aware of the advantages.

Pointing out that in many cases destinations focus on the promotional functions without properly defining their comparative advantages and planning for the development of appropriate products, Kotler et al (2002) identify a three-phase charter for the planning group:

- define and diagnose the community's condition-the "place audit";
- develop a vision of long-term solutions based on a realistic assessment of the community's problems-a vision founded on a combination of factors that are unique and commercially viable, upon which a value-added process can be implemented; and
- design a long-term plan of action that involves several intermediate stages of investment and transformation.

Destinations have what Butler (1980) termed tourist area life cycles-in essence the product life cycle analysis applied to destinations. The cycle-comprising the emergent, growth, stagnation & decline stages-can be over in a decade or can be extended with appropriate product and market development over centuries. Few new and emerging destinations adopt the strategy of targeting the whole tourist market catering for the mainstream beach or general interest touring segments. It is simply too difficult to create and sustain a differentiated positioning and image. Instead, destinations increasingly seek out their comparative advantages and develop their marketing strategy on these opportunities.

Cluster Development

Of particular relevance to newly developing destinations is the grouping of attractions and facilities into "clusters". This provides the economies of scale and scope to justify promoting the destination and serves as the magnet to "draw" visitors to the area. The most effective partnerships relate to "clusters" of tourism attractions and operations, reflecting the fact that a destination tourism product is comprised of many separate but interdependent components. Clusters can be developed for a geographic area or for a group of firms engaged in similar or related activities within a national economy-what are called "value chain groupings of tourism activities-in which case geographic proximity is not the defining characteristic. For example, in tourism clusters can be developed for all the golfing facilities within a destination to maximise penetration with the targeted golfing market segment. Using a clustering approach can help speed-up the cluster's members to competitiveness. This growth can be especially dramatic when supported by public:private sector cooperation. The critical advantage of clusters is that it allows members to cooperate and compete.

Public:Private Partnerships In Product Development

Put simply, tourism is a private sector activity but the activity (and, thus, operations in) tourism by virtue of interacting with local societies and their environments requires guidance and direction from the relevant authority. Additionally, the peculiar characteristics of tourism requiring the creation of destination awareness and a positive perception in the marketplace involves central government in marketing and promotion of the country. There is then a strong prima facie case for close collaboration between the public and private sectors, as observed by many writers-including Hall (2000), Bramwell and Lane (2000), Jeffries (2001) and the WTO (2000).

Drawing together the findings of a number of WTO studies the following points and issues represent a useful starting place for a consideration of the application and operation of public:private partnerships.

1. Public:private partnerships are a "natural" process in tourism because the roles (ie Government-policy, planning and regulation; private sector-investment and operation) are at the same time non-interchangeable but complementary;
2. The areas most suitable for public:private cooperation seem to be what WTO terms the AMPM model ie:
   - improving a destination's attractiveness (A),

- marketing (M),
- productivity (P),
- management (M) of its tourism system;

3. More sophisticated forms of cooperation entail long term partnerships between local tourism clusters, with governments or other central authorities, and with international organisations
4. The attractiveness component is crucial as it acknowledges that increasing destination competition makes it ever more difficult for destinations to differentiate themselves and to afford the investment needed for marketing and managing their tourism sectors-certainly it is beyond the means of developing countries and even established tourism destinations of relatively small scale eg Malta. Pooling resources in order to achieve good value for effort is essential-nothing must be wasted or duplicated, and consistency based on consensus must be the approach.
5. In developing the specific form of a partnership each party has to recognise its roles which can be summarised as:

Public Sector

- has a vision for tourism,
- provides an enabling environment for tourism,
- ensures adequate infrastructure development and maintenance,
- creates sufficiently open market conditions to stimulate tourism investment,
- provides support facilities and facilitation services, along with appropriate incentives,
- guarantees stable regulations and fair taxation,
- provides a regulatory framework to protect and enhance natural and socio-cultural environments,
- assures the well-being of local communities and visitors,

- undertakes and distributes market research and information for investors and operators.

Private Sector

- understands the environmental and social concerns of government and local communities,
- provides the expertise and access to finance to develop and operate tourism facilities,
- assumes collective responsibility for laying down industry standards,
- contributes to preserving culture and heritage and protect the environment,
- involves local communities in tourism development and ensures they enjoy their fair share of benefits,
- undertakes industry training to achieve excellence of service,
- works with governments to ensure the safety and security of tourists,
- contributes to improved research and the development of statistical databases,
- harnesses technology to improve the efficiency of tourism operations, marketing and service.

6. Each country differs so the structure of any partnership will be unique to each destination, while roles and responsibilities change as a country's tourism sector develops.
7. Key critical success factors can be identified as:
   - the need for a balanced structure within the partnership with clear roles and responsibilities for all partners,
   - shared leadership between the public and private sector with well-defined, shared goals, realistic expectations and the identification of benefits for each partner,
   - a flexible approach on the part of all partners, combined with a willingness to understand each other's needs and to contribute to shared resources,

- understanding between all partners that tourism development must be sustainable-economically, socially and environmentally,
- a long term commitment combining a strategic vision and plan with shorter term goals and measurable initiatives,
- periodic evaluation of the efficacy of each partner's role,
- good communication between partners and from partners to all stakeholders.

8. The question of financing public:private partnerships is the issue which causes most problems. Various approaches and formulae have been used depending on the nature of the collaboration eg incentives for tourism development projects so that adequate levels of investment are attracted, tax holidays or special sales taxes levied on the tourist to fund marketing partnerships.

The private sector may not always do what destination Governments, host communities and NGOs with a "fair trade" or "pro poor" agenda might want, but without their investment of resources and the ability to operate on a commercially viable basis sustainable tourism cannot be achieved since no tourism facilities will be developed or operated under circumstances which prevent tourism businesses from types of development which enable them to make a profit.

In the great majority of developing country destinations the negative consequences of zero tourism development would far outweigh instances where ridding a destination of tourism might benefit the people of those destinations.

The fundamental truth that should never be forgotten by planners, lobbyists or others seeking to determine the shape and rules of engagement of the sector, is that it is overwhelmingly a private sector activity. The key to successful public:private partnerahip in tourism is to understand the motives and methods of the private sector-particularly of the foreign operators with which the destination does business-and to enlist the cooperation and commitment of the private sector:

— in pursuing practices which are mutually beneficial to both operator and destination-short term priorities-and

— in the realisation of strategies determined by the destination-a longer term goal.

Through fostering a partnership approach, tour operators can be-and are being-persuaded to adopt practices that are leading to sustainable development in destinations, as evidenced by the Tour Operators' Initiative for Sustainable Tourism Development and the Association for Independent Tour Operators' (AITO's) Responsible Tourism Guidelines.

PROMOTION

Focussing on the promotion element of the four Ps, good communication is the key to effective marketing. Potential customers go through a purchase cycle: pre-transactional (i.e. before a purchase), transactional (ie at the time of purchase) and post-transactional (ie after the purchase has been made). The AIDA model encapsulates this sequence and can assist in the planning of any communications campaign:

A-*awareness/attention*-making the consumer aware of the product and getting his attention

I-*interest*-generating interest in the product/service on offer

D-*desire*-creating a desire for your product /service-on two levels: first, related to the target's needs/wants; and, second, relative to your competitors

A-*action*-stimulating the target to purchase the product/ service

Effectiveness of communication can be judged against the customer's stage of development through the purchase cycle. In general, the objectives of communication will be from one of the following three categories:

- *Informing*-giving information, building awareness that a product/service exists, what its attributes are, where it can be obtained etc
- *Persuading*-creating a favourable attitude, providing a stimulus to favour one brand over another etc.

- *Reinforcing*-dispelling doubts about a purchase decision already taken, building support/loyalty, ensuring a good climate for future sales.

Consider what happens when you encounter a new product for the first time-say a destination like the Cook Islands in the South Pacific. Your initial contact may be via a magazine/ newspaper or television feature, a casual web surf, a conversation with a family member/friend/work or study colleague etc. You use clues to determine how you respond to this new destination. These include: the type of feature/ information about the destination, the type of tourist products it offers, image portrayed, apparent quality, price and packaging (though some of these items of information will have to be sought out after the initial awareness has been created). Of course, your own experience of other, comparable destinations is used as a filter.

A stimulus-response model of buyer behaviour illustrates five processes: first, the stimulus input ie the product offering-or menu-in travel and tourism which provokes the sense of wanting to take a holiday trip; second, the communications channels comprising the full range of communications paid or otherwise orchestrated by product/service suppliers plus and in conjunction with the influence of friends, family, reference groups, guide books etc; third, the buyer characteristics and decision process ie the communications filters of perceptions built up from diverse sources, learning and past experiences; together these link with the whole range of physical and psychological dimensions to determine needs/wants/goals ie the motivation; and, finally, the response to the first four stages is the purchase choice made.

Marketing communications media fall into two groups: personal and non-personal. In travel and tourism, personal marketing communications are principally through telephone/ email, website (which, as shown later in this Unit, can be a highly effective personalised means of communicating) and trade fairs and exhibitions (central to many destinations' need to create a clearer identity for their attractions, products and services and to make them more accessible. Participation at tourism fairs in main tourist generating markets is the centrepiece of many destinations' marketing and promotional programmes, often on a cooperative basis with other regional destinations (eg the Caribbean and South Pacific villages at shows like the World Travel Market each November in London and the International Tourism Bourse in Berlin in March). The regional approach to marketing has been favoured in the past by aid donors like the European Union for financial support.

Another personal form of communication especially relevant to tourism is the familiarisation visit. This involves the destination (and its tourism operators) hosting visits of invited individuals in travel companies in main tourist source markets, these being selected on the basis of their significant influence on consumer choice (either through offering tour programmes featuring the destination or offering advice and guidance to consumers as travel counsellors).

Not only does the familiarisation trip deliver first hand experience, it can also be relatively inexpensive if organised to use spare transport and accommodation capacity. The key for effectiveness, however, is to select individuals with genuinely strong influence on tour programming and consumer counselling. Even a small destination like the Cook Islands attracting just 70,000 tourists a year organises familiarisation visits for around 300 tour operator/travel agent/travel media groups a year amounting to more than 1,000 individuals.

The primary non-personal marketing communications tools are: advertising, public relations/publicity, sales promotion, brochures and other printed material and sponsorship. An effective example of the use of publicity for pre-transaction, awareness creation was the case of the Cook Islands which in conjunction with its participation at the World Travel Market arranged for one of its dancers to briefly "stop London's traffic" by posing in Kensington High Street clad in traditional costume.

The Cook Islands tourism officials had tipped off the main media about their plan and the photographs appeared in a number of national dailies the next morning, creating a highly positive impression among millions of Britons at their breakfast tables and registering the Cook Islands as a prospective future holiday destination.

Note that websites are in essence electronic brochures but because of the interactive facility that can be built into their design and the immediacy of information (through regular-even daily-updating), they move from being a non-personal to a personal means of communication. Keeping to our example of the Cook Islands, even this small destination records an average of three-quarters of a million hits a month on its website.

Looking at the destination marketing process for national tourist offices (NTOs), the need is for NTOs to act as the implementer of government policy, to constitute the bridge between government and the private sector, and to be both an executor of marketing and promotion and a facilitating agent for the private sector's own marketing and promotional efforts. The NTO has no specific product/service to sell-though, of course, it may have a small retail activity in posters, maps, videos and the like and some are acting as booking agents thereby generating commission earnings.

The NTO's prime marketing and promotional tasks are twofold: first, the creation of awareness of, and interest in, the country as a desirable tourist destination within particular target markets/segments, and help shape a distinct and coherent image; and, second, to enable more cost effective individual product promotion to take place ie acting as an umbrella, or-to use another analogy-preparing the field for the seed to be sown. The emphasis in countries with well-established tourism sectors is the second of these areas; while for developing countries with emergent tourism sectors the focus is on those activities which address the first two of the AIDA principles ie awareness and interest.

The range of facilitation processes for NTOs can include:

- Providing a flow of research data to the private sector
- Operating representative offices in main generating markets
- Organising and facilitating participation at overseas trade shows and setting up associated trade workshops
- Organising familiarisation trips for travel trade personnel from source markets, and coordinating

arrangements for visits by media people developing features on the destination

- Preparing and disseminating comprehensive and up-to-date travel trade manuals-in hard copy and increasingly on-line
- Participation in joint marketing and promotional schemes with the tourism private sector
- Providing support for new tourism products, through dedicated printed or on-line materials (eg small-scale indigenous tourism enterprises for which the costs of marketing to potential segments in inter-regional source markets is prohibitively high)
- Operating an information (and reservations) system
- Providing consumer assistance and protection
- Acting as an intermediary between government and tourism private sector

PUBLIC: PRIVATE PARTNERSHIPS IN MARKETING

In tourism destinations, the marketing goals of the public and private sectors marketing goals are broadly in line-namely attracting the greatest volume of tourists from the targeted segments (and maximising their expenditure in the country). The NTO seeks to devise appropriate strategies, develop an image for the destination and use the menu of communications tools to realise goals set; while the local private sector looks to build on the foundations created by the NTO to attract the maximum levels of business for its own operation. For both the public and private sectors, the strength of the market's perception of the destination is of paramount importance-and their commitment to the destination is total. This is not necessarily the case for those foreign travel and tourism doing business with and supplying tourists to the country and its tourism facilities.

These differing levels of commitment to the destination would not matter if it were not the case that the great bulk of tourism-particularly to developing country destinations-are organized through companies in the source market countries.

Distribution is a key component of marketing. As discussed later "place" (in effect how products/services are made available to consumers) is one of the four Ps of marketing communications. Traditionally travel overseas by the residents of major tourist generating countries has been organised through companies of the source country. Distribution is controlled by the North with little self-determination or control of destiny lodged in the South. Consider how the would-be tourist would go about booking a holiday, who would he/she buy tickets or package tours from. The channels used (ie tour operators, airlines, hotels, travel agents) and individual companies using those channels are invariably from the tourist generating country rather than from the destination. In this regard travel and tourism distribution IS strongly similar to the distribution of primary produce in systems developed in colonial days with everything-including price-determined by the large organisations in the North. Providers in the South of accommodation, ground transport, local excursions, tourist attraction operators are largely dependent on the distributors from the North. If they demand price increases, they risk being dropped in favour of competing destinations.

It is apparent with such a wide range of destinations featured in their programmes there is little commitment to specific destinations for many operators. The bottom line for the operator is that the customer should buy a holiday from its organisation rather than from a competitor. Whether the customer buys a tour to Greece, Turkey or Spain is of little concern to the operator who is keen to gain maximum bodies on seats and in beds to which he is committed. "Commitment" in this instance means the charter air capacity he has programmed for each destination and the rooms he has confirmed at the final "release" date in each location. To "win" the customer, the tour operator provides brochure and electronic information that enable the prospective tourist to compare and contrast. Operators, therefore, exert pressure on hoteliers to offer facilities comparable to those of other destinations. At the same time, they want all destinations to appear attractive-why otherwise would they have incurred the costs of including it in their programme? "Homogenised and canned paradise" would sum the approach of many operators. This is clearly an unsustainable approach for small destinations, and to be fair it is not widely practiced by tour operators in their dealings with such destinations. However as tourism grows to the developing countries, so there is the risk that this approach could become more common.

In marketing, despite the intensification of destination competition many NTOs are having their budgets cut, as central governments contend that the principal direct beneficiaries from tourism-the private sector, and the stakeholders in the localised economies receiving tourist income-should take on more of the responsibility of tourism marketing. This position is supported by aid donors like the European Union which, after providing over a 15 year period nearly 24 million Euros principally for marketing activities to the South Pacific Tourism Organisation (SPTO)-a regional inter-governmental body, determined in 2000 that it would no longer do so and instructed the SPTO to focus on private sector member recruitment so as to design and undertake future marketing campaigns on a collaborative basis.

This principle of demanding a greater commitment from the private sector is both more logical and easier to put into practice for established tourism destinations already with a clear national identity and a thriving private sector than it is for emerging destinations where the central marketing task remains that of creating awareness of, and interest in, the destination. In that respect, it is clear why the USA disbanded its national marketing arm in the late 1990s, devolving responsibility to the States. However, the consequence of the EU's decision in respect of the SPTO is that while the more established member destinations like Fiji, French Polynesia (Tahiti) and the Cook Islands are not materially affected, any cut back in generic SPTO marketing activities will hurt the smaller islands without a significant tourism private sector and weak market awareness (eg Samoa, Tonga, Solomons, Tuvalu, Kiribati).

Joint venture promotions with the private sector are being increasingly used to maximise the effectiveness of the promotional dollar. The most extensive example is France's La Maison de la France (MDLF) which has taken the joint venture concept furthest using government money to attract the private sector and provincial tourism administrations to take part in individual thematic or specific product promotions. Created in 1987 the MDLF has grown to more than 1,200 members with a budget in 2004 of Euros60mn, over half being contributed by the private sector. The most prominent private sector partners were four transport companies, 13 "departements" and Eurodisney. A presentation on the MDLF's strategies and operations is included on the resource disk.

Public:private marketing partnerships are led by the tourist office with a formula specified governing the tourism industry's participation. This can be done on a negotiated basis within a broad framework or to detailed guidelines as in the case of the State of Wisconsin.

While more destinations are looking to the private sector to provide a greater portion of the country's marketing budget, the process is advancing relatively slowly-both because of the reluctance of the private sector to collaborate with government agencies which it regards with apprehension bordering on scepticism, and the unpreparedness of governments to relinquish control. Jordan is an example where the Jordan Tourist Board, set up in the late 1990s, was found by the private sector to remain largely controlled by government and ineffective vehicle for it to work through for most of its marketing effort. To an extent these difficulties are part of the normal digestion process of what constitutes a major change in the way of doing things. The WTO's survey of NTO marketing budgets found that in 1996 some 20% of promotional budgets of 27 European NTOs came from private sources. This proportion has continued to grow though the fact that major destinations like Singapore with high marketing spend receive all funding from government means the overall share of the private sector is still less than one-third.

Public:private tourism marketing partnerships are more advanced in established tourism destinations like North America, where they exist at sate/province and municipal levels.

Getting the right balance is the key, argue Millington and Cleverdon (1999). They cite two examples: Sweden where the State left the responsibility for tourism marketing entirely to the private sector for a number of years but then stepped back in when it found that its disengagement had led to a total loss of control of the country's image and marketing themes; and the US State of Colorado which found that when marketing is turned over to the private sector, the large companies (often multinational) tend to dominate, resulting in a substantive leakage of economic benefits from the locality. These factors are often compounded by the belief that the cost of private sector funding is passed onto the consumer in the form of higher prices. In addition, without the balancing effect of public sector promotion, there is the danger of "over-promotion" of certain "honeypot" areas leading to congestion and excessive pressure on the environment.

THE CONSUMER'S INCREASED ROLE

Maybe the consumer has a greater role in forcing public:private marketing partnerships. Research undertaken a decade ago for a British tour operator, Owners Abroad, revealed that:

> *"Holidaymakers seeking sunshine, sea and sand are more concerned about the price of the package than the resort... Research revealed at a British travel industry conference...suggests that many of them do not even care which tour operator they travel with and almost one in five does not even read the glossy brochure...It found...price outweighed choice of destination as the crucial factor in picking a package." (London Evening Standard, 6th September 1993)*

At any current international gathering of tourism officials responsible for tourism policy and planning of the sector, platform talk is dominated by the need for sustainable tourism that does not harm the environment or cause deleterious impacts on the people of the destination. During the coffee breaks, however, the emphasis frequently switches to the numbers game-the growth rate in arrivals over last year, promotion aimed at achieving inroads in new markets or getting "approved destination status" from the Chinese Government, new hotel capacity coming on stream this year, or next. It is almost as if public espousal of sustainable tourism serves to cleanse the soul. Once done, developing country governments can revert to the pursuit and pleasing of the foreign tour operator and tourist.

The danger of bowing to the demand of foreign interests is the homogenisation of destinations and standardisation of facilities. Large-scale mainstream tour operators' interests are served by being able to show attractions and facilities which focus on quality, comfort and accessibility/convenience. Their customers like to be able to compare so if the images are all of similar features like destination beaches, resort hotel buffets and local shows etc, they make their choice principally on perception and price. For the undecided, the importance of price is paramount. Fiji is this week's special offer-but it might be Bali or Barbados!! But the signs are that more consumers are changing their destination evaluation and purchasing methods, obliging tour operators to change their attitudes, practices, and values if they are to win these consumer groups' business.

To maximise advantage from these trends, destinations can develop tourism development strategies that serve their long term socio-economic and environmental interests, based on their individual distinctive features and advantages. Of course, the chosen tourism development strategy needs to meet the economic goals set for the sector and the product mix has to be marketable-but there is no incompatibility here. Tourism based on the people and natural resources of the country can certainly generate significant economic benefits, and do so over the foreseeable future if, as more recent research than the Evening Standard piece referred to above suggests, the traveller is becoming more educated and aware in the choice of destination and holiday:

> *"Just over half of consumers (52%) would be more likely to book a holiday with a company that had a written code to guarantee good working conditions, protect the environment and support local charities in the tourist destination. This proportion has risen from 45% when Tearfund first conducted the poll two years ago... When Tearfund last polled holidaymakers two tears ago, three in five of those questioned (59%) said they would be willing to pay more for their holiday if the money went*

to the preservation of the local environments, good wages and working conditions for workers, or to a local charity." (Worlds Apart: a call to responsible global tourism. Tearfund. February 2002).

The key questions are: do the public's actions match its avowed intentions-will consumers "walk the talk?" will the conversion rate between intention and action grow in the way Tearfund indicates or remain limited to a minority? and will the private sector embrace and support sustainable socio environmental practices, or only do what they have to?

Wheeller (1993) has long argued that, like giving to charity, people's ready acceptance of sustainability "makes us feel better" and that when it comes to holiday choice the prevailing sentiment is "concerned with maintaining our status, massaging our egos and appeasing our guilt than with addressing the actual issues involved." Josephides (2002) responding to the Tearfund survey also sounds a negative note about consumers' preparedness to pay more to ensure the destination's environment is not harmed.

Reporting that only 8% of his company's (Sunvil's) client base indicated that they were encouraged to patronise the company by its environmental initiative, he stressed that: "With the exception of a handful of niche players, environmental awareness among operators does not result from pressure from clients but from our wish to educate them. Customers simply want a comfortable holiday in a five-star hotel on an unspoilt beach, and they don't care how it is achieved...they also want it cheap and to hell with who or what is exploited to get the price down."

Nonetheless it is clear that, while it is a slow, gradual process, consumers are changing their travel motivations, their attitudes towards destinations and their behavioural patterns- a process which has been accelerated by the widespread media coverage of the suffering and need for the return of tourism for the populations of the areas devastated by the recent tsunami. The 2003 National Geographic/Tourism Industry Association of America survey found 35% of US foreign travellers could be classified as geotourists ("tourism that sustains or enhances the geographical character of a place-its environment, culture, aesthetics, heritage, and the well-being of its residents"). It appears then to be a question of scale and speed of conversion of motivation, attitude and behaviour.

WTO (1999), citing numerous studies in North America and Europe, states that 12 to 15% of international, discretionary travel is for non-mainstream tourism, based on a genuine interest in the socio-cultural and environmental attributes of the destination visited.

This proportion is undoubtedly expanding at a faster rate than mainstream tourism. If we take 3.5% a year growth in mainstream tourism and 7.5% for discretionary tourism more in line with sustainable development principles, then by the end of the present decade, while the 85:15 ratio will have changed to 81:19, the additional annual volumes of tourists in the two categories over present levels will be 113 million mainstream and just under 50 million non-mainstream.

Extended for a further decade at these same rates of growth the ratio between mainstream and non-mainstream will be 74:26 by 2020 and the extra annual volumes will be 193 and 168 million respectively-in other words mainstream tourism is still expanding faster than non-mainstream tourist activity. More extreme growth rates are unrealistic taking account of the economic factors (and specifically personal discretionary disposable income levels-in other words lots of people will still have their holiday choice determined by what they can afford) and the structure of the international tourism distribution system, which may evolve but will not be completely dismantled from the present pattern.

Specifically addressing the question of how to encourage the consumer to demand tourism products that are sustainable, the UNEP workshop report (pp25-36) Marketing Sustainable Tourism Products (2005) rates various marketing and promotional tools in terms of their effectiveness of supporting the marketing of sustainable tourism products ie moving sustainable tourism products from niche to mainstream (what it terms "normalisation potential"). The workshop report concludes:

1. Destination marketing organisations and tourist boards have a great opportunity to mainstream sustainable tourism, as long as they can manage the process of giving preferential treatment to companies meeting the standards, and to encourage others to work towards them.
2. Normalisation or mainstreaming potential depends on the ability of these distribution channels to reach niche markets that appreciate sustainable tourism products. In this sense the number of tour operators, internet retailers, guide books, travel fairs, travel sections in the media and certification programmes either fully or partly dedicated to sustainable tourism is growing fast. However, their volume of operations is still comparatively low.
3. Sustainable tourism, ecotourism, fair trade tourism claims are not regulated, and a good part of the mainstreaming potential comes down to the ability to bring in criteria that are measurable and verifiable, without increasing the cost of the product beyond the customers' willingness to pay. There are examples of individual distribution channels implementing these criteria in their chains of supply, mainly voluntarily, and focusing more on the environment than social issues.

RESPONSIBLE MARKETING AND ECOSELL

Tour operators say-reasonably-that their success depends on providing what the public wants. They respond to trends and changes in demand. The argument, then, is that the tour operators should help "shape" demand for tour products that are more sustainable and "fairer" to the destination by disseminating information through their brochures and advertising that shows:

— the contribution that their visits and spending make in respect of raising living standards, and

— the need for tourists to adopt appropriate behaviour, in respect of purchasing local goods and avoiding actions that might damage the environment or cause socio-cultural disruption.

It is difficult for tour operators to "sell the dream" in their advertising, which is after all designed to win them customers, without claims that exaggerate or verge on the misleading. The call is for responsible marketing. The main area of concern is in respect of the way ecotourism is marketed, a problem that arises because of the lack of a universally accepted definition as to what ecotourism comprises. The problem is that the marketing weight of the term ecotourism encourages many operators whose products are not true ecotourism products to describe their offerings as such.

Wight in Cater and Lowman, eds. (1994) presents details of the spectrum of language used to market ecotourism, classifying the terms used in four groups along a continuum from "non-specific, sell-oriented" to "specific, values-oriented". She develops a segmentation model. The commercial ecotourism sector-even those pursuing responsible marketing approaches and combining with local communities and conservation groups-is characterised by relatively low local involvement and high negative impact; while the not-for-profit sector, though clearly much smaller in scale, is generally beneficial for the destination. Destinations can, however, seek to structure their ecotourism operations-through access fees levied on tour operators-to channel some of the monies generated from commercial operations into those forms of ecotourism which involve scientific research, conservation etc. The model overleaf illustrates the relative scale of demand for the various types while indicating the level and focus of interest, dividing these into "soft core" and "hard core", the former serving to contribute towards the costs of the research needed for the latter.

Wight (op cit) points out that the marketing activities of the range of players involved in ecotourism reflect their motivations and can be exploitative of the resource base through eco-sell, or can neglect to market their operation's commitment to environmentally responsible activities. She argues, however, that they need not act as two forces pulling in fundamentally opposite directions. Through complementary integration, the conservation and profit-making perspectives can reinforce and strengthen each other, providing there is:

- a strategic and proactive approach

- better understanding of the linkage and potentially symbiotic relationship between conservation and marketing
- reconciling environmental marketing with industry commitment to environmentally responsible action
- taking a supply management perspective which acknowledges resource values and accepts resource constraints and limits, as well as seizing resource-based opportunities
- development of understanding and partnerships between host communities, governments, non-governmental organisations and industry
- greater discrimination in client selection through identification of market segments which better match the range of ecotourism products
- development of formal or informal product and performance standards
- promotion and acceptance of a tourist and operator code of ethics, and guidelines for responsible travel practices and behaviour (Wight 1994)

MODEL OF NATURE-BASED TOURISM

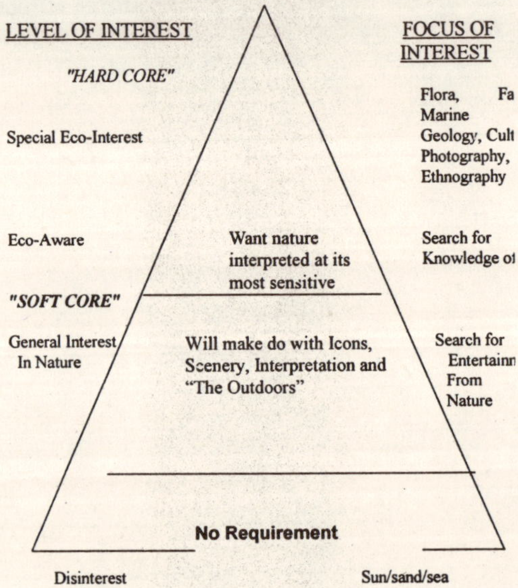

INCREASING MARKETING'S ROLE IN RESPONSIBLE TOURISM

There are four possible responses to the question: "what is marketing's role in responsible tourism?"

— it is peripheral-inconsequential

— it is a necessary evil-and potentially dangerous as it may lead to too much tourism or the wrong type of tourism, or both

— it is operational function-vital for creating business

— it is a central determinant-acting as a safeguard for responsible tourism-remember our car driving analogy from Unit 3 with the vital roles of the brake, accelerator, gear control and steering wheel!

Without marketing there is no possibility of managing the scale and type of business attracted to a location, facility etc. It is important to recognise the fact that too little tourism of the right type is just as damaging as too much tourism of the wrong type, since the latter can be addressed through de-marketing. No marketing strategy, image positioning or communications programme can be developed in a vacuum. The market-and segments within it that are being targeted-has to be receptive in principle to the marketing campaign directed at them. This is part of a market-as opposed to production or sales-oriented approach to marketing. Similarly in respect of responsible tourism marketing, it will be increasingly effective in circumstances where the consumer has greater awareness of, and interest in, it.

A major research study conducted through a collaboration by the European market research organisation-ESOMAR-and United Nations Environment Programme, Division of Technology and Economics-UNEP TIE-investigated why "marketing appears to have failed the sustainability agenda." In respect of consumer attitudes the study's findings are that:

- consumer concern for sustainability issues is high, but the strength and depth of attitudes (level of belief) is low which accounts for the perception that the rate of progress towards a sustainability culture is less than desirable;

- high public concern does not necessarily mean that sustainability issues are the highest priority for most people so potential activities may be subordinated to other concerns;
- although information is widely available, the necessary ingredients for cultural change are absent: the level of belief is low, there is no effective feedback on achievement, there is contradictory advice on actions and a lack of role models-all of which make it hard for people to make the emotional connection required for behavioural change; and
- people are fed up with the unfulfilled 'fear' factor.

From the research perspective, the study finds that much research is not well-directed because:

- current methods of categorisation of consumers may be over-estimating the level of commitment by measuring low levels of activity rather than underlying attitudes to behaviour and biased question formats are inflating responses;
- the level of debate about sustainability issues is uninformative ie one-sided arguments, vested political interests and exaggeration for effect serving to devalue the strength of the case and allowing people an opt-out for their behaviour; and
- a failure to recognise the existence of a disconnect between attitudes and behaviour, leading to measurements that do not distinguish between importance, level of concern and propensity to act and, in consequence, make interpretation difficult.

Marketers show reluctance to promote a sustainability platform because of the lack of a clear and agreed terminology for encompassing the sustainability issue. Short hand communications like green labelling confuse rather than help when used indiscriminately. In addition, product benefits for sustainability are usually secondary to the main evaluation criteria for purchasing decisions-usually to product performance and value for money. Marketers and other decision-makers in the corporate environment have no special access to sustainability information-they pick it up in the same way that consumers do.

The ESOMAR/UNEP TIE study states that it suspects that people need to have confidence that the supplier organisation is doing its bit within the constraints of the current levels of knowledge rather than looking for products that are specifically sustainable. Clear statements about products cannot be made with certainty since there remains more to learn technically about the interactions and inter-dependencies of sustainability issues-there are almost always counter-arguments and there may never be an answer that is not a compromise.

The report concludes that marketers need to take a more holistic view of the business and engage in the underlying business strategy to develop a sustainability position for the organisation and to attach it to the brand image. Brand attributes tend to fall into one of three categories:

- essential ie you can't compete at all if you don't have these
- differentiating ie those that account for market performance and typically define how you can compete
- focus ie those factors that matter to certain segments only.

At present, sustainability is a focus level factor and the segments are relatively small. If it were to be raised to a differentiating factor, the collective marketing efforts the world would achieve considerably more than the present level of social marketing can achieve.

To be able to make this desirable shift, however, researchers and marketers need better methods of measuring where individuals stand on the spectrum of a customer decision-making continuum in terms of propensity to act something that would enable better measurement of the effectiveness of communications. Working with social psychologists, researchers need to better define the framing to obtain more meaningful measures. The study concludes that benchmarks need to be established and trends monitored in order to set reference points for marketers. At the same time, the role of marketers in the strategic planning process and their connections with

activity on sustainable production, research and development and process issues within the organisation needs to be better understood. Also needed are internal studies in organisations to identify how they apply their knowledge at work and to align internal and external brand perceptions. This sets the agenda for the next stage of the UNEP research on this topic.

The key is seen by UNEP TIE spokesperson Solange Montillaud-Joyel as understanding the consumer:

> *"..when considering environmental and sustainability issues, there has been little or no consideration about what drives people to consume. Environmentalists have always looked at rational equations. But, it is not because a product is greener that, for humanity's sake, the consumer will buy it. If enhancing the sense of guilt and fear can sometimes be successful in some governmental education campaigns, when it comes to purchasing behaviour, functionality, price but also irrational factors such as emotion, pleasure and peer pressure can have a great influence on the final decision. We need to make sure that the 'sustainable' concept-at least in the marketplace-is associated with an appealing and positive message in order to help shift current consumption patterns. And to achieve that, more research needs to be done on the psychology of the consumer...Key topics could be: what prompts him or her to buy this product rather than another? How can we adapt the sustainability message to the unconscious expectations of the consumer? And how should marketing strategies be adapted to the promotion of green products and services without becoming sermon-like and ultimately resulting in commercial failure."*

In some respects, tourism is at the forefront of this exercise in that it has been long acknowledged that emotional factors (and, of course, price or perceived value-for-money) play a central role in decision-making. Psychographic research is enabling those consumers most likely to be sensitive to the sustainable or responsible tourism message to be identified and "ring-fenced" as targets for product offerings and marketing communications as witnessed by the TIA/National Geographic geotourism study. Conversion of their interest into business and spreading the awareness to other segments are the key challenges-and the ESOMAR/UNEP TIE study shows that this should not be approached through hectoring or haranguing the consumer.

PROMOTING TOURISM INVESTMENT

Many public sector tourism departments or agencies have responsibility not only for attracting tourists but also promoting tourism investment. Before leaving the subject of the promotion component of the marketing mix related to tourism, it is worthwhile to consider approaches to the promotion of tourism investment opportunities. Clearly, the framework within which the tourism authorities and promotion investment agency can work will be set through a development and/or investment code, possibly outlining incentives available for prospective investors-either offered generally or specifically for types of investment in the tourism sector. The validity of incentives in tourism is high because of the fact that most tourism ventures involve extremely high capital costs with only a gradual build up of income. Few tourism investments achieve profitability until 3 to 5 years. The waiving of import duties, tax holidays and soft loans are the main means by which destinations assist new developments and rehabilitation projects.

Investment promotion typically takes the form of a combination of a set of promotional material (in both hard copy and electronic format). This is supplemented in respect of foreign investment through the organisation of special events such as trade fairs or roadshows; while the encouragement of local small/medium scale entrepreneurial development specialist agencies to work with prospective parties are established, guiding them through the processes and assistance schemes available.

PRICING

The third element of the marketing mix is that of pricing-the accelerator or brake. Pricing is the prime tactical marketing tool, most typically used in times of weak demand (ie off season) to create demand that would otherwise not be realised eg in the low season, in the aftermath of a negative development such as a natural disaster, incident of civil disruption, health scare.

The target for price promotion fall into two broad camps: those who would otherwise not be able to afford to come to the destination; and those who consider standard prices to be too high under the prevailing circumstance of, for example, less than ideal climatic conditions, concerns about disruption to the visit arising from the local difficulty being encountered. The need for tactical pricing arises from the inflexibility (or rigidity) of supply in tourism. Scheduled transport services cannot be changed on a daily basis to suit demand, so incentives are offered to fill the plane etc-"bums on seats"; similarly, the volume of hotel beds cannot be changed rapidly so if demand is in danger of falling below capacity, price inducements are offered-"bodies in beds".

Tactical pricing should be engaged in with caution. It is necessary to conduct sufficient research to ensure that the price cuts:

1. will achieve the desired result-it would be self-defeating to offer cuts which are availed of only by those who would have come in any case; and
2. will attract those market segments that fall within the targets for the destination-remember other tourists are part of the destination experience and there can be incompatibilities between different segments, possibly resulting in a primary market segment turning against the destination because a different segment had been attracted through the price cuts.

Price is perceived by tourists in terms of value for money. How a tourist sees a destination as offering good or poor value for money is highly personal and dictated to a large extent by his/her prior expectation of how expensive or cheap the destination would be. Take a simple example, Japan has long been perceived as an expensive destination and India a less costly one. If a tourist had been expecting to pay $200 a night for his hotel room in Tokyo and $100 in Delhi, but found they were both $150 his reaction would be likely to be that Japan was better value for money than India! Price and the market's perception of price needs, therefore, to be handled knowledgeably and carefully within the marketing mix.

The Development of Appropriate Tourism Distribution Networks and Partnerships

Distribution is an organised activity which, given the nature of the tourism product, is a vital and costly element of the sector's marketing mix. Middleton and Clarke (2001) identify eight factors that, apart from the opportunities opened up by the web, focus increasing attention on developing distribution channels in travel and tourism:

- the growing size of businesses
- the increasing number of units within a group or chain (under one ownership, or linked via strategic marketing alliances) that opens up distribution options
- the growth of long haul travel, and the consequent need to provide reassurance about facilities in those less well-known destinations
- the importance of reaching and drawing in more first-time visitors in order to make a business grow
- the even greater need to provide the most convenient forms of access for repeat or loyal customers
- growing competition for shares of markets where there is excess capacity in a destination
- the need to sell capacity ahead of production to optimise business cash flow and operational planning
- the need to maximise use of the sales promotion and tactical pricing opportunities afforded by modern distribution channels, especially in response to yield management programmes focussing on weak booking periods.

Travel and tourism principals (ie transport operators, hotels) have the basic choice of selling direct to the customer or channelling sales through intermediaries (eg travel agents). These can be developed into five main choices:

1. Principal → Customer (on producer's premises) ie producer acting as own retailer
2. Principal → Customer (in customer's home) ie via producer reservation system
3. Principal → Owned retail outlet → Customer (on producer's premises) i.e. vertically integrated operation
4. Principal → Independent retail outlet → Customers (on retailer's premises) i.e. on the basis of principal commission payment to agent
5. Principal → Tour operator'Independent retail outlet → Customer (on retailer's premises) ie bulk sale to tour operator.

Tour operators are hybrid organisations as they are wholesalers but combine the products/services of other principals to devise a new product. They then have the choice of 1-4 above. There are many variants within the basic system of distribution outlined above, as the two designated readings for this topic illustrate. The key to successful distribution revolves around the exploitation of electronic technology applications. Distribution raises a quite different set of questions for tourism destinations. Consider the players in the tourism distribution system for destinations:

- the destination tourist office BUT it has nothing to sell
- the destination facilities BUT they are physically remote from the prospective tourist
- the national airline-a major supporter for the destination's tourism BUT over half (much more in some instances) traffic to developing country destinations is carried by foreign carriers
- tour operators from source markets-key providers BUT nearly all are foreign-owned with little commitment to the destinations they feature in their tour programmes
- travel agents in tourist generating countries-major influence and intermediary BUT again these are all owned in source countries and there is little difference to them whichever destination their clients purchase.

OVERSEAS MARKET REPRESENTATION

Destinations have a number of choices in determining how they should be represented in primary tourist generating markets, the choice of the most appropriate method being a function of the scale and form of market opportunity, and the type of marketing communication necessary to achieve maximum realisation of the identified opportunity.

The range includes:

- No representation, with everything handled from head office where the market opportunity is low;
- Appointment of an individual public relations officer where awareness needs to built up and potential is low-to-moderate;
- Appointment of a public relations company where awareness needs to built up and potential is medium-to-high;
- Appointment of a marketing representation company to coordinate a marketing and promotional campaign, where awareness of the destination is developed and opportunity is high;
- Appointment of both public relations and marketing representation companies (or a company which combines these roles) where there are image concerns but where the potential is high;
- Establishment of the destination's own tourist office, staffed by personnel drawn either from then generating market or the destination, to handle a full programme of public relations and marketing and promotion.

To be effective, there are three requisites for the personnel representing a tourist destination in overseas markets: first, an intimate, up-to-date and accurate knowledge of the destination-its resources, facilities and developments; second, a high level of understanding of the way travel distribution functions in the generating country, including a large number of personal contacts in travel agencies, tour operators and airlines; and, third, excellent communication skills (ie pleasant, outgoing personality, good speaking voice, and appropriate linguistic ability). In the case of the appointment of public relations and/or marketing representatives, it is important to study the customer portfolio of candidate companies, avoiding those which have destinations of similar profile and attributes. It is also crucial that a strong system of activity reporting is put in place to ensure that the appointed representative is allocating sufficient resources to the destination being represented.

Choosing the appropriate form of representation is complicated for countries with established tourism sectors spread across states or provinces which have a high degree of autonomy. Do you leave all overseas representation to the national tourism office? or do you market yourselves autonomously?

Models include the USA, where the States market themselves independently (indeed there is now no national promotional agency), and Australia, where the national marketing effort (through the Australian Tourism Commission) acts as an overall umbrella for the individual States' marketing and promotion campaigns. In regional marketing organisations like the Caribbean Tourism Organisation the focus of all activities is the geographic region in question, with individual member states carrying out their specific marketing activities (often) separate from, but building on the foundations laid by, those of the regional body. In China, the CNTA is the regional organisation, creating awareness of, and generating interest in, China as an overall destination. It is then up to the individual province to develop its tourism products and to communicate to targeted market segments for such products using effective messages, symbols and icons in the various key media for such segments.

In broad terms, having own overseas offices-whether at street level to serve the public, or off street to deal with the travel trade-is highly costly and can only be justified for fully-established destinations.

ELECTRONIC TECHNOLOGY

Up to the end of the 1970s travel distribution was effected through telephones and pin boards-now electronic systems dominate. This gives rise to questions such as: what has been the technological revolution and how has it impacted on the travel industry and the traveller? Is on-line direct sell the inevitable way forward or do travel agents have a future? What role will relationship marketing and "personal agents" have in travel and tourism? how has the worldwide web and internet affected tourism marketing?

At the end of 1999, 9 million British consumers had home access to the internet, the volume having doubled in just a year. By the end of 2002 a further rise of almost a quarter had taken place to 11.5 million, and the further close to 20% a year rises in the proportion of the population being on-line has led to almost one-in-five Britons currently buying their holidays through the internet (Mintel, 2005).

Despite the huge take up of electronic technology, there is still a marked difference in the use of the internet to research a holiday (or other form of trip) and to book one. The former is more than double the latter, because of a combination of fears about the security of on-line purchasing-a concern for 13% of the UK public-and the need for reassurance about the destination the customer is considering. This "hand-holding" function has been what has kept the great bulk of package tour sales being sold via travel agents, and the proportion is only slowly declining from the 80% mark. A Thomas Cook survey of the British public in 2000 found that 53% consider it important to deal with a trusted high street brand even when shopping on-line!

The advantage of the internet is the reduction of barriers to entry for destinations and their operators alike. The cost of setting up a high quality website is modest-significantly less than a single television spot on CNN for example-while its maintenance is similarly inexpensive. Furthermore websites enable the most up-to-date information to be posted, as well as giving immediacy in responding to consumer queries and requests. The problem is that there is no search engine dedicated to tourism, so many smaller operators for whom the website potentially represents a means of direct access to prospective customers at low cost are not identified on any of the initial pages of the search using major engines like google or yahoo.

This is now changing thanks to the April 2005 allocation by ICANN (Internet Corporation for Assigned Names and Numbers) of the.travel domain to Tralliance Corporation. Tralliance will oversee the.travel domain registration programme in conjunction with the sponsor, The Travel Partnership Corporation (TTPC). TTPC, a non-profit corporation, will assist in policy development. It claims that over 100 international travel trade associations are committed to participate, on behalf of their members, in the new domain. The.travel domain will allow the travel industry to substantially improve their internet visibility, communications and transactional capability with travel consumers by lifting their companies out of the anonymity of a.com Web. For consumers, the.travel directory is likely to enable a better match to be achieved between buyers and sellers by delivering more precise results to the would-be purchaser's online travel queries, resulting in increased purchasing from travel suppliers.

CENTRAL LEVEL PLANNING: LOCAL LEVEL ACTION

The establishment of the political and regulatory framework for tourism, and the necessary facilitative measures to bring about the desired form and scale of development can only be carried out at central level, albeit based on consultation with the full range of stakeholders. However tourism takes place in specific locations-almost always where other people live. The need for the involvement of the local level participants in planning and presenting the image in marketing with which they are happy is clearly strong.

The obstacle to the greater involvement and control at regional and sub-regional level within a country in tourism development and marketing strategic planning is twofold: weak institutional capacity, and inadequate financial resources. South Africa is a good example and details are given on the resource disk.

Destination marketing is changing. As competition grows, with virtually every country or territory actively seeking to encourage in bound tourism, so the way in which destinations organise and undertake their marketing and promotional programmes is evolving. The reason is straightforward-

destinations, especially developing nations, are unable to devote the scale of increased financial resources to the marketing budget which the growth of competition necessitates. To do so would literally "break the bank" with no guarantee of success. As destination marketing becomes a growing babel of activity, shouting louder is not a valid option.

The successful destination will increasingly segment its markets and devolve responsibility to the various stakeholders involved in tourism for the key marketing tasks-those of creating awareness and interest, converting such interest into desire to visit the destination, achieving sales, and providing stimulating and satisfying experiences which lead to repeat (and recommended) visitation. The NTO can no longer carry the burden for all these tasks, especially given the EU's policy resolution to phase out its assistance for tourism marketing and promotion: the private sector, and provinces and states down to the municipal level, each have increasing roles to play in line with the rewards they obtain from tourism.

There are four distinct aspects that can be combined in making the case for increased local level marketing intervention:

1. money from the centre is tight. Central government, in seeking to reduce the dependence on it to finance the country's tourism marketing, is pushing responsibility for marketing "down the line" to provincial/local administrations and the private sector operating in the localised areas;
2. need for tightly focused niche marketing on a highly targeted basis. Local input can be crucial in developing a differentiated message for targeted segments;
3. counterbalance to the international tourism distribution system's push for standardisation in destination tourism products. This increasing commoditisation of tourism products can be slowed through the development of marketing messages that stress the unique features and attractions of individual localities (again requiring strong local level involvement); and,
4. exploiting growing consumer trends. In the globalisation: localisation continuum, the opportunities in tourism

destinations offered through growing consumer interest in local cultures and features necessitate marketing action at the local level to be fully realised.

It is only at the local level that the differentiation that is necessary for long term survival as distinct and distinctive destinations can realistically be achieved. It is only at the local, micro level that the importance of differentiation is of the greatest priority as it is in the direct interests of a given location's tourism stakeholders to ensure the durability of its tourism sector. That said, it will remain appropriate for countries with emerging tourism sectors to lend substantive marketing support from the centre to create a strongly positive image for the destination in source markets (ie addressing the Awareness and Interest dimensions of the AIDA marketing sequence).

The ability of any destination to decentralize marketing responsibility depends on sufficiently developed institutional capacity at provincial and local level to take on the devolved task. In developing an agenda for local level destination tourism marketing action, the following key factors need to be considered:

- coordination (national-provincial-local)
- organisation (local administration-private sector-community)
- product development and marketing strategy
- attracting, informing and satisfying the tourist

There are few instances where a region or locality within a country can operate on a "stand alone" basis-Bali being one of the few truly successful examples in a developing country; neither is it a desirable route because it can lead to fragmentation, inconsistency and internal competition within a country. Coordination with national policy and strategy is, therefore, a priority. It is vital to ensure that local level marketing initiatives:

1. are consistent and compatible with tourism product development and marketing strategy at national and provincial levels-at best they should represent the "hands on" implementation of the country's overall goals for tourism, interpreting them in the local context; and

2. "piggyback" to the maximum extent possible on national and provincial programmes and schemes in order to achieve local level objectives.

A formal means of coordination between national-provincial-local levels in tourism planning and marketing. The exact specification will vary from country-to-country depending on government structure and present institutional arrangements. The need is to avoid creating unwieldy bureaucratic structures while giving stakeholders at individual local level a "voice" in plans and strategies developed for the country and the regions within it.

Furthermore, this "voice" needs to be based on sound, technical knowledge of tourism, and to be representative of the divergent views about tourism development and marketing which are frequently found in communities.

At the local level, it is important for a means to exist by which the various stakeholders in tourism (including community representatives such as leaders from traditional society, church/religious groups, residents etc) are consulted and account taken of their opinions and demands. Under the auspices of the local administration, a Tourism Committee (or other appropriate nomenclature) should be established with participants from the local private sector-both those directly involved in tourism and those that supply goods and services to tourism operations-and the community.

The Tourism Committee could operate at two levels: first, strategy and planning for tourism development and marketing (including liaison with national and provincial levels); and, second, overseeing the execution of local marketing activities. As noted, the chair of the Tourism Committee could be the local representative in the national-provincial planning system for tourism. Competence in tourism techniques rather than political figurehead should be the criterion driving the selection of this person.

The principal barrier to local level tourism marketing is the "distance" (ie physical and psychological) to the potential tourist market. Local tourism marketing plays a limited role in direct marketing to consumers through advertising and promotion though some local authorities have sufficient resources to participate (under the auspices of the NTO) at overseas trade fairs, and in joint promotions. The key areas of operation at the local level are in:

- organising special events and attractions to draw tourist to the locality-the list of possibilities is endless with examples including flower and fruit festivals, arts and music events etc
- providing state-of-the-art information services to prospective and actual tourists
- giving tourists "added extras" to make their experience of the destination special and memorable

Information services are a crucially important component of locally based marketing. There are three elements: the range and quality (and presentation) of the information itself; the physical resource-the information center, bureau or kiosk; and the staff who provide the information to tourists.

Information should include: multilingual printed materials (ie maps, guidebook, thematic brochures and items for sale like posters, postcards, books, video); web site, linked to that of the NTO; good interpretative at the locality's key tourist sites; clear and distinctive signage to tourist attractions and features; and tour guides drawn from the local community, who are fully versed in the locality's tourist product, have appropriate linguistic ability and possess social skills making them effective communicators to tourists.

The locality's tourist information center(s) should be in easy-to-find locations, use local artifacts and materials in construction and décor, be kept clean and tidy with use of fresh flowers in the reception area, be stocked with a good range of information materials (along with quality items on the locality and its tourist features for sale), and be staffed with welcoming, linguistically competent, helpful, and well-informed personnel.

It is important to create strong first impressions, so all communications (both in person and by mail/email) should be dealt with promptly, informatively and personably.

The question of satisfying and creating strong word-of-mouth recommendation for a specific location depends on a wide range of variables. Invariably, however, a single bad experience (like being overcharged by a taxi) or special good experience can play a major role in the memory that a tourist takes away from a destination. Local tourism administrations need to establish a local code of practice-overseen by the Tourism Committee but largely achieved through peer pressure. At the same time, good experiences will arise "naturally" out of good practice, but can also be "created".

The Mayor of Giza in Egypt has a practice of receiving tourist groups for tea. This undoubtedly creates a positive impression on tourists who see a destination that values them highly. Opportunities to create such high profile, strongly positive events, involving local dignitaries and personalities, should be actively sought.

8

INTERNET TOURISM MARKETING: POTENTIAL AND CONSTRAINTS

The Internet has increasingly become a popular medium for marketing. This paper attempted to investigate the potential of the Internet for tourism marketing and the current constraints on the full realisation of such potential. Through an examination of the advantages of the Internet as a marketing tool and the characteristics of the tourism industry, the paper found that the Internet was ideal for marketing tourism. It then analysed the main Internet applications in tourism marketing and explored the key factors that were attributable to the current low level of travel sales an the Internet The paper concluded with a brief discussion of the major strategic issues in the implementation of Internet tourism marketing.

INTRODUCTION

The Internet is the global 'network of networks" of interlinked computers operating on a standard protocol which allows data to be transferred between them. As an information exchange system, the most important aspect of the Internet is its connectivity, the ability to allow everyone to access the network (Young et al 1999). The potential of using the Internet for marketing activities is derived from its general use as an information exchange system in the digital age. The information can be stored, indexed, retrieved, restructured and redistributed automatically by software and without human intervention. The Internet connects companies with companies, companies with customers, and people with people without regard to time, space and hardware/ software platforms (Mathur et al 1998).

Although the Internet originated in the 19605, it is only in recent years that it has become a buzz-word. Internet services fall into two broad categories: communication services and information services. Communication services such as e-mail, and e-mail-based discussion lists and net news, allow the direct exchange of information between Internet users. Information services, including Telnet, Gopher and anonymous FTP (the File Transfer Protocol), allow users to access data that has been made available by other users. Since 1993, the Internet has been transformed completely by its newest component the World Wide Web (WWW or the Web). The WWW not only integrates other file transfer protocols like Gopher and FTP, but also allows the user to access hosts through Telnet, read newsgroups and use e-mail. Through an Internet browser, a user can link to any web sites and may explore the Internet resource in an unprecedented way for both leisure and commercial purposes. Moreover, the Web's capability to blend text, pictures, sounds and video clips into multimedia documents played the key role in popularising the Internet beyond its traditionally academic boundaries and become an effective communication means in business and everyday life. Indeed, the WWW has been so successful that it changed the appearance of the Internet and for many it even become synonymous with the Internet itself (Hafner and Lyon 1996, Kehoe 1996, Maler 1997, Poon and Jevons 1997). In this paper, the WWW or the Web is also used loosely and interchangeably with the Internet or the Net simply because most marketing activities carried out on the Internet are based on the World Wide Web.

The rapid growth of the Internet, especially the WWW, has attracted a great deal of interest among both academic researchers and business practitioners, especially in the fields of Information Technology (IT) and marketing. There are also an increasing number of publications on Internet tourism marketing, in the last few years. The works of Bender (1997), Sheldon (1997), Inkpen (1998), Richer and O'Neil-Dunne (1998), Buhalis and Schertler (1999), Marcussen (1999) and O'Connor (1999), among others, have provided the necessary background and some in-depth discussions of the various issues of marketing tourism on the Internet, in particular its impacts on tourism distribution. However, this field of research is, by and large, still in its infancy and much more effort must be made to improve our understanding of the Internet's role in tourism marketing and the ways through which tourism organisations and destinations can exploit its full potential.

This paper intends to investigate two fundamental but interrelated issues in Internet tourism marketing-the potential of the Internet for tourism marketing and the current constraints on the full realization of such potential. The 'potential" issue is addressed in three parts: the paper first discusses generally the advantages of the Net as a marketing tool in comparison to the conventional media; it then demonstrates that the Net is ideal for tourism marketing largely through an examination of the characteristics of tourism; and finally it explores the main areas of Internet application in tourism marketing. The "constraints" issue is tackled through an assessment of the conditions of the four major forces-demand, supply, technology and government-which jointly determines the current shape and future prospects of internet-commerce. Based on the understanding of the potential and constraints, the paper concludes with a brief discussion of the strategic issues for successfully conducting Internet tourism marketing.

ADVANTAGES OF THE INTERNET AS A MARKETING TOOL

The Internet is widely recognised as an extremely valuable marketing tool. It is generally held that the Internet offers substantial advantages over traditional means of communication: reduced costs of information exchange; increased speed of information transfer and retrieval; increased customer involvement in and control of transactions; and greater flexibility of using the marketing mix. Its main business uses include communications (both internal and external), market research, customer services, market penetration, product development, cost savings through process reengineering, direct marketing, advertising and product delivering (Cronin 1996, Ellsworth and Ellsworth 1996). The following paragraphs examine the main features of the Net, in comparison with conventional media and with relevance to marketing, as an effective and efficient communications means.

Addressability

The Internet has the unique quality that, through its addressibility, can transform the prominent marketing communication paradigm from one-to-many to one-to-one or from broadcasting to narrowcasting. The traditional media, such as print, radio and television, follow a passive one-to-many communication model, whereby a company reaches many current and potential customers through the broadcasting of the same message. This approach to communication has three problems:

1. uncustomised message to every consumer,
2. wasted exposures to uninterested audiences,
3. and "noise" distraction from competing and conflicting messages.

In contrast, the Internet enables a company to individually "address" consumers in its marketing communications because each time a user visits its web site, its server has a record of the user's electronic address. The company can then "narrowcast"-send tailor-made message content-to a smaller target audience or an individual consumer (Heinen 1996, Hoffman and Novak 1996).

Blattberg and Deighton (1991) argue that this kind of addressable marketing is not new; the mail, telephone and personal selling have also been the addressable tools in marketing for many years. What makes the Internet so special in this regard is its low-cost and high-speed information transmission and retrieval. The addressability of the Web provides the opportunity for marketing to create individual relationships, managing markets of one, and addressing each in terms of its stage of development. In essence, it represents the opportunity to customise and tailor the product and/or the marketing effort to one consumer at a time. Pitta (1998) argues that this Internet-enabled one-to-one marketing reconfigures the familiar four Ps into one element-the relationship. It represents the ultimate expression of target marketing-a market of one-or at least one at a time. Therefore, well designed Internet communications, through web sites, emails and news-groups, can match the effectiveness of personal selling. In fact, Internet marketers can do what a sales-force can but with much more flexibility, better memory and less cost (Kiani 1998).

Interactivity

Another feature of the Net that distinguishes itself from traditional communication media is its ability to respond to user inputs, i.e. interactivity. The Internet is capable of giving feedback in response to the actions users perform on the computer, resulting in the sense of engagement with the computer (Shili 1998). This two-way dialogue forms an important component of relationship marketing, and is an important factor in building customer loyalty. Customers are effortlessly communicate with companies to find product information and conduct transactions with a few keystrokes while companies can easily contact customers to clarify their needs or inform them of new products. Features such as Email, web forms and Java applets positively encourage marketers to interact with consumers (O'Conner 1999). Moreover, in contrast to traditional communication channels like newspapers or television, on the Net the customer is an active participant and is in greater control of choosing and processing information about the firm. It is the customer-and not the marketer-who decides with whom to interact and how to interact. In other words, it is entirely in the customer's power to decide whether to surf the net, which web site to visit, which web page to browse, for how long, how often and how much information to obtain.

In addition to the company-to-consumer and consumer-to-company interaction, Kiani (1998) examines the consumer-to-consumer and company-to-company communications and argues that in an interactive media like the Net, a marketing activity can employ a combination of the above communication patterns. The company-to-company interaction not only provides competitive intelligence but also provides opportunities in partnering and co-operation, especially in improving supply-channel and distribution-channel relationships.

The consumer-to-consumer communication helps to establish cyber or virtual communities, which has significant implications for marketing segmentation and customer service. These online "clubs" can be an important venue for consumers to exchange information or experiences, for example opportunities in time-sharing accommodation, as well as for companies to improve the understanding of consumer behaviour.

Flexibility

The Web is a much more flexible marketing medium than the traditional mass media. A web page can be considered as an electronic billboard, electronic advertisement, or electronic catalogue that provides information on products or services plus contact information for interested consumers. But a virtual advertisement or catalogue is much flexible than a physical advertisement or catalogue. It can gather fresh and updated information based on the direct feedback received from consumers. A virtual catalogue can be gradually developed and organised based on the actual interest of consumers (Kiani 1998). It can also keep consumers constantly informed of the company's new product offerings, latest price changes and sales promotion initiatives.

In the travel business, the Web's flexibility and instantaneousness in information transmission is invaluable, since where the brochure is the main means for marketing package tours. UK tour operators, for example, produce about 120 million holiday brochures a year, 40% of which are not used at all. For some holidays it takes, in average, 28 brochures to generate a booking. In addition, large tour operators usually launch their main summer holiday brochures 10 months in advance (Holloway and Robinson 1995). Obviously, the preparation and distribution of holiday brochures is a costly and lengthy process during which the demand conditions and competition situation could change greatly. With the print medium, tour operators have to issue supplements to the main brochures, adjusting prices and availability. With the Web, all changes to the electronic brochures can be made instantly and at little cost. The online brochure can also be linked to inventory data, so that the user can immediately see whether a particular holiday is available or not. Moreover, the electronic brochure can be indexed in many ways and the user can be provided with search facilities to locate items quickly. They can also be associated with relevant free information and services for the consumer who visits the page.

Accessibility

As a communication medium, the area in which the Internet has overwhelming advantage over any other media is its permanent exposure and global market reach. The Net greatly improves, both spatially and temporally, the information availability and user interaction. With an effective web site, a company is on business on a global spectrum 24 hours a day, 365 days a year. Any web user in the world can access its marketing information at any time that is convenient for him. This extends greatly the place and time utility of companies which traditionally rely on distribution channel members to perform. The round the clock accessibility is extremely important especially in international trade where business is conducted across different time zones.

The global exposure is particularly desirable for tourism destinations which up until the mid-1990s had to depend entirely on promotion agencies in tourist generating regions to market its products. The Web has enabled tourism destinations to market themselves with well constructed and well promoted web sites. Furthermore, the Web facilitates doing business overseas by avoiding regulations and restrictions that companies must follow when they are physically present in other countries, for instance in many countries, foreign travel companies are forbidden from organising or selling tours. Finally, compared with the traditional media, the Web not only provides virtually unlimited access for hundreds of million users but also delivers unlimited amount of information on the Web as there is practically no restrictions in terms of the "space of advertisement"-the number of pages a web site can accommodate or the "bytes" of data a online database can hold. For example, the global distribution system (GDS) Sabre's data centre has a capacity of 60 terabytes of electronic storage-equivalent to over 15 billion pages of information (Sabre 2000).

Service Improvements

The Web helps companies to improve service quality at all stages of customer interaction-pre-sale, during sale and after-sale. De and Mathew (1999) identified that the Web provides four tangible improvements in customer service: first, larger accessible choice set for customer since a web site can display a vast set of product options and service options; second, faster payment processing for customers-through automatic processing of cyber-cash or credit card charges; third, reduced delivery time for many products such as online software and music distribution; and fourth, easier, faster and greater availability of support literature, and more detailed and particularised help. In tourism the web-based distribution systems can satisfy consumer needs for easy access to transparent and easy to compare information on a wide variety of choices of destinations, holiday packages, flights, lodging and leisure services. They also provide immediate confirmation and speedy documentation of reservations providing a greater degree of flexibility and enabling prospective travellers to book at the "last minute" (Buhalis 1996).

Increasingly, tourists' satisfaction depends on the accuracy and relevance of tourism information as well as the promptness of responding to consumers' requests. As a Delta Airlines executive said: "Most people will tolerate misconnects and changes when they occur in the airline industry what they won't tolerate is not getting timely and accurate information. The airline business today is much more than a transportation business-it's an information business, prefaced with an 'e'" (Yahoo 2000). Many airlines are using the Internet, especially through mobile phones, to provide aggregate information in real-time to business partners, employees as well as customers. Across the tourism industry, the improved access to information covering all aspects of tourist activities has provided marketers with the opportunity to offer personalised services at price levels comparable to those of standard packages.

Cost Savings

The cost saving effect of the Internet derives mainly from five areas. First, the streamlining and electronic processing of booking and payments cuts down sales cost. Second, automation and the deskilling of tasks reduce the labour intensity and staff training cost. For example, the web-based travel reservation systems (using windows and is menu-driven) are much easier to use than the traditional viewdata systems (using DOS and was command driven where a sales clerk has to remember all the commands and the airport codes). Third, by offering direct links between the producer and the consumer, the Net helps the producer to save huge distribution costs through the disintermediation process. Fourth, the ability of the Net in narrowcasting and electronic communication leads substantial savings on promotion in both "above and below the line" costs. Finally, cost savings in the form of reduced office and sales space, furniture and decoration outlay, and administration overheads.

The cost of setting up a promotional web site (i.e., without the booking facilities) is relatively low. An average computer user, given a proper software package, such as Microsoft FrontPage can build a basic company web site in days. The marginal cost of adding an extra web-page to the site is negligible. The more comprehensive and powerful web-sites, such as a destination site offers complete information, a tour operator site with a virtual multimedia brochure to include thousands of product offerings, and a site which integrates information, reservation and transactions, will cost more and take longer to develop. However, compared with the tens of millions of dollars spent by airlines, tour operators and hotel chains on TV and magazine ads, the Web is a low cost medium for promotion. The simple web-presence, by providing information on the Net, and allow customers to find answers to their inquiries themselves can also help to reduce telephone charges based on toll-free numbers.

The Internet has also great potential for saving distribution costs. Distribution, the selling and marketing of tickets, is one of the biggest cost items in the airline industry. At British Airways, for example, distribution accounts for about 18% of its total costs of £8.5bn and a share of about 20 per cent is typical among big carriers. The chief executive of Swissair sees that the Internet can potentially save 50% of the airlines distribution cost (Dones 2000). Airlines web-based ticket sale operation can at least eliminate the key distribution costs of an airline seat-travel agent commission (standard 5-10%, with override, another 1-2%) and GDS fees US$3.20 gross (Richard and O'Neil-Dunne 1998). Internet-based supply-channel management can also save procurement costs for businesses.

British Airways aims to increase the share of online purchasing from the current 25% to 80% in two years time and achieve a estimated saving of more than 5% of its annual £3.5 billion purchasing budget (Tyler 2000).

THE CHARACTERISTICS OF TOURISM MARKETING

Travel and tourism products are ideal for marketing on the Internet. This is because tourism is an information-intensive industry and the Internet is the most effective and efficient means in information exchange worldwide. The Net can greatly facilitate the promotion and distribution of tourist products and potentially enable tourism destinations and enterprises to compete on a level playing field.

Tourism is an Information-Intensive Industry

Tourism is very information-intensive and information is often dubbed the "life-blood" or "cement" of the industry which holds together the different producers within the travel industry-airlines, tour operators, travel agencies, attractions, car rental, cruise lines, and other supplies. "In few other areas of activity are the generation, gathering, processing, application and communication of information as important for day-to-day operations as they are for the travel and tourism industry" (Poon 1993:154). The perishability of tourism products and the often erratic tourist demand make the task of balancing tourism supply and demand far more significant than any other sector. That is probably why tourism became one of the first industries to widely apply IT and conduct electronic commerce from the 1960s in the form of computer(ised) reservation systems (CRSs) and then global distribution Systems (GDSs).

However, the traditional CRSs and GDSs had only improved the information communication between tourist businesses, originally between airlines and travel agents, as they do not directly interact with consumers. The systems are also expensive to both the tourism producer and the retailer. For instance, the GDS cost accounted for an average 8.1% of the International Air Transport Association (IATA) member airlines' distribution cost in 1996 (IATA 2000), and the major GDSs charge around US$600 a month to put a terminal in a travel agency. Moreover, the systems are flawed with incompatibility between each other, especially in the lodging sector, where "switch" companies such as THISCO (The Hotel Industry Switching Company) was needed to connect hotels with all the major GDSs to facilitate room reservations by travel agencies worldwide (Sheldon 1997). With the effective use of the Internet, these problems can be addressed effectively and cheaply. In addition to its traditional function, a web-based GDS can increase the speed of information transmission, improve the quality of information delivery (from the old viewdata to the window-based computer screen), reduce the cost to the user as no special connections are necessary, and most important of all, has the potential to interact with all web users in the world. Having realised the tremendous potential of the Internet, GDS companies already started to develop new and web-based systems which could transform the whole tourism distribution landscape in the near future. For example, Amadeus launched Amadeus Pro Web in January 2000, which is a browser-based reservation tool allowing travel agents to service customers worldwide without a dedicated communications line and at a greatly reduced cost. In fact, with this system any Internet user can become an online travel agent within a week (Amadeus 2000).

Tourist Products and Services are Difficult to Evaluate

As a service industry, most tourist products are intangible services, they are experienced and cannot be touched, tasted, smelt or seen and therefore

difficult for tourists to grasp and evaluate. Furthermore, the spatial fixity of tourist attractions and amenities means that a tourist cannot really assess their quality until he arrives at the destination. Tourists have, for a long time, relied on limited information from holiday brochures and other literature to evaluate tours and destinations. Comprehensive, relevant, timely and accurate information is essential in tourists' holiday decision making process. But they were not readily available to tourists until the emergence of the Internet, especially the wide use of the Web.

With the Internet, virtually unlimited amount of information can be stored at a web site and an unlimited number of users can retrieve it at any time from anywhere in the world. The Web can not only provide more information but also provide it from a much wider range of sources; while in the past, tourists are almost exclusively dependent upon representations and descriptions by the travel trade.

The Web can also deliver the information in a greater variety of formats, from text to photos, graphs, audio and video clips, whereas in the past, tourists primarily relied on the printed brochures as the limited copies of videos of a limited number of tourism destinations or holidays were only available to the major travel agents.

The web-based electronic brochure can also facilitate the complex process of choosing among the hundreds of holidays using browser-generated selections from back-end databases linked to web servers whereas the printed brochures are usually arranged and indexed by one way, often by destination. Through Internet video telephony, tourists can also "test drive" a prospective holiday by viewing real-time scenes through cameras placed in hotels, clubs, restaurants, scenic spots and other sites in the destination and transmitted via the Internet. Video clips can also show episodes and scenes of festivals, art performances and service delivery to facilitate tourists in the comparison and evaluation of intangible services, the quality of which is otherwise difficult to assess in advance.

Tourism Distribution has Physically Nothing but Travel Tickets to Deliver

Since in tourism, it is the tourists who travel to the destination, rather than the tourist product be transported to the market. When a tourist books an airline seat, a hotel room, or a package holiday, he acquires the right to use that seat, room or holiday in the specified time period. After the tourist completed his journey or holiday, he takes nothing home but experiences (though often together with some photos and souvenirs). In the whole process, from the booking, through the out journey to the return journey, the only things being transported are travel tickets and the tourist himself. This unique characteristic offers tourism a great advantage in Internet marketing as the only cost of online sale will be the transaction processing expense plus a little postage cost; in contrast, for manufactured goods, the delivery cost is often substantial.

'With the increasing popularity of electronic-ticketing (c-ticketing) or ticketless-travel, especially among airlines, online tourism distribution over the Web may one day have no physical goods (not even a ticket) to deliver at all. Ticket-less travel means that check-in is achieved by proof of identity and a booking reference number. This saves the cost of ticketing for the airline which would usually include stationery, printing and postage and speeds up the check-in process at airports by enabling passengers to self check-in at check-in machines with a credit card. Worldwide, there are more than 30 airlines offer e-ticketing in at least some routes in its networks (IATA 2000). About 60% of United Airlines' passengers are now using c-tickets. British Airways has even announced that from May 2000 travellers will be charged £25 for a printed ticket where e-ticketing is available for the flight. It could also cost the traveller £50 to replace a lost paper ticket. Obviously, c-ticketing is a key development that will accelerate the acceptability and convenience of booking air travel via an on-line travel agent. Since such a web-based e-ticket seller has no physical ticket to deliver, it can potentially sell from anywhere in the world to anyone in the world (Richer and 0'Neil-Dunne 1998).

The Tourism Destination Product is Fragmented

As a place product, tourism includes all the elements a destination has to offer to tourists, including the social, cultural and physical environments as well the "touristic" components of tourism supply such as attractions, transport and lodging facilities, and other travel related services. Pollock (1999) highlights the difficulties in tourism destination marketing which are attributable primarily to two factors. First, tourism is fragmented in that while the tourist looks at a holiday as a complete "experience", it is sold in the market place "in bits" as beds, meals, tours, seats, etc. by a plethora of independent suppliers that operate independently of one another. Second, no one agency controls or can deliver content about a destination's tourism product as the marketing of a tourism destination is shared by another plethora of organisations such as tourist information centres, regional tourism boards, national tourism organisations and national tourist offices overseas located in main generating markets.

The Internet provides the effective means for a destination to develop a sustainable electronic "infrastructure" that is capable of establishing a comprehensive and multi-lingual destination web site. This site can present existing and potential tourists with up to date information, from a variety of sources, about the destination in all aspects of tourism-tourist attractions, transportation, accommodation, tour operators, travel agencies, shopping and leisure facilities-as well as the background of its people, culture, history, economy, climate. The master destination database can be integrated through hyperlinks with individual tourism companies as well as with suite of applications which enable tourists to pick and mix to make their own holiday "packages". As such a mega-site could be the "portal" or the "home page" of the web sites of all tourism enterprises in a destinations, it is a great deal easier for the destination to establish itself in the already crowded web-space. From this first stop-of-call, an visitor can search for all the information he needs to make a decision as to whether to visit the destination, what facilities to use and to arrange for reservations and transactions online. In comparison, with the traditional media, in order to get the relevant information of a destination a tourist often needs to go to a travel agency to get a brochure, to a bookshop to get a guide book, and may also contact the destination's national tourist office to get some promotional literature. Furthermore, the printed literature the tourists get is often outdated while a properly constructed and maintained web site can provide right-to-the-minute information.

The Vast Majority of Tourism Enterprises are Small in Size

The fragmented tourism industry is also polarised in that on the one hand, there are a few large multinational airlines, tour operators, hotel chains and theme parks; on the other, there are millions of small and often family owned businesses, especially in the travel retailing, tour guiding, hotel and catering sectors. For example, in Scotland the average size of the accommodation establishment in the Bed and Breakfast sector was 2.5 rooms in 1999. For the small tourism enterprises, the Web is probably the first effective and feasible medium for them to carry out professional marketing function beyond the basic sales and operating activities.

The Internet has opened the door for small businesses with little capital to reach a worldwide market. Open access results in lower entry barriers so that virtually anyone can both access and provide content to the Internet. Travel retailing is one of the sectors m the economy that requires very little initial capital investment.

The Net also re-defines economies of scale, allowing small firms to achieve low unit costs for products and services in markets (such as tour operating) dominated by large companies. In the hospitality sector, small firms could also have more cost-effective marketing through the destination's web-site than the printed tourist directory. In essence, the Web "levels the playing field" (Hoffman and Novak 1996). For this reason, Inkpen (1998:178) goes so far as to praise the Internet as a marketer's "dream" because it enables companies of different sizes to compete on more equal terms. This analysis also applies to tourism destinations (as resorts, regions or nations). For example, a strong web presence may substantially increase the exposure of many small and developing destinations in the Western market where the high cost of mass media advertising made such exposure practically impossible in the past. Nevertheless, it must be noted that although it costs little to achieve a web exposure, the development of a fully functional marketing and sales site and especially the promotion of the site to increase visitor numbers require huge investment. Therefore, the Internet provides a level playing field for all sizes of companies only at the point of entry-that is, to establish a web presence.

APPLICATIONS OF THE INTERNET IN TOURISM MARKETING

The Internet as a marketing media can be of great benefit to virtual all areas of marketing, from marketing research, through market segmentation, targeting and positioning, to the effective use of the marketing mix, and marketing organisation and control. The following discussion does not attempt to provide an exhaustive list of the Net's use in tourism; rather, it simply intends to exemplify its common applications in and main implications for tourism marketing.

Marketing Research

The Internet does more than automating online business transaction, it can "informate" in that it provides a vast amount of information which was previously unavailable. Marketing is essentially an information-processing activity which links an organisation to the external environment in which it operates. The Internet is an invaluable source of low cost but up-to-date marketing intelligence which can be sourced through a company's own site (for details of its customers) and other web sites (for information on competition situations, market conditions and the general environment). The Internet is extremely useful in build a customer information database. With the use of proper software such as Aurum Software's Web-Trak (and even with simple means like cookies, web forms and email feedback) it is easy to gather systematic data about all users who visited the company's web site. This information can be used to identify prospects, understand customer needs and customise resources to give greater levels of service to customers (Heinen 1996). A database of online transaction histories can be the primary marketing resource of tourism companies, determining what kind of travel products they can deliver, what market segments they serve best, and what is the lifetime value of each customer to the firm.

By searching other web sites, a company can get valuable information about market demand, supply, competition and economic, demographic, legislation and technological changes in the domestic and international markets. Web sites of government agencies, media companies and non-profit organisations usually provide large amount of information free on general issues; while commercial sites are good sources of information on new technologies, best business practices, and industry initiatives. Scanning competitors' home pages helps companies to track competitors' marketing strategies and tactics. For example, from hotel chains' web sites, one can easily locate information about the chains' main business activities, financial performance, new hotel openings and investment plans, and key marketing strategies; whereas airlines' web sites often show such useful data as business and financial analysis, strategic alliance groups, new routes development and fleet expansion plans, frequent flyer programmes and (where a online GDS is available) the fares and availability of flights between any two destinations.

Market Targeting

An important feature of the Web as a medium is that it is the consumer who is actively searching for information about products or brands in which they are interested. In effect the consumer is "pre-screened" and shows both interest and involvement in visiting the web site. While on the Web, the consumer can also provide instantaneous feedback to the marketer (Stern, 1995). All the feedback, and indeed, every "click" or "hit" the user makes can be memorised by the web server. Through the application of the IT data mining technique, companies can find patterns within their internal customer data and make sense of data or turn data into meaningful marketing information.

For instance, the visitation record of an online brochure may show the total number of hits, the distribution of the hits among the pages and across time, the order of the pages been accessed. The user's visitation data can be easily combined with user profile information from user registrations through online visit cards or questionnaires and used to uncover the consumers 'interest and the patterns of demand and buying behaviour. This in turn leads to identification of likely target segments, often niches based on specific benefit sought. Armed with such information, organisations can refine their targets and develop specific means to achieve true one-to-one marketing (Pitta 1998).

The appropriate use of user profile and surfing behaviour data can improve the effectiveness and efficiency of market segmentation and targeting. This is because the traditional approach to market segmentation is often based simplistically on geographical, demographic and economic variables while the psycho, behavioural or lifestyle data is costly to collect and difficult to measure and compare. In Internet marketing, it is easier to collect these data from potentially each and every user of the company web site, though tangible rewards such as free prize draws and free membership, are often needed to attract users to fill in web forms. It is even a great deal simpler and more effective in market targeting as the email messages and even tailor-made web-pages can reach the intended receiver with little cost. It is possible to set up 'virtual" or cyber-communities for each target market niche in the form of news-groups through which consumers with similar interest and behaviour patterns can be sent with relevant product offering and other information from the marketer. Members of such Internet communities can regularly exchange information between them and strengthen a sense of belonging.

Product

One of the major advantages of the Internet in marketing is that the tourist can here be a value creator for tourism companies through redefining the labour division between the marketer and the tourist in providing tourist experiences (Dellaert 1999).

This is because, on the one hand, tourists can provide individual preferences for or specifications of holiday packages through feedback in the forms of web forms, email messages or simply the 'clicking' patterns, which the tourism marketer can use to development new products or tailor-make existing products to suit the needs of particular consumer(s). In this sense, the Internet has accelerated a shift in the nature of products from mass produced and tangible to customised and information based.

On the other hand, the self-servicing tourist can not only conduct transactions online and reduce costs of sales for the supplier but also actively participate in the production process itself. Provided with choices, a tourist can now assemble his own product according to the specifications desired. This is especially useful in the production and marketing of package holidays. Tour operators, for example, can offer modular products or services, such as flights, rooms, tours, car hire and performances on their web sites, and allow the user to participate in the development of the specific holiday packages using a menu of options, ie., 'pick and mix" his own package. As tour operators negotiate with the providers of these separate holiday items and buy in bulk, The economies of scale will enable the operators to offer lower "parts" prices to individual consumers than they buy directly from the different producers of the travel products. At the meantime, since the booking engine is integrated with the product inventory, it is easy for the operator to adjust in real-time the prices of different holiday components in response to their relative popularity and demand patterns. In this way, tour operators can effectively provide the market with low cost and flexible (rather than the conventional rigid) package tours This is what both marketers and consumers have long dreamed for-high quality products made individually at a unit cost level of mass production-all enabled by the power of the Internet.

Internet technologies can also contribute to the improvement of current products on offer or development of new products and services that redefine the company's strategic position. For instance, Boeing announced on 27 April 2000 plans for a network which will allow passengers to use the internet, watch TV and receive other data while flying. Called Connexion by Boeing, it will use satellite technology to provide broadband services to aircraft, which could greatly improve passengers' flight experiences. The introduction of electronic ticketing (e-ticketing) and flight information exchange through mobile phones by many airlines in recent years also improve customer services. The Internet also give tourist attractions such as museums and galleries wider format options for electronic presentation and show web collections which are physically impossible to construct (Taylor and Ran 1995). Zoos and aquariums can improve its product offering through 'live" camera links using web sites like whale-watching to show views of animals not in captivity (Benhow 1997).

Pricing

The role of the Internet in pricing is based on its ability in processing and exchanging large amount of data instantaneously with a great number of people. This information processing capacity enables a company to analyze relevant pricing data effectively and quickly. The information exchange capacity enables firms to set and change prices in real time and also facilitates online bidding and flexible pricing. Both of these qualities of the Net are extremely useful in tourism marketing.

The major tour operators in the UK, for example, produce some 2,000 to 3,000 brochure pages annually, most pages feature a price panel with perhaps 100 separate prices, making a total of about a quarter of a million individual prices (Holloway and Robinson 1995). The sheer number of prices, together with the fact that most brochures are launched 10 months in advance of the holiday season, mean that pricing in the travel industry is extremely difficult Since it is unpractical to set the prices for such a great number of holidays on the bases on demand analysis or competition research, most operators simply follow a cost-plus policy with little regard to the market changes in the months to follow.

Even an operator wishes to adjust its holidays prices it is a costly and cumbersome process as new price panels have to be printed and distributed to the travel agencies. With the help of a web-based reservation system, the task can be a great deal easier. A tour operator can make real-time adjustment to its thousands of holiday prices at a touch of a button in response to competition moves and demand changes. A special late-booking section can also be included in the main web site to promote 'left-over" holidays at the last minute to solve the problems of over-supply or under-demand in the package tour industry which has become a chronic issue in the UK during the last decade or so.

In Internet marketing, the potential for price discrimination is diminished given the enhanced capability of consumers to identity the least expensive source, regardless of supplier or location. The skilled consumer could have the "perfect knowledge" of market prices, which could facilitate the realization, to certain extent, of 'perfection competition" at the national and global markets. This will lead to the increasing standardisation of prices across companies or even borders, especially for the undifferentiated products such as airline seats, beach holidays and city breaks. Other applications of pricing on the Web including bidding and flexible pricing-many web-based businesses allow customers to bid for products on their sites. Customers commit to the sale if the price is agreed upon. The bidding locks in customers to the sale and the committed price. This is a flexible pricing strategy where the buying capacity of the customer reflects in the eventual price. Companies such as Ebay.com and Bid.com have developed a model where other vendors can place products up for bids (De and Mathew 1999).

Airlines could sell seats on over-demanded flights or routes through online bidding to the highest bidders to generate extra revenue. Tour operators may use online bidding in a different manner to market special holidays the demand for which may be extremely difficult to estimate in advance. For example, a tour operator can put on its web site the details of a package holiday to the moon and the total cost (including profit margins) for a group, say 50 travellers, the more people bid the lower the price for each traveller. This way of pricing could well enhance the operator's image and profitability, as it is both an innovative marketing and sound financial approach.

Place

The uniqueness of the Internet as a means of distribution is based on the fact that it exists in "cyberspace" thus physical phenomena such as location and distance are less significant or even irrelevant. For the producer, the Web enables it to have direct links with consumers at a low cost therefore provides it with the opportunity of "disintermediation". For the retailer, the Web threatens its livelihood and changes its critical success factor from location, location, location to access, access, access. For the wholesaler, web-based business means it can bypass retailers while at the same time risk being bypassed by the producers.

The foremost role of the Web in tourism distribution is the direct electronic reservation and transactions between tourism product supplier and consumers. Aldridge et al (1997) argues that direct marketing is the name of the game on the Internet, offering both consumers and marketers greater control and lower potential costs of access due to the conveniences of the Net. Because direct channels may be producer-direct or intermediary-direct, the potential for channel conflict will be magnified. In order to assuage channel conflict and price competition between direct-sellers and retailers, both producers and intermediaries will have to develop augmented product features and unique benefits. For example, direct online booking of airline tickets often carries special benefits not available from travel agents, such as extra frequent-flyer miles; while purchasing an airline ticket from an online travel agency may also benefit from such services as hotel reservations and travel insurance.

Airlines are among the first industry to invest in and develop CRSs and GDSs to exploit the potentials of IT. The Web offers the airlines even greater opportunities in streamlining and shortening the distribution channel. The no-frills or low-cost airlines emerged in the last few years are already heavily relying on the Web to distribute flight tickets directly to customers. The major global airlines have also started to believe that the Internet offers a unique opportunity to drive down costs and restore profitability to the sector which is troubled with financial losses across the globe (e.g., the 266 IATA member airlines as a whole made an accumulated loss of US $800 million during the first 8 years of the 1990s) (IATA 2000).

British Airways, for example, launched an e-business strategy recently which places the Internet at the centre of its efforts to transform relationships with both customers and suppliers. It is planning to invest £90 million during the next two years to develop its web-based operations with the aim of increasing the share of tickets sold over the Internet from less than 1% in 1999 to 50% by 2004. It is also preparing to operate via mobile phones and interactive television. Major airlines have also started to use the Internet to manage the supply channel and reduce procurement costs. For instance American Airlines, Air France, British Airways, Continental Airlines, Delta Airlines and United Airlines have agreed to jointly create and operate a web site that will handle supply purchases with US$32 billion a year (CNET News 2000).

The biggest change to tourism distribution brought by the Web could, in the next 5 to 10 years, be the noticeable shrinking of the travel agent sector. Agents are squeezed by both a decreasing market as more and more consumers go online and book directly from airlines and operators and by airlines' declining commission levels. The Association of British Travel Agents (ABTA) believes that the Internet will not cut out the middleman, but it will certainly put their added value under scrutiny. It warns that High Street travel agents that do not excel in what they do may not survive the competition. Nevertheless, the travel agent sector will not be doomed to extinction. How far and how soon the role of travel agent will diminish in the future is dependent upon how flexible and innovative the travel agents can be and how fast the Web can dominate both business and everyday life (Liu and Jones 1995). The Travel agency will have to reinvent itself to suit the new Internet era by transforming from a travel ticket seller to a travel information manager.

For tour operators, the potential disintermediation has a dual effect. On the one hand, they can be bypassed by the producer as airlines and hotels that directly sell their products to the travel agencies and consumers; on the other, tour operators could benefit from its own direct sell operation by eliminating the travel retailers. It is hard to estimate the full impacts of the two. But one thing is sure to say that the tour operators, more than travel agencies, have a future in the Internet era.

This is based on the understanding that tour operators are not purely intermediaries as they do perform some production function in assembling the various parts of tourism products into a marketable package. Through this value-creating activities, tour operators can provide convenience and better value for consumers, by passing on to them some cost savings gained through bulk buying the separate components of the package, than they would otherwise get from the individual tourist product providers. The major tour operators (in the UK) are also 'backward" integrated and have their own charter airlines thus major schedule airlines' direct selling is not much as a threat to them as to travel agents.

Promotion

Arguably, the component of the marketing mix being most quickly transformed as a result of Internet usage is promotion.

The Internet provides a labour-efficient and cost-effective way of distributing information almost instantaneously to millions of potential clients in the global markets. Internet promotion combines mass media's reach with the personalization inherent in two-way dialogue-previously only possible in personal selling. It can be used for corporate visibility, brand name recognition, advertising, public relations, corporate sponsorship, direct sales, sales promotion, customer support and technical assistance. There are three main issues in the application of the Internet to tourism promotion.

First, present the promotional information on the company's web site. The Web enables more information to be transmitted to (potentially) more people cheaply, instantly and with multimedia effect. The key to achieve these benefits is a well-designed and maintained web site which is attractive, informative and interactive. Through its multimedia capability, a good web site can and should incorporate information as accurate and detailed as brochures or timetables, photos and graphs as glossy as magazine ads, and videos as entertaining as TV commercials.

The site can and supply as much promotional information as possible as there is virtually no capacity constraints or advertising space limits on the Web. By hyper-'inking pages together in an appropriate fashion, the Web marketer can create an ultra-comprehensive brochure to include everything a user wishes to know. For instance, a tourism destination web site may become a 'information mall" which provides the users with all the basic information about it such as the exchange rates, local traditions, weather, what to buy, etc. and, through the hyperlinks to the sites of tourism firms, details of flight schedules, tour prices, park opening times, late offers, and so on. A company web site with email links or even telephone numbers and address will enable users to contact it for further and often more personalised information.

Second, promote the web site itself to increase its exposure and visitation since a company's web site has to compete in the clutter of thousands of other web sites selling similar products and services. This can be achieved through a number of ways. A memorable Internet address to help user locate it on the Web, usually the company or brand name or a catchy word or phrase. Links "from" other web sites, by registering with search engines and online directories and paying relevant sites for click-through links or banners ads, are particularly important if the company's site is not well known. Links 'to" other sites, such as those offer news or entertainment services and those offer complementary products can also make the site more interesting as well as providing more relevant and up-to-date information for the users. Promoting the web site through the traditional media is also important, especially when it was first set up. For example, expedia.co.uk launched a £4 million promotion campaign on British TV and Press recently. The company's web address should also be included on all its media messages "to drive consumers to the Web" (Pardun and Lamb 1999).

Third, use the company's web site as a platform for advertising sites or products of other businesses. Through "banners" and banner linked web pages, a company's web site can also generate revenues by becoming an advertising medium for other organisations. Indeed, the effectiveness of the Web as a medium for advertising has already made online advertising a boom business itself.

The Internet Advertising Bureau's research shows that online advertising revenue reached US$4.62 billion in 1999. It also finds that banner advertisements is the predominate type of advertising, accounting for 56%, sponsorships at 27%, interstitials at 4%, email at 2%, and other rounding out the category at 11% (IAB 2000). Increased Web advertising will reduce the attractiveness and spending on some traditional forms of promotion such as direct mail, outdoor displays and radio advertising. Fletcher Research (2000) predicted that the online advertising spending in the UK would soar from £50 million in 1999 to £625 million by 2004, while expenditures on direct mail could see a 33% fall in the same period.

THE CURRENT CONSTRAINTS ON INTERNET TOURISM MARKETING

The Internet has created great opportunities for tourism marketing. However, the current level of online travel sales is low though most researchers expect it to increase rapidly in the next few years. For example, it was estimated that purchases of travel products represent just 6% of overall Internet sales and 0.5% of all travel and tourism spending (Smith and Jenner 1998). In the US, Jupiter Communications forecasts that online travel bookings will grow from US$2.2 billion in 1998 to US$ 16.6 billion by 2003, representing a market share of total travel sales of 1.7% and 9.6% respectively (Bates 2000, Tyler 2000). In the UK, Thomas Cook predicts that one in five package holidays and 40% of all flights will be sold via the internet or digital television in the next three years (Banerjee and Mayling 2000). Obviously, the comparative advantages of using the Internet in tourism marketing is compelling but its full potential as a marketing tool will only be realised if a number of well-documented limitations are successfully addressed.

Demand Factors

Consumer demand is the fundamental determinant of all forms of businesses. Whether an industry is initially supply-led or demand-driven, consumers are the key force in deciding the scale, structure, style and speed of its development. The small size of Internet business transactions in the world economy at present is caused to a great extent by insufficient demand, though more limited by consumers' willingness than their ability to shop on the Net.

First, the penetration rate of computer using and Internet connections is still low worldwide. In the main developed countries, about 30-50% of the adult population are Internet users while the global average is about 1-2%. One estimate shows that in 1997, there were 50.2 million web-users, of which 60% were in US and 20% in Europe; the world total web-population in 2001 was predicted to be 174.5 million, the US and Europe account for 54% and 18% respectively (Juliussen and Petska-Juliussen 1998).

Although people with Internet access tend to be more affluent, better educated and younger than the average consumer, the small number of web-population does reveal that globally it is still a relatively small market. Furthermore not all web-user are frequent users. In the UK for example, a quarter of the 15 million adults with Internet access surf the

Web less than once a week, and only a fifth of web-users have actually ordered something via the Internet (Fletcher Research 1999). At the well publicised travel web cite-lastminute.com-only 6% of its 1.5 million register users have ever purchased anything there.

Second, the low frequency of web surfing is mainly caused by high access cost, especially in countries outside of North America. In the UK for example, local telephone charges are still metered, though the Internet subscription fees has largely gone from last year. Most consumers find it is an expensive hobby to surf the Web, especially when the search task is complicated by low speed and difficulties in locating the desired information. The main UK Internet service providers (ISPs) have recently launched unmetered packages which will be available from mid-2000. This new development could see a surge in web visitation in the country.

Third, The vast majority of users access web sites for information or entertainment purposes rather than for online shopping. Among the Net resources, email is the most frequently used, news and sports sites attract more visitors than commercial sites, and sex and MP3 are for many years the most searched key words. Although Internet transactions offer the potential benefits of convenience and cost savings, due to factors discussed later, consumers still believe traditional shopping methods are more reliable and sometimes more economical. A recent survey of 50,000 Internet users in the UK show that 80% used the Web to access email while less than a third had bought online (Fletcher Research 1999)

Fourth, concerns over privacy, information abuse, web crime, payment security and undelivery or late delivery, are often cited as the main inhibitor to online shopping. There is a lot of trust involved in online shopping. A web users has to trust that he receives the product he orders as well as trust its quality to be as described. He also wants to be sure that his private information such as address and credit card numbers is handled sensitively (Ratnasingham 1998). However, there is at present no special legal provision to protect consumers' interest in web transactions and according to a Consumers International survey: 6% of the items ordered took more than a month to arrive and at least 8% never did; many sites did not give clear information about delivery charges; only 13% of sites promised that they would not sell customers' personal information on to a third party; and only 53% of the companies had a policy on returning goods (BBC 1999a). As a result, in average less than 1% of those 'looking" are actually 'booking" at the web site.

A recent MORI survey of package holidaymakers in the UK also found that only 45% of the respondents answered 'Yes" to the question of "In principle (if you had access) would you be prepared to book a holiday through the Internet?" while 46% answered "No"; and 9% answered "Don't know" (Martin 1999). A report on travellers' use of the Internet in the US, which has the most advanced Internet businesses and Internet users, shows that 52.2 million people used the Internet for researching travel in 1999 but only 16.5 million (32%) of which actually made their travel reservations online (Tyler 2000).

Finally, consumers' anxiety over safety and security in online shopping is further exacerbated by frequent media reports about web security breaches and frauds, and insufficient knowledge of the matter itself. Most of the security worries are caused by people who are not sufficiently aware of the possible protection that exists (Furnell and Karweni 1999). Although the Web is generally considered to be user friendly and even 'foolproof", a user without the proper IT knowledge and skills will certainly encounter more problems and feel less confident in conducting web-based transactions.

Technological Factors

Many of the current constraints and problems of conducting web-based business are caused by the Web technology itself. 'Web technologies consist of the hardware, software and networks that enable individuals and organisations to connect with and interact with the World Wide Web. Hardware consists of the client terminals, the server, the gateway, the router, and hubs. The software consists of operating and application software, including the browsers and application software on the client side, database servers, web servers and other application servers on the server side, and network operating systems and managers on the network side. The networks consist of cables, either leased or proprietary, and message carrier services" (Dc and Mathew 1999:432). The main causes for concern over the ability of the Web in implementing c-commerce are as follows:

The Web's slow speed, often dubbed as the 'world wide wait", slows down the growth of the web-based businesses as users are often not prepared to wait for too long to see the information appears on the screen. The slowness of the Web is a combined results of three factors: the increasing number of Internet users, the increasing frequency of use, and the increasing richness of the information (from simple text to full colour pictures and videos) being transferred over the Internet (O'Conner 1999).

Technology will not reduce these growing demands on the Web, on the contrary, technology will constantly expand the Web's capacity for accommodate and even stimulate the increasing demand. For example, the new digital broadband service, due to be introduced in the UK this year, could offer instant and always-on high-speed (10 times faster) Internet access. It will not only enable much faster Internet access but also enhance facilities such as interactive digital TV and video e-mail. The advent of broadband and mobile accessibility is creating a second wave in Internet development (after the WWW in 1993). Research shows that a broadband customer will stay online four times as long as a narrowband customer, and spend nearly three times as much on c-commerce BBC 2000).

Functionally, the Internet is close to fully operational for commercial purposes. The main remaining impediment to maximum use of the Internet for c-commerce is the concerns for information security. The securing of information includes the protection of: (1) confidentiality-providing confidentiality in the transmission (and sometimes the storage) of data; (2) authentication-proving the identification of the individuals both transmitting and receiving the data; certifying that all parties to a transaction are indeed who they claim to be; and (3) non-repudiation-providing proof that the transaction actually took place, establishing an irrefutable time stamp on the sending and receiving of the message (Liddy 1997). In particular, there is an urgent need for an integrated financial transaction system that is suitable for an open electronic marketplace such as the Internet. How the consumer will pay for goods and services and how the provider will receive the payment securely over the Internet are issues which are being seen as some of the most important success factors for Internet commerce. A survey of US corporations revealed that 75% of the executives lacked confidence in the Internet as a vehicle for electronic commerce, primarily because of the vulnerabilities. The risks in electronic commerce are shown in poor security such as: from the short-cuts in the software development process, shortcomings in the popular operating system, deficiencies in the Internet protocols and problems inherent in managing the Internet (Ratnasingham 1998).

Related to security is the issue of 'cyber' crimes. Internet crimes include not only fraud and theft-related activities, which simply represented the extension of traditional crimes into the electronic environment, but also new and more advanced forms of abuse such as hacking and computer viruses (Furnell and Warren 1997). Web scam and online credit card fraud are also increasing rapidly.

Visa International says that half of all credit-card disputes are about Internet transactions, despite online transactions making up just 2% of Visa's overall business. Visa found that across the EU only 5% of consumers trust e-commerce (BBC 1999c). Web technology does not cause the web crimes but these cyber crimes are more difficult to prevent and detect as they are committed in a virtual space. Unless the IT industry can come up with some effective solutions to the security problems in web-commerce, consumers will have to either take a high risk in or stay away from Net-shopping.

Furthermore, the 'unorganised" nature of the Web, makes it difficult to locate the information users desired. The Web offers an uncontrolled and vast universe of information: there are now about 5 million web sites with some 1 billion web pages. However, there is no overriding structure and control over information, no single entry point to the Web, and no centralized directory of content. Although the development of search engines and online directories has made finding information somewhat simpler, it i~ still easy to get distracted or lost during a search and much precious time can be wasted in gathering information. Ironically, this may negate the productivity benefits that derived from its use (Soh et al 1997, Hormozi et al 1998).

The other problems of the Web can be seen from Internet Industry Almanac's "Top 10 pain in the Net"-junk email, slow web sites with too many images to load, web sites with white text that you can't print, cookies, broken links, interstitial ads, hard-to-read tiny text, web sites with no basic company information, old forgotten web sites, and the server is not responding (Juliussen and Juliussen 1998).

Organisational Factors

The low level of web-based business is also attributable to the failure of business organisations in implementing the Web technologies in operation and marketing. Most business leaders did not realise the potential impacts of the Web on commerce until very recently (some still do not). A survey of US hotel managers found that they believe the Internet will 'someday" become an effective marketing and communication tool but not at the present time. Ironically, respondents with greater exposure to the Net rated its present usefulness lower than those with no net experience. On the other hand, those same experienced users gave the Net's future prospects a much higher rating than the inexperienced respondents (van Hoof and Combrink 1998).

Many companies, even with recognition of the advantages of the Internet in marketing, failed to exploit its full potential due to the lack of management commitment, investment capital and the qualified technical and managerial personnel. This is particularly the case for small tourism businesses. In the UK for example, travel agents are not using the Internet to provide better service to customers because of perceived investment and access costs and fear of new technology. Sabre (UK) recently discovered that fewer than half of its agency customers had an email address (Fox 2000). On the other hand, some large travel corporations failed to develop web-based operations wholeheartedly due to both complacency about their market leader positions and the vested interest in their highly vertically integrated business structure. The top three tour operators in the UK-Thomson, Airtours and First Choice-for instance, did not have a formal Internet strategy until March 2000. They probably overlooked the potential of the new Internet start-ups since the Net-commerce had a slow start and the travel web sites were mainly selling airline seats instead of package tours. The major tour operators were also concerned with the impacts of web-based operation on their own travel agent chains because the "disintermediation" in travel distribution saves operator side cost at the expense of losing businesses at the agency side.

As a result, not all tourism companies are on the Web. When they are on the Web, most of their web sites are PR or promotion sites that provide merely the companies a presence on the Net or little more than advertisements for their products and services. With the few comprehensive sales and transactions web sites, users were often asked to phone an operator or offered a brochure in the post. Just a fifth of the UK's top 40 tour operators have a real-time booking facility on their Internet sites. A recent survey also shows that 62% of the travel companies which have facilities to sell via the Web or email have less than 1% of its total business is conducted through online booking (TTG 2000).

Even when web sites are fully operational in real-time transactions, such as many airlines owned sites, they often offer limited choice. Consumers increasingly want to use the web, and they want the convenience to see all the options in one place, no matter which airlines or tour operator is involved. However, most of the travel products on sale over the Net are stored at various web sites owned and operated by individual companies, such as airlines, tour operators, travel agencies and ferry companies.

Another problem is that the Web does not always offer the lowest prices compared with the traditional distribution outlets. Research by Express Money (1999) shows that booking holidays and flights through the Internet is not cheaper and traditional, low-cost outlets offer lower prices for several popular destinations. This is particularly the case for airlines as where a single flight could have over 50 different fares, the cheapest fares are usually given to flight-brokers or consolidators. Since most web users consider 'price" as the most important factor in buying an airline ticket, they will certainly be discouraged from booking directly on the Web when they realise that the traditional agents offer better deals.

Governmental Factors

The nature of the Internet enables no one to control its structure and content, while as a recent phenomenon, laws and standards are yet to be developed and adopted to facilitate and regulate its commercial use. Some of the problems highlighted above are partly attributable to or greatly escalated by the lack of effective government involvement in promoting, facilitating and regulating e-commerce on the Internet.

Governments across the world have been slow in realising the potential of the Internet for economic growth and even slower in providing the necessary regulatory framework appropriate for conducting Net-based business. Although existing business laws and regulations are applicable to e-commerce, the particular nature of Internet-based business does requires special treatment, especially in the areas of security, fraud, sabotage, and data and consumer protection. Without the confidence and trust of those participating in the process, it will be impossible to achieve sustainable growth in e-commerce. However, censoring indecent and potentially criminal material on the Internet were often the main reasons chosen for regulation. In the UK, one of the advanced Net-economies, the Government put forward a draft Electronic Communications bill last year which deals with a wide range of issues central to the healthy development of e-commerce, including consumer protection, information security, authentication and digital signatures, confidentiality, encryption, taxation issues, intellectual property rights, technical standards, illegal content and so on. The problem is, the bill remains to be a draft bill until the Parliament passes it through a lengthy process that could last for years.

As the Internet is a global computer network and e-commerce is essentially global business, the establishment of international standards and legal provisions for its smooth function is also critical. International bodies like the Organisation for Economic Cooperation and Development (OECD) and the European Union (EU) started to address some of the key issues in e-commerce from 1998, such as building trust in electronic commerce by ensuring the security and privacy of information and the protection of consumers; establishing ground rules for electronic transactions; and enhancing the information infrastructure through common interoperable standards, and access to open networks (BBC 1998). However, progress is lamentably slow. It appears that each country will have to create their own Internet acceptable use policies, and figure out how to enforce them. Until then, the Internet will be a lawless frontier where anarchy and vigilantism are alive and well (Thomas et al 1998, Westphal and Towell 1998).

Legislation is of fundamental importance, but legal provisions only mark the boundary of unacceptable business practices and protect the consumer by redressing any illegal treatment. Consumers want to buy from companies that are not only law-abiding but more importantly are reliable and offer quality and value. Nevertheless, it is extremely difficult, if not impossible, to judge a company by its web site. Therefore, other (non-legal) measures must also be taken to boost consumer confidence in online shopping.

The UK Government is trying to promote the ideas of 'e-hallmarks" which will guarantee that its users are legitimate traders offering assurances on security of payments and communications and giving accurate information on goods, prices and a returns policy. A new body-TrustUK-will be set up to accredit c-commerce codes and there are plans to market the c-hallmark internationally (BBC 1999b). However, many business organisations oppose the idea, wanting instead to rely on self-regulation without government intervention.

For example, ABTA aims to clamp down on Internet sales by creating regulations for online travel transactions. It plans to publish a single revised code of conduct for agents and operators in May 2000, with a new section on Internet sales. It will require members to have a secure payment system if using the Internet to take bookings, and to observe the same ABTA rules as for other types of advertising.

The government can also play an active role in e-commerce by providing the necessary infrastructure for conducting Internet business. After all, the Internet was first started by Government-the US Department of Defence-in 1969 as ARPANet and only became commercialised in 1993 (Krol 1994). Uncertainty in many countries with regard to policies for investment, ownership, technology selection and general public access to the Internet has restricted the development of Net-based business and the penetration of Internet itself. Especially in the developing world, the huge investment required to establish the network and to make full use of it is out of reach of many businesses. In such circumstances, government could provide start-up funding for small companies. The UK government is also trying to close the gap between technology haves and have-nots and has launched an initiative to make computers available to low-income families for as little as £5 a month.

CONCLUSIONS

This paper has so far examined some of the key issues related to the marketing of tourism on the Internet. In particular, it has highlighted the main features of the Internet as an effective and efficient communication medium, including its addressability, interactivity, flexibility and accessibility, and its role in improving customer service and reducing costs. It has also analysed the unique characteristics of tourism which make it perfect to be marketed on the Internet and further explored the main areas in tourism marketing where the Internet could play a significant role and provide substantial benefits for both the marketer and the consumer. In an investigation of the key forces which drive Internet commerce, it has found that a wide variety of factors, grouped conveniently in four broad categories demand, organisational, technological and governmental-could both enable and restrict the application of the Internet in tourism marketing.

With regard to the future of Internet tourism marketing, there appears to be little question that the Internet will permeate into every aspect of tourism business and every area of marketing activities. Indeed, the Net could become the dominant platform and instrument for tourism promotion and distribution in five years' time. This is based on the author's belief that Internet marketing has now survived its infancy and is ready to accelerate the transition from the introduction to the growth stage as more and more people and organisations are recognising its unique and great potential for marketing.

The increasing power of computers, decreasing surfing cost, and higher level of computer literary and web skills will make web surfing as a necessity in everyday life to an increasingly large population, especially in the developed world. Many of the current technological constraints could also be overcome (though new problems will inevitably emerge) in the next few years with the high quality broadband access via optical fiber or satellites to improve speed; the wide application of constantly improving firewalls, encryption and digital signature software to enhance security; the development of more sophisticated search engines and 'intelligent agents" to simplify web search task; and the Wireless Application Protocol (WAP) technology linking mobiles to the Internet to extend the range of services available to the public.

At the same time, governments are increasingly involved in the expanding e-commerce through providing incentives to small businesses, facilitating infrastructure development and establishing the regulatory framework which supports and protects all those concerned.

It is obvious to the current writer that the key to the future growth and improvement in Internet tourism marketing lies in tourism organisations. The market conditions and web technologies are improving steadily and a conducive legal and social environment is starting to take shape, it is now up to tourism organisations to seize and exploit the opportunities created by such changes to its full potential. Therefore, the crucial question for academic researchers and practitioners in future research is how tourism organisations can take advantage of the changes and opportunities brought about by the Internet. To offer a prescriptive list of policy recommendations is neither feasible, because it requires a thorough understanding of all relevant issues including expertise in technology, tourism, marketing and a keen awareness of all new developments in both IT and tourism, nor necessary since different tourism businesses have different resources and operate in different settings. Instead, an attempt is made here to discuss issues that are both important and with wide applicability. Three interwoven cognitive issues are highlighted below to emphasise the significance of changing the mentality of tourism organisations to preparing for the new virtual business environment.

In order to market tourism products successfully on the Internet, a tourism organisation must first of all have a strategic vision whereby it can fully comprehend the changing market space, from physical to both physical and virtual, and the underlying forces shaping this new marketing space. The Internet has altered forever the tourism marketing system and its environment, no tourism business can escape its impacts but companies willing to become engaged in Internet and embrace Net commerce should find more opportunities while those still pretend that the internet is a bad dream, such as some travel agencies, will be left with all the threats.

Whether a organisation likes it or not, the Internet is here to stay and is going to dominate tourism marketing. Andy Grove, the Chairman of Intel, has been widely quoted as saying that in five years' time all companies will be Internet companies or they won't be companies at all. Second, the Internet must not be treated as just a promotion aid or distribution device, but be seen as a major force in itself that profoundly changes the way tourist business is conducted. 'Marketers will need to rethink fundamentally the processes by which they identify, communicate, and deliver customer value. They will need to improve their skills in managing individual customers and allies. They will need to involve their customers in the act of codesigning their desired products" (Kotler 1999:206). Indeed, tourism marketers should change their business paradigm and marketing practices to suit the new Internet era.

Third, as the Internet alters the critical success factors in many businesses, tourism organisations must use it effectively to create new competitive advantages. For example, tour operators (in the UK) were obsessed with gaining control of distribution through vertical integration with travel agencies in the last decade, but with the emerging web-based online sales companies, control of how they let the product be distributed now supersedes control of actual distribution.

In responding to the threats from airlines direct sale, the major GDSs have been using the Internet to develop web-based GDSs and to diversify their product base to include hotels, car rental, cruise lines, tour operators, etc. Clearly, tourism organisations have to adopt a technology management policy that will assist their competitive strategy and usefully leverage the technology innovations to their advantage. Strategic Internet partnerships or alliances, especially those between tourism companies, and between tourism and IT companies, are also a major source of competitive advantage.

9

TOURISM DESTINATION MARKETING

INTRODUCTION

Over the past twenty years, the tourism industry has evolved dramatically. Changes in the environment, economics, technology, and tourists' beliefs and activities have caused the mass tourism which dominated the 1970s and 1980s to give way to the "new tourism," involving new tourists, new technologies, and new management practices (Poon, 1993). Marketing is an important activity for any business that wishes to become and remain competitive and successful. This is certainly the case in the rapidly changing tourism industry, and therefore tourism destination marketers must constantly review and revise their marketing goals, images, strategies and plans.

This chapter explores the importance of marketing in the tourism industry. It begins by outlining the general marketing system, then examines the special characteristics of tourism, including a discussion of how general marketing processes must be adapted when marketing tourism destinations. Next, a review of tourism marketing materials is undertaken. This includes consideration of consumers' access to, and use of, the marketing materials, and the role of images of space and place in these materials. The chapter closes with a review of examples of tourism marketing.

THE IMPORTANCE OF MARKETING IN THE TOURISM INDUSTRY

The tourism industry encompasses many businesses, such as accommodations, attractions, transportation, and restaurants, each of which may undertake marketing efforts. That is, there are different scales at which marketing can occur, from large-scale marketing of individual businesses or attractions (such as a horse-and-carriage tour operator, a hot dog stand, a whale watching business), to small-scale marketing of regions or entire countries.

The focus of this research is on the small scale marketing of destination regions, because it is at the regional, or community, level that "successful tourism planning is likely to take place" (Heath and Wall, 1992:6) and at which "most of the impacts of tourism, both positive and negative, occur" (Murphy, 1983, in Heath & Wall, 1992:6).

Tourism is the largest industry in the world. It is a very competitive industry with a highly volatile product. Destinations in vogue today often are out of fashion tomorrow. Marketing is one of the main ways for destinations to inform and entice potential tourists and to gain competitive advantage. However, many service industries such as tourism have traditionally used marketing less than manufacturing firms, as they felt it was too expensive, time-consuming, unnecessary, and unprofessional (Kotler et al., 1996), relying primarily on an established reputation to attract business.

And there are still those who consider marketing unprofessional, particularly within the area of advertising. Such detractors hold on to the belief that marketers will do anything to sell their products or services, with their number one goal being the making of a "quick buck." They are seen as having a complete lack of respect for customers' opinions, desires and intellects, and the environment or society as a whole. But this is an unfair view of many of today's marketers, because in a true marketing philosophy, customer satisfaction is key (Ibid).

Some have noted that marketing also can be used to protect the environment, improve quality of life, and help society as a whole. Marketers can use demand management to increase, decrease, or shift demand for a product or service either temporarily or permanently (Ibid). In the case of tourism, demarketing can be particularly useful, as it can be used to even-out demand (i.e., increase off-season visits, and limit high-season visits, thus reducing congestion, crowding and environmental impacts), to restrict access to sensitive areas, and to inform and educate tourists about problems facing various areas. Tourism destinations that adopt a modern marketing philosophy "that focuses on the satisfaction of tourist needs and wants while respecting the long-term interests in the community" (Mill & Morrison, 1985:360) will benefit not only themselves, but consumers, the environment, and society. This is corroborated by Poon (1993:7) who believes that "[n]ew tourism can play a leading role in providing and promoting more sustainable patterns of development and in saving Planet Earth." Thus, tourism marketing can and should assume an important role in education and conservation, because in the tourism industry, there is much more to gain (or lose) than just profits.

In these days of increased amounts of leisure time, higher standards of living, greater quality of life, higher expectations, and increasing choices (at least in so-called "developed countries"), tourism destination marketers must work harder to provide tourist satisfaction and to ensure they obtain and retain their share of the market. But tourism marketers should be sensitive to the new situation in which they are marketing. They must realize that tourism can and does have a sizeable impact on the environment, and tourism should not be promoted without full knowledge and understanding of that fact.

Certainly not all regions are ready or willing to accept and develop tourism. Nor should they, as tourism does not always have a positive effect (Richardson & Cohen, 1993; Ringer, 1996). But in many areas, tourism marketing can make a significant contribution to the quality of life of residents and tourists alike. Destinations that have chosen to embrace or at least accept tourism as a valuable industry must find a way to compete and succeed, and to protect the environment from the negative impacts of tourism. Adoption of a marketing philosophy is the key to success, and tourism marketers that adopt the societal marketing concept will be better off in the future, as consumers are becoming more educated and concerned about choosing products and services that benefit rather than harm the environment.

THE BASICS OF MARKETING

Marketing is defined most simply as "providing the right products [or services] at the right price in the right place and promoting them in a way that will appeal to the target market" (Weichard, 1992:2). More specifically:

> *"marketing is a managerial process involving the setting of organizational goals and objectives, analysis, planning, and implementation. It is a set of activities that results in the formulation of plans and programs. Through these activities an organization seeks to bring about a voluntary exchange of values by providing benefits to its clients and potential clients and, through this, benefits to the organization and its constituent parts or members" (Heath & Wall, 1992:7).*

Marketing can be visualized at three levels (see Figure 3.1). Firstly, any "exchange" of products or services in order to satisfy needs and wants is considered marketing (Weichard, 1992; Kotler et al., 1996). Secondly, marketing is a "system," which includes the providers of goods and services (i.e., the industry), those purchasing the goods and services (i.e., the market), and those responsible for delivering goods and services from the producers to the consumers. The marketing system also encompasses the flows of money, communications, and information between the industry and the market, and the surrounding environment in which these flows occur (Kotler et al., 1996).

Thirdly, a marketing "management philosophy" is one of five management philosophies, including the "production concept," the "product concept," the "selling concept," the "marketing concept," and the "societal marketing concept" (Ibid), that may be adopted by organizations involved in exchanges with consumers.

Organizations that focus on providing their products and services in the most efficient manner possible are said to have a "production" orientation, whereas organizations that concentrate their efforts on producing the best product possible have adopted a "product" orientation. The "selling" philosophy involves "large-scale selling and promotion effort[s]" in order to stimulate purchases (Ibid: 17).

A "marketing philosophy" involves "determining the needs and wants of target markets and delivering the desired satisfactions more effectively and efficiently than competitors do" (Ibid: 19). Some companies go further by adopting a "societal marketing concept" in order to "deliver the desired satisfactions more effectively and efficiently than competitors in a way that maintains or improves the consumer's and society's well-being" (Ibid: 20, emphasis added).

According to this philosophy, marketers should make every effort possible to find out what it is that consumers really want and need, and then endeavour to provide these products and services in an ethical and socially-responsible way. One example of the societal marketing concept for tourism can be seen in the case of bike tours of Africa (www.ibike.org/bikeafrica). The tourist experiences the outdoors, improves his/her well-being by obtaining exercise, learns about the history, culture, ecology, and economics first-hand, all the while avoiding the pollution and environmental damage that would be produced by renting a vehicle.

The marketing system comprises many complex, interrelated elements and processes (see Figure 3.2). Despite the fact that the individual, specialized elements in a marketing process vary, and the order in which the steps should be followed is flexible (in fact, many of these "steps" occur simultaneously and repeatedly), there is a general consensus on the process to be followed regardless of the product or service being marketed.

Strategic marketing planning is the first step in the marketing process, and involves developing the business portfolio, creating the mission statement, determining goals and objectives, and designing functional strategies for each department of the business (e.g., human resources, accounting, purchasing). A business portfolio is "the collection of businesses and products that comprise the company" (Kotler et al., 1996:41). The mission statement is a statement of a company's overall reasons for doing business, and provides guidance for all the various departments, products, and services which make up the company. Goals and objectives are set in order to help the company and its various departments fulfill the mission statement, and to provide direction for every aspect of the business. Functional strategies are plans which help each business unit to achieve its goals and objectives.

Another major step in the marketing process is the selection of the target market, defined as the group of consumers sharing similar characteristics or needs that the company has chosen to satisfy. This in turn is made up of four steps: "demand measurement and forecasting;" "market segmentation;" "market targeting;" and "market positioning" (Ibid: 266).

Demand measurement involves determining whether or not there exists a market for the product or service at the present time, and forecasting is used to estimate the demand for the product or service in the future. As it is nearly impossible to satisfy every consumer with a particular product or service, market segmentation is performed to identify "distinct groups of buyers with different needs, characteristics, or behaviours who might require separate products or marketing mixes" (Ibid: 48). The selection of the particular markets to be satisfied by the company's product or service is called market targeting, and is followed by marketing positioning, which involves determining the distinctive position (e.g., most luxurious, most economical) the product or service will occupy in the market relative to competing products or services.

The development of "competitive marketing strategies" (Ibid: 50) requires the examination and evaluation of competitors so as to discern "areas of potential advantage and disadvantage" (Ibid: 51). This is followed by the development of the "marketing mix," which is "the set of controllable tactical marketing tools-product, price, place, and promotion-that the firm blends to produce the response it wants in the target market" (Ibid). The marketing mix is of great importance as "[i]t determines how the marketing budget is allocated, forms the foundation of the marketing plan's strategy, and provides the marketing manager with the techniques to optimise his [sic] budgetary expenditure" (Holloway & Robinson, 1995:32). "Product" refers to the product or service that the company has chosen to offer to its target markets, and the "price" is the amount that consumers will have to pay to obtain the product or service. "Place" refers to the physical location in which consumers may access the product or service, and encompasses the distribution of the product or service. Lastly, "promotion" involves the activities that the company undertakes in order to make consumers aware of its products and services.

Businesses also must undertake the management of their marketing efforts, which includes analysis, planning, implementation and control. Marketing analysis involves "complete analysis of the company's situation... to determine which opportunities it can best pursue" (Kotler et al., 1996:54). Through the process of marketing planning, a company develops a marketing plan, which "will help the company attain its overall strategic objectives" and includes an "executive summary, current marketing situation, threats and opportunities, objectives and issues, marketing strategies, action programs, budgets, and controls" (Ibid).

The third step in marketing management is implementation, which involves "turn[ing] marketing strategies and plans into marketing actions to accomplish strategic marketing objectives" (Ibid: 57). Lastly, marketing control is used to evaluate the performance of the plans and strategies against preset goals. In this way, marketers may analyse the performance of their plans, and then take "corrective actions" in order to improve future performance (Ibid).

The preceding description of the marketing process highlights the fact that marketing is a complex, time-consuming, and expensive undertaking, made even more so because it occurs in an environment that is constantly changing, and involves competitors that are trying to gain competitive advantage. Businesses (and tourist destinations) must realize the importance of their marketing efforts, and continually monitor and modify their marketing strategies and plans in order to survive in this competitive environment.

TOURISM MARKETING

Marketing involves the creation of an image of a product or service. In the case of tourism marketing, the product is "the destination itself" (Sinclair & Stabler, 1991:124), or "an experience of place (location and people) at a particular time" (Wheeler, 1995:39). Thus, the purpose of tourism marketing is to create a desirable image of the tourism destination in the minds of potential tourists, with the goal of enticing tourists to select the destination for their next holiday. As Ashworth (1991:122) affirms:

> *"the demand for holidays emanates from a consumer reaction to perceptions of anticipated tourism experiences which are inextricably place-bound... the tourism product is a set of such experiences packaged as a destination place and marketed largely through images of that place."*

Murphy (1987:418) agrees, stating that "tourism is built upon imagery." However, a desirable image is not enough. Kotler et al. (1993) stress that destination images must also be simple, appealing, distinctive, believable, and above all valid, as deceptive or unrealistic images can lead to tourist disappointment and dissatisfaction, loss of repeat business, bad "word-of-mouth" advertising, and a poor reputation. Thus, the formation of a desirable and realistic image of the tourism destination is of the utmost importance in tourism marketing.

Despite the unusual nature of the product, the principles of tourism marketing are the same as for the marketing of other products and services, however, "differences occur in the application of the theory" (Middleton, 1988:31, emphasis in original). Tourism is a service, and must be marketed accordingly. Services are "products purchased through an exchange transaction that does not confer ownership but permits access to and use of a service at a specified time in a specified place" (Ibid: 25). Hence the four special characteristics of tourism: "intangibility," "perishability," "inseparability," and "heterogeneity" (Mill & Morrison, 1985; Middleton, 1988; Laws, 1991; Weichard, 1992; Holloway & Robinson, 1995) (discussed in Section 2.3-see Figure 3.3).

Middleton (1988:28-30) discusses three other important characteristics of tourism services, namely "seasonality and demand fluctuations," the "interdependence of the tourism product" and the "high fixed costs of service operations." Demand for tourism products and services varies on a daily, weekly, monthly, and yearly basis (termed "seasonality"), mainly as a result of varying climatic conditions and the patterns of the school and business year. "Interdependence" occurs because when tourists visit a destination their experience is made up of several services, such as accommodation, transportation, and attractions. Tourism services have "high fixed costs," meaning that in order to perform a tourism service, the fixed costs are practically identical regardless of how many people use the service. For example, to operate a hotel, overhead costs are virtually the same, regardless of whether there is 30% or 70% occupancy on a particular day.

Wheeler (1995:41) describes the tourism industry as "volatile," because it is "affected by world events and the health of national economies." The horrible incidents of September 11, 2001 are an extreme example of the tourism industry's volatility. The terror attacks significantly impacted tourism in New York, which suffered a loss of almost $1 billion (NYC & Company, 2002), and in the entire travel sector (World Tourism Organization, 2002).

Due to the preceding factors, the tourism "product evolves over time to become... a totally different product" (Ryan, in Wheeler, 1995:41). This has been described as the "non-standardization" of tourism (Schwainger, 1989, in Wheeler, 1995:41). (See Figure 3.3.)

When marketing tourism, the marketing mix (which includes the variables of product, price, place, and promotion-the "4 Ps") must be applied appropriately and may be expanded to include "people" and "physical evidence" (Weichard, 1992). Within tourism marketing, the marketing mix elements are important because they communicate to consumers what type of tourists particular destinations are trying to attract (Mill & Morrison, 1985). The marketing mix is closely related to the "scale" of tourism to be marketed, as each of the marketing mix elements will vary depending on the scale of the tourism product being marketed. Obviously, the overall marketing mix, including such things as price and promotion will differ greatly, depending on the scale of the tourism product. For example, a souvenir store (large-scale) versus Canada as a tourism destination (small-scale).

As discussed earlier, the "product" of tourism is different in nature than other products. The product of tourism is "a satisfying experience at a desired destination" (Jefferson &

Lickorish, 1988:4) and "a bundle of benefits" (Heath & Wall, 1992:129), and is intangible, inseparable, perishable, and heterogeneous. Furthermore, "the tourist travels to the destination area where the product is experienced" (Heath & Wall, 1992:126). More generally, the product of tourism is space and place, and tourism destination marketers can be considered "place marketers" (Kotler et al., 1993), or "experience" marketers.

The "price" of tourism is highly variable due to the interdependent and seasonal nature of tourism services. Heath & Wall (1992:141) state that, "[u]nderstanding the composition of and interrelationships among regional tourism products is... an important prerequisite to the development of an effective pricing strategy." Variable pricing strategies play an important role in demand management, as lower prices can be used to attract tourists to various destinations during their "off-seasons." In the same way, higher prices can be used to limit visitors in peak seasons.

The element of "place" in the marketing mix refers to the distribution of the product, and includes "the location of all the points of sale which provide prospective customers with access to tourist products" (Middleton, 1988:59, emphasis in original). As discussed earlier, tourism services are perishable, and cannot be stored for sale at a later date. This affects the distribution of tourism services, as they must be marketed in a way that minimizes lost capacities (e.g., empty seats on an airplane, vacant rooms in a hotel).

The fourth 'P' in the marketing mix refers to "promotion," which is the most visible element in the marketing mix, because "advertising and other promotional activities are the primary means of communication with tourists in target markets" (Heath & Wall, 1992:153). Promotion consists of personal selling, sales promotion, public relations, and advertising.

"People" refers to staff who deal with customers, and the customers (or tourists) themselves. "Physical evidence," the sixth marketing mix element, includes "physical characteristics" that influence "a company's atmosphere, image and identity and can affect consumers' judgments and perceptions about the service product they receive and about the service organisation itself" (Weichard, 1992:41).

Integrated marketing communication should be used to coordinate all direct and indirect contact that consumers will have with a company's message. In integrated marketing communication, the "4 Ps" become the "4 Cs"-consumers (rather than products), cost (rather than price), convenience (rather than place), and communication (rather than promotion) (Entarga, 2002).

The above discussion highlights the complex nature of the tourism marketing process, and perhaps provides reason for the claim that "good marketing practice is rare" (Holloway & Robinson, 1995:3). In fact, "[m]any communities, including those whose economies are dominated by tourism, do not have tourism plans, marketing plans, or even tourism or marketing components in a general plan" (Heath & Wall, 1992:5).

Failure to recognize the importance of a dynamic tourism marketing plan and to implement it will lead to the loss of (or failure to attain) competitive advantage, tourist dissatisfaction, and possibly environmental degradation.

TOURISM MARKETING AND PROMOTIONAL MATERIALS

The most visible tourism marketing materials are those involved in the process of promotion, as its purpose is to create and increase awareness of a business' products or services and involves communicating with prospective clients. Promotion encompasses the areas of personal selling, direct marketing, sales promotion, public relations, and advertising and of these, advertising is usually the most obvious as it is conducted on a larger scale than the other four.

Personal selling consists of one-on-one interactions between a company's salespersons and their prospective clients, and is one form of direct marketing, which involves communicating with potential customers, usually by direct mail and telephone, and measuring the response. Public relations involves "building a good reputation and image" (Weichard, 1992:106), and "handling or heading off unfavourable rumours, stories, and events" (Kotler et al., 1996:492). Sales promotion includes "short-term incentives to encourage purchase or sales of a product or service" (Ibid: 491), such as rebates, coupons, or contests.

Advertising can occur through a number of different media, including print materials (such as brochures, magazines and newspapers), direct mail (flyers, announcements), television commercials, videos, radio advertisements, window displays, and through the newest communication channel: the Internet. These advertisements usually consist of pictures, graphics, drawings, videos, maps, animation, and text, in varying amounts depending on the advertising channel employed.

Consumers access marketing materials by either seeking them out, coming across them while pursuing other activities, or receiving them directly from the company undertaking the advertising effort. Once discovered, they can choose either to ignore the information, to express interest, to request further information, or to put the information to use (e.g., to make comparisons, to help with decision-making, for fun or educational use, for personal interest or armchair travel, or to book a holiday). In addition, marketing may be either direct or indirect. Direct marketing is that which attempts to make a sale immediately, whereas indirect marketing is aimed at making a sale eventually (Levinson, 2002).

Images of space and place play a prominent role in promotional materials, as their goal is the creation of a desirable image of the destination region, with the hope of causing consumers to seek further information and eventually select the destination as the site for future tourism experiences. Images are created through textual description, pictures, drawings, graphics, maps, music, audio, video, and animation. Even the overall "look and feel" of the promotional materials, the choice of promotional methods, and the communication channel used, may influence the image of a destination. However, there are other factors which may influence images of place. Indirect influences (both positive and negative) on place images include movies, television shows, web sites, books, magazines, clothing, sporting events, music, posters, myths, rumours, stories, legends, and word-of-mouth from family and friends.

EXAMPLES OF TOURISM ADVERTISING MATERIALS

Tourism advertising materials are used to communicate images of tourism destinations to potential tourists. As humans are mainly "visual beings" (Gifford & Ng, 1982) these materials usually contain many pictures, maps, animation, and video. Textual descriptions are rich in adjectives and adverbs, and sounds or music elements are used to complement the images created by the visual elements.

Print advertisements include those in magazines and newspapers, and tourism brochures and flyers. The "Official Vacation Planner [for] Victoria and the Islands" (Figure 3.4) is a typical example of a tourism brochure. It is filled with pictures, maps, lists of, and advertisements for, attractions, accommodations, and restaurants, and rich textual descriptions of Victoria and the surrounding area. These elements, including design elements such as text font, page layout, and background colours all work together to create the overall image of the destination in the tourist's mind, as the following excerpt demonstrates:

"With the mildest climate in the country, Victoria is perfect for visiting at any time of the year. Spring begins as early as February when residents count the number of blossoms in their gardens and a total for the city is tabulated. Summer, with its lush, vivid gardens, is warm and dry, never too hot to be out exploring. Fall begins in late September and is a lovely transition as deciduous trees change from green to gold" (Tourism Victoria, 1998:4).

The brochure attempts to portray Victoria as a multicultural, "super-natural," British, garden city, with a rich heritage, perfect at all times of the year. While the image created is positive, believable, and fairly valid, not everything in Victoria is as "perfect" as the brochure makes it seem!

Television commercials also endeavour to create desirable images, and due to television's visual nature are largely focussed on video images and pictures of the destination. Music is played, and while text is minimal, verbal descriptions and commentary are common. Most commercials provide a toll-free telephone number which you can call to obtain a brochure, and many recent commercials also refer watchers to their web site.

Radio commercials for tourism are less common, mainly because radio is a "nonvisual" form of communication, thus making it harder to create an image of the destination. Radio advertisements are more commonly used to announce current specials or promotional offerings by various tourist agencies and transportation carriers, rather than to promote destination regions.

The Internet is the newest and perhaps most powerful tool available to tourism marketers. The World Wide Web, the graphical interface through which users may navigate the Internet, has multimedia capabilities and, therefore, is a valuable device for creating images of tourism destinations. Tourism destination web sites may consist of pictures, videos, sounds, animations, graphics, maps and interactive maps, charts, text, games, and even programs, such as distance calculators and currency converters.

CONCLUSION

The tourism industry is highly competitive, and tourism marketers must constantly review and revise their marketing goals, plans, strategies, and images. Knowledge of the special characteristics of tourism, and how these affect traditional marketing methods is crucial.

Goodall & Ashworth (1988:ix) state that:

"Destination regions have to work increasingly hard to create or maintain a share of the tourism market. Not all can be, indeed [most] will not be, successful. Much depends on how destination regions market their 'images,' i.e. whether they are successful in persuading potential tourists that they will enjoy 'the holiday of a life-time' if they choose a particular destination."

The communication of a desirable and realistic image of the tourism destination to potential tourists is crucial as nothing will convince potential tourists to visit a destination unless they possess a desirable image of that destination. And unless the marketing process is successful in attracting tourists through the creation of such images, the rest of the marketing process has been a waste of time, money, and energy.

10

Images of Space and Place in Tourism Marketing

INTRODUCTION

As discussed in the previous chapter, people travel for many reasons, but regardless of the motivation, the choice of a destination is dependent upon the tourist's perception of the ability of that destination to satisfy the "need" for travelling (Mill & Morrison, 1985:15).

The creation of a desirable place image, "the sum of beliefs, ideas, and impressions that a people have of a place" (Kotler et al., 1993:141) is an important concern for place marketers, as the ability to attract tourists spells success or failure for the destination (Ashworth, 1991). Tourism destination marketers must project the right image of their destination in order to entice the potential tourist to consider the site for a future vacation or business endeavour. The key here is the creation of a desirable place image of the tourism destination in the mind of the potential tourist.

However, the mental images that tourists create (i.e., the perceived images, or brand images) are rarely, if ever, identical to the images projected by the destination (i.e., projected images, or brand concepts), as there are many other forces which influence images of space and place. (Space and place are discussed in more detail in Section 4.3 below.) Therefore, in order to understand why tourists select certain destinations it is necessary to identify the influencing factors, and examine how people perceive, and then create mental images of, space and place.

This chapter focuses on the role of images in tourism destination marketing. It begins with a review of the process of environmental perception, followed by discussion of how these perceptions are translated into evaluations, judgments, and images of space and place. The chapter then turns to an examination of the "holiday selection process" (Goodall, 1988) in which tourists make travel decisions based on images of the tourism destination. Lastly, the chapter considers the tourism marketing process in order to determine how images of destinations are created and projected so as to entice potential tourists.

ENVIRONMENTAL PERCEPTION

The process of perception has been defined as "both the response of the senses to external stimuli and purposeful activity in which certain phenomena are clearly registered while others recede in the shade or are blocked out" (Tuan, 1974:4). During interaction with the environment, the senses of sight, hearing, smell, taste, touch, and the sixth sense of "feel" (Goodey, 1982), constantly and selectively sense and collect information about that environment, in the process known as environmental perception (Gifford, 1987).

A concise explanation of the environmental perception process is provided by Goodey (1974:8, emphasis added):

> *"In operating within any environment, man [sic] is involved in the 'image system.' He [sic] perceives, selectively, certain information by means of his [sic] various senses and adds this information to his [sic] store of mental images. Images from other environments, as well as the image of the environment under consideration, will be 'consulted' before behaviour is decided upon. Behaviour itself will be varied by motivation and the play of social, political and economic factors, but when it does take place the environment itself will be affected and the individual's information on that environment will be supplemented. During and after activity within the environment, perception by the individual will continually change."*

Berlyne (1971:111-4) notes that "perception is gradual and takes time... involves difficulty and effort... has emotional accompaniments... [and] can be rewarding and pleasurable." For the purpose of this research, this type of perception is considered 'on-site' perception.

It may be argued that there are three different stages of perception: pre-visit perception, on-site perception, and post-visit perception. Pre-visit perception is that which occurs before direct, on-site perception has occurred, and is a result of information collected (both consciously and unconsciously) from sources other than the environment itself. On-site perception, as discussed above, is perception that occurs during interaction with the environment, but is influenced by pre-visit perception. Post-visit perception occurs after interaction with the environment, and is influenced by various information sources. Post-visit perceptions may continue to change, as memory tends to be selective and may fail over time.

An image is defined as a "mental conception, perception or idea" of something (Stabler, 1988:134), and is the product of the perception process (Pocock, 1974:6). As Porteous (1977:216) explains, "the personal image one has of the phenomenal environment is said to be one's perception of the environment." However, "the perceived environment or image is more than the sum of direct perceptual experiences" (Pocock, 1974:3, emphasis added), as additional, indirect, information about environments may come from "... simulative exploration, cinematic and photographic displays, sketches, drawings [and] replicas" (Wilson-Hodges, 1978:5).

All three stages of perception, and therefore also the image an individual has of the environment, are influenced by numerous factors, including physical and mental ability, gender, age, familiarity with and affection towards the surroundings, socioeconomic status, religion, ambitions, education, time, weather, fashion, and the political situation (Bell et al., 1978; Gifford, 1987). Images are influenced further by the media, television, radio, the Internet, movies, books, magazines, advertisements, stories, myths, legends, and rumours, and discussions with friends and family.

As individuals interact with the environment, the information they receive may be used for: classification and description; appraisals involving emotions, meanings and values; or "predictions and inference which give to the image a depth, continuity, pattern or meaning beyond that justified by experience of a particular scene alone" (Pocock, 1974:6-7). Once information about the environment has been collected, from both direct and indirect sources, and during all three stages of perception, the process of environmental cognition organizes, stores and recalls the information when necessary (Gifford, 1987).

Thus, personal perceptions, evaluations, preferences, attitudes, aesthetic judgments, appraisals and images of the environment are formed as a function of direct and indirect experiences, before, during, and after interaction with the environment (Bell et al., 1978; Gifford, 1987). These explanations reveal the intricate link between perception and the formation of images of space and place.

JUDGMENTS OF SPACE AND PLACE

Ringer (1996:952) states that:

"... an understanding of perceptions, and their role in influencing personal behavior and judgments about place, may be the most critical component of an effective, sustainable tourism plan for a destination community."

In order to understand how people make judgments about space and place, we must first examine the relationship between these two abstract terms. Tuan (1977:6) illustrates the link between them by explaining that:

"what begins as undifferentiated space becomes place as we get to know it better and endow it with value... From the security and stability of place we are aware of the openness, freedom, and threat of space, and vice versa. Furthermore, if we think of space as that which allows movement, then place is pause; each pause in movement makes it possible for location to be transformed into place."

In other words, space becomes place as we gain familiarity. In terms of tourism destination selection, space and place always play a role because tourism is "the experience and consumption of place" (Meethan, 1996:179), but this role varies in significance. Often it is the specific place, such as a specific city (e.g., Venice) which attracts tourists. However, in certain situations, the place is the deterring factor (e.g., a tourist who wishes to attend the Goodwill Games in New York but imagines New York to be an unsafe city). These may be considered a "real place" typology.

Alternatively, sometimes the specific place doesn't matter as much as the specific attribute(s) that the place possesses, such as the climate (e.g., sun, sand, surf); recreational resources (e.g., ski hills, golf courses, wilderness areas); status (e.g., most luxurious); special events (e.g., festival or type of sporting event); location relative to home; or even special pricing (e.g., a "hot deal" trip). These types of destinations are somewhat "interchangeable" because the desire for travelling could be satisfied by visiting any place that satisfies these criteria. These are similar to Tuan's (1974:114-8) "environments of persistent appeal" which include the tropical forest, seashore, valley, and island. In this situation, place plays a less prominent role. These are sometimes referred to as "generic place" typologies.

Judgments of environments are based on numerous criteria, both tangible and intangible. Tangible criteria involve such factors as air and water quality, noise pollution, recreation facilities, transportation systems, amount of green space, safety, crowding, remoteness, climate, natural resources, infrastructure, and tourist or recreation amenities (Daniel, 1976; Bell et al., 1978; Stabler, 1988). Intangible criteria upon which individuals form judgments of space and place include abstract concepts such as aesthetics, landscape quality, "style" or status, and the meanings or significance attached to place, such as biological, ecological, cultural, moral, economic, political, symbolic, and emotional (Lowenthal, 1978; Buttimer, 1980).

Perceived Environment Quality Indices (PEQI) have been developed in order to assess environmental quality (Craik & Zube, 1976; Bell et al., 1978) using measurements such as air and water quality, noise pollution, crowding, and even aesthetics. Traditionally, tangible criteria have been given more "weight" when judging space and place, as they are scientifically quantifiable, and therefore considered objective. Measurement of intangible elements is performed "indirectly, in terms of human experiences" (Daniel, 1976:29), and is therefore considered "subjective." But does this necessarily mean that they are less important, or perform a lesser role in the formation of environmental judgments? Craik & Zube (1976:29, emphasis in original) point out that:

> *"all indices of the quality of environmental components, however concrete and tangible the components may be, are based upon human perception and judgment. The identification of a component as a determinant of environmental quality, and the determination of appropriate standards of quality for that component, rest upon human (subjective) judgments."*

Generally, PEQIs have been used for decision-making by organizations rather than individuals. Personal judgments of space and place may be based on some of the same criteria as PEQIs, such as safety, climate, recreational amenities and aesthetics, but these judgments vary "with experience and perspective... novelty and familiarity... distance and memory," and are influenced by the intensity of feelings towards the environment, especially in crisis situations (Lowenthal, 1978:45-55). Furthermore, environments that are valued today, may not be valued tomorrow, as "value is a dynamic concept" (Gold & Burgess, 1982:5). PEQIs changes as a typology of place goes in or out of fashion. The media, societal trends, fashion and prestige change, as do variables such as safety (e.g., cancer from the sun, political unrest).

Recommendations and opinions from both formal (e.g., the media, travel agents, and tourism magazines) and informal (e.g., friends and relatives, myths and legends) sources play a significant role in the formation of personal judgments of space and place, particularly in the selection of a holiday destination.

Judgments and images of space and place depend on what individuals have done, are doing, or plan to do, in that space and place, their individual perceptions of that space and place (influenced by factors such as age, gender, beliefs, etc.), their experiences in and of that space or place, and the surrounding circumstances in which the judgments are formed (i.e., political situation, climate, culture). Therefore, it is obvious that images of space and place will affect decision-making, especially in the process of "holiday selection."

THE PROCESS OF DESTINATION SELECTION

As discussed earlier, individuals are constantly interacting with, and collecting information about, their immediate environment as well as distant places. When the decision

is made to plan a holiday, individuals will consult their personal images and information in order to begin the process of "holiday selection" (Goodall, 1988:2)

The first step is "problem recognition," and encompasses the factors motivating the individual to take a holiday. At that point, a "preferential image" (Goodall, 1988:3) is formed, based on the type of holiday the individual wishes to take and which he or she believes will best satisfy the reason for traveling. Obviously, this is subject to various constraints and outside influences, such as time, money, and peer pressure.

As an individual's information about the "total set" (Kotler et al., 1993:51) of holiday possibilities is limited, the individual undertakes an "information search" (Ibid: 48). Information is gathered from both formal (e.g., travel agents, brochures, travel magazines, Internet sites) and informal (e.g., friends and family) sources, and may be promoted or unpromoted (Ashworth, 1991). Unpromoted, informal information usually is judged by potential tourists to be more credible, as these sources do not have a "vested interest" in promoting a certain destination. In addition, perceived destination image is influenced by the communications channel through which the information is received and the environment in which the information is received.

Now that the individual has information on a number of different sites, forming the "awareness set" (Kotler et al., 1993:51), these are compared against the "evaluative image"

that the potential tourist has created (Goodall, 1988:3). The information gathered is used to form attitudes, preferences, and aesthetic judgments (Bell et al., 1978:21), and these in turn are used to form "naive or factual images" (Goodall, 1988:3) of each of the destinations in the "consideration set" (Kotler et al.,

1993:51). These images are continually compared against each other, the "evaluative image" and the reason for traveling, until the number of destinations under consideration is narrowed down to the "choice set" (Ibid). Other significant influences upon the consideration set include numerous trade-offs between, for example, time at the destination versus en-route travel time, destination versus cost, and cost versus length of holiday.

From the final choice set, the destination which is expected to "exceed the aspiration level by the greatest amount" (Goodall, 1988:5) is chosen, unless the decision to travel is aborted.

Goodall (1988:10) articulates the essential role of destination images in the holiday selection process:

> *"... unless a given destination figures amongst a would-be tourist's current set of mental images it has no chance of being selected as the holiday base. [W]here it does figure in the tourist's image set a very positive image of that destination must be projected in the tourist's mind for it to be selected in preference to an alternative. [W]here the tourist is successfully enticed to a destination it is equally important that the satisfaction derived from the holiday at least matches the expectations created by the image-otherwise the tourist will not wish to return and will not recommend that destination to friends (indeed, the dissatisfied tourist may be instrumental in implanting a negative image in the minds of friends)."*

Destination marketers must be aware of their image as perceived by potential tourists. If this image is not positive, place marketers must attempt either to alter or to recreate their image. But this should be done in an ethical manner. With large amounts of money at stake, place marketers sometimes "stretch the truth" in order to persuade and attract tourists. Deceptive or unrealistic images can lead to tourist disappointment and dissatisfaction, loss of repeat business, bad "word-of-mouth" advertising, and a poor reputation. As Kotler et al. (1996:727) state: "[n]o amount of advertising and public relations can fool the public for long if the reality fails to match the image." Therefore, destination marketers must strive to create and project desirable and realistic images of their destination.

PLACE MARKETING

As stated earlier, "contacts and communication are vital elements" of tourism (Jefferson & Lickorish, 1988:3). Within the tourism marketing process, communication refers to transferring an image of the tourism destination through various promotional channels to potential tourists. The purpose of this is "to create, maintain, or change attitudes or behaviour toward particular places" (Kotler et al., 1996:729), and:

> *"to persuade the potential tourist to make a holiday purchase where none was made before: to induce a change in holiday behaviour by getting the tourist to purchase a different destination or type of holiday; or to reinforce the tourist's existing behaviour by maintaining the purchase of a given holiday 'brand'" (Mill & Morrison, 1985:218-9).*

Destination marketers must first conduct research in order to determine how consumers view the destination. As different markets have different needs, wants and, therefore, different images of the destination, the consultation must be performed within the chosen "target markets," the groups of consumers sharing similar characteristics that the destination has decided to attract and "serve" (Kotler et al., 1996), in order "to avoid the problem of unstable or inconsistent images" (Kotler et al., 1993:144).

If the image is unsatisfactory, destination marketers will have to determine why the projected image is inadequate. Does the image need to be coordinated, enhanced, altered, or completely recreated? Was the marketing emphasizing the wrong things? What is the nature of the desired image? How will the new image be created and promoted? How will the current political, economic, and technological environment affect the creation and promotion of the projected image? Kotler et al. (1993:55) outline the various strategies that may be adopted by tourism marketers in order to improve a destination's image. First, the actual, physical attributes of the destination may be improved, a process termed "real repositioning"; or tourism marketers may undertake "psychological repositioning" to influences people's beliefs about the destination. "Competitive depositioning" and the highlighting of "neglected attributes" of other destinations may be employed, in order to influence beliefs about competing destinations. Finally, they may change the "importance weights" by "persuad[ing] buyers to attach more importance to the attributes in which the place excels," or attempt to "shift the buyer's ideals" (Ibid). Selection of the appropriate positioning method is dependent upon the natural, competitive, social, cultural, political, technological, and economic environments in which the destination exists.

If planned carefully, an image promotion campaign may be successful in influencing people's beliefs and perceived images of a destination. In order to be effective, projected place images must be simple, distinctive, appealing, believable, and valid. As tourism services are "interdependent" (i.e., they are made up of several services) the coordination of the images of these services is necessary for the creation of a simple and distinctive image. This prevents tourist "confusion" and aids in distinguishing the destination from competitors (Kotler et al., 1993).

The image must be appealing and believable in order to attract tourists, and then must be valid in order to avoid tourist dissatisfaction and disappointment (Ibid). To achieve a simple, distinctive, and appealing image, tourism marketers may employ "slogans, themes and positions," "symbols and branding," or "events and deeds" (Kotler et al., 1993; Schmitt & Simonson, 1997).

Aesthetics play an essential role in the creation of a destination's identity, and its image as perceived by target markets. This argument is forwarded by Schmitt & Simonson (1997:3-4):

> *"Aesthetics is not esoteric. The vitality of aesthetics in customers' lives provides opportunities for organizations to appeal to customers through a variety of sensory experiences and thereby benefit both the customers and the organizations through customer satisfaction and loyalty. These opportunities are not limited... Any organization whatsoever, in any industry, for any customer base, for profit or not for profit, governmental or private, consumer, industrial or service can benefit from using aesthetics."*

Projected images, including the aesthetic qualities of these images, may be considered important "pull factors" for tourism destinations. That is, they may attract or "pull" tourists toward a certain destination (Gartner, 1993). Place marketers must understand the image formation process, and the role of aesthetics in this process.

After tourism marketers have decided on the nature and design of the image they wish to project, they must decide how, and through which channels, this image will be projected or communicated to potential tourists.

An important concept regarding marketing communications, known as the "AIDA model," (Awareness, Interest, Desire, Action) is identified in the literature (Laws, 1991; Getz & Sailor, 1993). Before a tourist selects a destination, they must be aware of the destination and have the interest and desire to visit the destination. Interest and desire may be created through the design and delivery of a positive place image to potential tourists. At this point the tourist may choose to perform the required actions to visit the destination, but this will only happen after a desirable image has been formed in the mind of the potential tourist and that image has out-bid all other potential destination sites in the choice set (see Figure 4.1). No matter how good the marketing strategy, how low the price, how available the product, and how visible the advertising, if a consumer's image of the destination is not sufficient to make the choice set, nothing will convince them to choose the site as a tourism destination. This awareness, interest, desire, and action may be created through promotion of the destination region, but marketing and promotional efforts will differ depending upon which phase of the AIDA model the tourism marketer is trying to address.

Promotion encompasses personal selling, sales promotion, public relations and advertising. Each of these elements can influence perceived images of a tourism destination, however, advertising is the most visible factor as it is undertaken on a larger scale than the others. Both informative and persuasive advertising may be used to increase awareness of, and demand for, products and services, including tourism (Kotler et al., 1996). Informative advertising is generally used to increase awareness of new products, features, or destinations, whereas persuasive advertising is an attempt to convince consumers that the destination will best satisfy their "need" for traveling (Ibid). Promotional materials and information about tourism destinations may reach consumers through a number of "communication channels" (Weichard, 1992; Kotler et al., 1993), including television and radio, print ads in magazines and newspapers, brochures and flyers, and most recently, through the Internet.

Although tourists may obtain a "virtual" tourism experience through videos and web sites, in reality the tourism product is 'intangible.' Therefore:

> *"[t]o reduce uncertainty [and increase tangibility], buyers look for 'signals' of service quality. They draw conclusions about quality from the place, people, price, equipment, and communication material that they can see" (Kotler et al., 1996:716).*

It is essential for tourism marketers to realize that not only does the quality, design, and timing of these materials have an influence on tourists' images, but the communication channel itself can play a role. The Internet is the newest and most powerful communications and research tool available to tourism marketers. Use of the Internet may make tourism information available to a larger audience, as the Internet is quickly spreading worldwide. Moreover, a well-designed, informative web site that provides information and value to potential tourists may help to create a positive and professional image of the destination.

CONCLUSION

Tourism marketers can use image marketing to promote destination regions. This involves creating and projecting a desirable, valid, simple, distinctive, and believable image of the destination to the target markets of potential tourists. But projected images are not necessarily the same as perceived images.

As consumers receive both promoted and unpromoted information about a destination, they form images and opinions about that destination. Perceived images are dependent upon a number of different factors, such as mental and physical capacity, previous experiences and images, and the environment in which the perception occurs. Often consumers have images of destinations before they receive any promotional information about the destination. These may be based upon myths, stories, legends, impressions, and images communicated by family and friends. Thus, destination marketers have the difficult job of identifying, creating, altering, changing, or completely reinventing the destination's image. Knowing how people judge space and place, and upon which criteria they base these judgments, is extremely important for tourism marketers.

Although image creation and promotion play a significant role in tourism destination marketing, it is only one of many important elements of a comprehensive marketing process.

As Ashworth (1991:140) warns:

> *"Place image promotion... should only be undertaken as part of a wider series of measures, including product development. Image promotion that loses touch with changes in either the product or the market is at best futile and at worst counter-productive, which, given the essentially volatile nature of both market requirements and product positioning, necessitates flexible and responsive marketing strategies."*

The challenge for tourism marketers is to create and promote desirable images of their destination, while actively analysing, planning, implementing, and controlling all other elements in the marketing process.

11

Online Survey Results

INTRODUCTION

In this chapter, the results of the online user survey are presented, by survey section. A review of the results to the background questions is presented in Section 7.3. The ratings and comments provided for each web site, and the maps found within each web site, are summarized in Sections 7.4-7.8. Under each heading, design suggestions and key findings relating to the particular web site and map are listed. The participants' final thoughts are reviewed in Section 7.9, and the overall site and map rankings are presented in Sections 7.10 and 7.11. For reference, the entire survey is located in Appendix G. A complete list of survey questions and the associated responses are listed in Appendix J.

Responses Collected

A total of 210 responses were collected during a six-month period from September 17, 2001 to March 22, 2002. Of the responses collected, 88 were complete and 122 were incomplete. The large number of incomplete responses may have been due to the length of time it took to complete the survey. Although the survey was designed to be completed in approximately 30 minutes, it became clear that many respondents took much longer. A few of the respondents commented on the length of time it took to complete the survey, either partway through, or in the Final Thoughts section. In addition, comparison of the email submission times for the first and last pages of the survey showed that most took longer than 30 minutes.

BACKGROUND QUESTION RESULTS

Approximately half of all respondents were from the cartography or geography community (111 in total), with the remainder from the public at large (99 in total). Respondents distributed reasonably uniformly over age cohorts, and 49% of all respondents were female.

The majority of survey respondents reported that they use the Internet every day (70%). In addition, 96% reported that they have searched the Web for tourism-related information. Of these, 55% responded that they search "occasionally" for this type of information. Most respondents (99%) have looked for this type of information on the Web before a trip, with 21% searching after a trip, and only 11% during a trip.

When asked to list the type of information they expect to find on tourism destination web sites, the most common responses were attractions (70%), accommodations (66%), maps (50%), transportation (35%), general information (34%), and cost (32%).

Examination of the results of the online survey revealed that users of Internet-based tourism destination marketing find maps to be extremely valuable and needed, with maps rated as "very important" components of travel destination web sites by 82% of respondents. It is interesting to note that, by comparison, pictures were rated as "very important" by only 50% of participants, and sounds and/or music are considered "very unimportant" (53%).

Maps were stated to be useful for many different reasons, including orientation (57%), navigation (42%), preparation (32%), visualization (22%), and to reduce anxiety (15%). There also was majority consensus that online maps included in travel destination web sites should be interactive (50% "somewhat important") and easily printable (58% "very important").

The few participants who responded that maps are not important reasoned that online maps are limited (4%) or they are not needed because there are other sources for maps (3%).

Maps that are included on tourism destination web sites should load quickly, as the majority of participants (49%) are willing to wait for less than 30 seconds for online maps to load.

OVERALL MAP RANKING

Using the ratings provided by survey participants on "map usefulness" and "map design," an overall ranking was determined for the nine sample maps, listed below from highest to lowest.

This "static interactive point location" map obtained the highest ratings for both usefulness and design quality, and received a majority of positive comments. User comments reveal that it is a pleasing map which provides a good progression of detail and lots of information. Several participants provided a comment like "it makes me want to go walking in Scotland right now." A few participants mentioned they would like more detail and more maps. We suspect that perhaps they did not find the detailed walking maps available after clicking on the initial walking map.

It is of interest to note that 86% of all respondents did not find this map when browsing the Scotland site, only encountering it when our survey pointed the respondents to it later in the survey.

This "static interactive chorochromatic" map garnered mainly positive comments. Participants noted that the map is useful for organizing accommodation information, has a pleasing design, suitable colours and makes good use of interactivity. The few negative comments provided relate to the fact that this map does not provide the ability to zoom in, obtain more detail on the map itself, or to see the location of each accommodation on the map. Again, this map seems to be hidden as the majority of the survey participants (62%) did not come across it initially while viewing the Scotland web site.

Mainly positive comments were provided by participants regarding this "static view only route map" from the Scotland web site. Participants mainly agree that it is a pleasing map-good quality, clear, and pleasing colours. 26% noted that the map is "informative," yet 18% state that they would like to obtain more detail. One participant noted the fact that "this map is not interactive, so why have it on the Internet?" As with the other two maps, 64% of respondents initially did not find this map within the Scotland site.

The majority of comments regarding this "dynamic interactive chorochromatic" map were positive. The design is pleasing, the map is useful, and there is good use of interactivity, as the regions are linked to further information. However, this map was designed using Flash, so anyone without the Flash plug-in cannot view the map. Pan and zoom options are available in Flash by using the right mouse button, but because there are no instructions provided, many users were unable or unaware of how to interact with the map. Furthermore, MAC users do not have a right mouse button, so they are unable to use the zoom and pan functions. Many participants (22%) commented that they would like more detail-perhaps they were unaware that they could zoom in, and they did not realize that another window opens with textual information when a region is selected. Some users liked the fact that the colours change as the pointer is moved over cities, and that the regions change colour and enlarge when selected. The interactivity comes at a price, however, and therefore the map is slow to load. Quite a few respondents commented on this. As with the Scotland maps, this map appeared to be well hidden, with more than half of the participants not coming across this map in their initial viewing of the Germany site.

This "static interactive route map" received more negative than positive comments. Participants state that the design is pleasing, yet the map has limited use because of the size and scale. Again, this map was designed with Flash, so many participants appeared to be unaware that they could zoom in and pan using the right mouse button. This may account for those who stated that the map is illegible and useless as well. One user suggested separating the transportation layers into separate maps to reduce confusion and to simplify the map. Yet again, more than half of the participants did not discover this map while initially viewing the Germany site.

The majority of comments regarding this "static interactive database navigation tool" map were negative. The map is clear, simple and pleasing, yet it does not contain enough information or offer enough detail. Participants stated they would like the ability to zoom in, and to have elements of the map linked to further information. Some respondents commented that this map is useful for locating Greece within the world, yet others stated that most people know where Greece is located and thus believe that the map is useless.

This "dynamic interactive global overview" map was the most controversial. It tied with the Barbados map for last place, and received the lowest rating for usefulness. This animated Flash map shows two aliens flying to earth and choosing Germany for their holiday. The animation received mostly negative comments, the most common of which were that the map is displeasing, stupid, or annoying. The animation is seen as silly, cheesy, gimmicky, and distracting. Note, however, that 33% remarked that although basically useless, this map was cute, fun or entertaining. Participants complained that the map is slow and a waste of time. It does not contain enough information or detail, and does not allow for interaction with the map.

This "static interactive point location" map received the lowest ratings for design quality, and earned 80% negative comments. However, 33% of participants rated it as "somewhat useful" for finding basic information regarding locations, and some appreciate the fact that it is interactive. Participants stated that it does not contain enough information or detail, the colours are ugly, and the symbology is unsuitable as it is difficult to differentiate between dot colours.

This "dynamic interactive database navigation tool" map from Singapore could not be included in the ranking as there was an unfortunate error in the html coding in this part of the online survey when receiving replies from respondents. Although responses were retrieved, there does exist uncertainty whether the entire response was captured. Thus, ratings for this map may be influenced by survey error.

However, comments retrieved from participants were mainly positive (55%) and indicate that the map has a pleasing design, nice colours, and is "eye-catching." It is somewhat useful (27%) and informative, but it is also slow to load and requires the Flash plug-in. Overall, participants appreciated the interactivity of this map, but disliked the animation. This map was also very difficult to find as 79% of participants did not come across this map during their initial visit to the Singapore site.

OTHER FINDINGS

It is crucial to note that there were no significant differences between the responses provided by both participant groups (i.e., "cartographers, geographers, geography students" AND "others") for each question throughout the survey. Therefore, maps are viewed as valuable and important elements of tourism destination web sites by cartographers AND non-cartographers.

A problem that became clear through the online survey was the fact that the maps contained within the sample of national travel destination web sites were difficult, if not impossible, to find. The majority of participants did not find the sample maps while exploring the sample sites, and they were only able to provide comments and rankings after being directed to the maps explicitly later in the survey. Respondents commented on this fact and expressed considerable frustration.

The lesson learned here is that the designers of tourism web sites need to put more thought into the location of maps within their sites. Respondents obviously find maps useful on travel destination sites. They comment that maps are powerful ways for organizing and accessing information about a destination. Thus, why not make maps a prominent part of the front page of a travel destination web site, and why not organize and hyperlink destination information using maps as organizational keys? Ironically, in this study it was discovered that the higher-rated the map, the more difficult it appeared to be to find. There is no intuitive or obvious explanation for this observation, but it is clear that tourism destination marketers need to put more thought into the use and implementation of online tourism maps. It is hoped that the information and suggested design guidelines presented in the next chapter will help in this area.

Bibliography

Abram, Simone: *Tourists and Tourism: Identifying with People and Places*, New York, Berg, 1997.

Ashworth, Gregory J.: *Marketing Tourism Places*, London, Routledge, 1990.

Baldacchino, G.: *'Global Tourism and Informal Labour Relations: The Small-scale Syndrome at Work'*, Mansell, UK, 1997.

Baum, T.: *'Human Resource Issues in International Tourism'*, Butterworth Heinemann, UK, 1993.

Bennett, O.: *Financing for Tourism Projects in Developing Countries*, England, Wiley, 1994.

Bevan, D. L., and D. W. Soskice: *Appraising Tourist Development in a Small Economy,* London, Heinemann, 1976.

Boissevain, J.: *Coping with Tourists: European Reactions to Mass Tourism*, Berghahn Books, UK, 1996.

Boniface, B.G. and Cooper, C.: *Geography of Travel and Tourism*, Butterworth Heinemann, UK, 1994.

Brogan, E.: *Human Resource Development in Tourism: The Scottish Perspective*, England, Wiley, 1994.

Bruce, David : *Tourism Strategies for Rural Development*, Sackville, New Brunswick, 1993.

Brunt, P.: *Market Research in Travel & Tourism*, Butterworth Heinemann, UK, 1997.

Butler, R., Hall, R. and Jenkins, M.: *Tourism and Recreation in Rural Areas*, Wiley, UK, 1998.

Chambers, Erve: *Tourism and Culture: An Applied Perspective*, Albany, State University of New York Press, 1997.

Conlin, M. and Baum, T.: *Island Tourism: Management Principles and Practice*, Wiley, UK, 1995.

Cooper, C.P.: *Progress in Tourism, Recreation and Hospitality Management*, Belhaven Press, UK, 1990.

Dane, Suzanne: *Share Your Heritage: Cultural Heritage Tourism Success Stories*, Washington, DC, National Trust for Historic Preservation, 2001.

Daniel, R.: *Recent Advances in Tourism Marketing Research*, New York, Hawthorne Press, 1996.

David W.: *Tourism Planning*, Chicago, Council of Planning Librarians, 1995.

David, L.: *International Tourism Policy*, New York, Van Nostrand Reinhold, 1990.

Davidson, R.: *European Business Travel and Tourism*, England, Wiley, 1994.

Deegan, J. and Dineen, D.A.: *Tourism Policy and Performance: The Irish Experience*, ITBP, UK, 1997.

Douglas, Pearce: *Change in Tourism: People, Places, Processes*, New York, Routledge, 1995.

Edward, M.: *In International Tourism: Identity and Change*, London, Sage, 1995.

Foley, M.: *In Tourism: The State of the Art*, England, Wiley, 1994.

Forbes, A. H.: *Tourism and Transport Policy in the European Union*, England, Wiley, 1994.

Frew, E.: *International Charter Travel—a New Opportunity for Australian Tourism*, England, Wiley, 1994.

Gimblett, Barbara: *Destination Culture: Tourism, Museums, and Heritage*, California, University of California, 1998.

Inskeep, E.: *Training for Tourism in Developing Countries*, Chichester, England, 1994.

James Makens: *Marketing for Hospitality and Tourism*: New Jersey, Prentice-Hall, 1998.

Kotler, Philip: *Marketing for Hospitality and Tourism*: New Jersey, Prentice-Hall, 1998.

Martinus J.: *Tourism by Train: Its Role in Alternative Tourism*, Philadelphia, University of Pennsylvania Press, 1992.

Ryan, Chris: *Recreational Tourism: A Social Science Perspective*, London, Routledge, 1991.

Victor T. C.: *Sustainable Tourism: A Marketing Perspective*, Woburn, Massachusetts: Butterworth-Heinemann, 1998.

INDEX

M

O

P

R

S

T

❑❑❑